CHILDREN
WITH CONDUCT
DISORDERS

CHILDREN
WITH CONDUCT
DISORDERS

A Psychotherapy Manual

PAULINA F. KERNBERG, M.D.
AND
SARALEA E. CHAZAN, PH.D.

WITH THE COLLABORATION OF
ALICE KROSS FRANKEL, M.D.   ROBERT S. KRUGER, PH.D.
JO ROSENBERG HARITON, A.C.S.W.
PATRICIA S. SAUNDERS, PH.D.   HANNAH H. SCHOLL, PH.D.

BasicBooks
A Division of HarperCollins*Publishers*

Library of Congress Cataloging-in-Publication Data
Kernberg, Paulina F.
    Children with conduct disorders : a psychotherapy man-
ual / Paulina F. Kernberg and Saralea E. Chazan ; with the
collaboration of Alice Kross Frankel . . . [et al.]
        p. cm.
    Includes bibliographical references and index.
    ISBN 0-465-01055-5
    1. Conduct disorders in children—Treatment. 2. Opposi-
tional defiant disorder in children—Treatment. 3. Play therapy. 4. Group psychotherapy for children. 5. Parenting—
Study and teaching.
    I. Chazan, Saralea E. II. Title.   [DNLM: 1. Child Behav-
ior Disorders—therapy. 2. Parents-education. 3. Play Therapy—methods. 4. Psychotherapy, Group—methods. WS
350.6 K39c]
    RJ506. C65K47 1991
    618.92'8914—dc20
    DLC   90-55665
    for Library of Congress   CIP

To our Parents

Isaac Fischer and Rebeca Ostray
P.F.K.

David and Ethel Engel
S.E.C.

CONTENTS

PART III
Play Group Psychotherapy

CONTRIBUTORS

Paulina F. Kernberg, M.D.
Director, Child and Adolescent Psychiatry
The New York Hospital-Cornell Medical Center
Westchester Division

Associate Professor of Psychiatry
Cornell University Medical College

Associate Attending Psychiatrist
The New York Hospital, Westchester Division

Saralea E. Chazan, Ph.D
Clinical Instructor of Psychology in Psychiatry
Professional Associate
Cornell University Medical College

Alice Kross Frankel, M.D.
Director, Child Development of the Jewish
Board of Family and Children's Services
120 West 57th Street
New York, New York 10021

Jo Rosenberg Hariton, A.C.S.W.
   Lecturer of Social Work in Psychiatry
   Cornell University Medical College

   Social Work Coordinator, Child and Adolescent Division
   The New York Hospital-Cornell Medical Center
   Westchester Division

Robert S. Kruger, Ph.D.
   Clinical Instructor of Psychology in Psychiatry
   Professional Associate
   Cornell University Medical College

Hannah H. Scholl, Ph.D.
   Research Associate
   Cornell University Medical College

Patricia S. Saunders, Ph.D.
   Research Associate
   Cornell University Medical College

PREFACE

THIS book grew out of the combined efforts of a group of clinicians striving to distill their therapeutic experience to advance teaching and research in psychotherapy with children. The focus on children with conduct disorders was a reflection of a common concern with a frequently encountered and difficult-to-treat clinic population. This clinical perspective was complemented by a theoretical interest in the means of transforming action-oriented behaviors into the language of subjective experience.

Our theoretical framework is ego psychoanalytic object relations theory. Attachment theory, learning theory, and the dynamics of group processes are included within this larger framework. We feel this integration of theoretical approaches contributes to the scope of our understanding. It was instructive to us that such a synthesis is not only possible and feasible but also enriching.

There are many individuals who assisted us in seeing this project reach fruition in the form of this volume, in particular our colleagues Fern K. Azima, Howard Kibel, and Robert C. Lane, who were helpful in many ways. A special thanks to Saul Scheidlinger who inspired our work with these children in therapeutic groups. Discussions with Fellows in Child Psychiatry clarified our formulations. The following student therapists assisted in the contribution of some of the clinical vignettes: Devra Braun, Birgit Elias, Erika Koshei, and Henry Schwartz. We are grateful to our editor Nina Gunzenhauser, who gave coherence and organizational continuity to the entire book, a task which seemed insurmountable. Our editor at Basic Books, JoAnn Miller, was untiring in her continuous support. We want to express appreciation to Ann Sandfur, who transcribed parts of the original manuscript, and especially to Louise Taitt, who typed and compiled the entire manuscript with outstanding efficiency in the final draft. The entire group wishes to thank their children and spouses for their understanding.

We also express our gratitude to the children and their parents who served as a source for our learning. The children described are in most cases a composite of several individuals. Therefore, a single example in most instances represents a condensation of experiences described as a single case. The comments of the children have been reconstructed and are not necessarily verbatim transcripts. In future works we hope to include recorded sessions that reflect more closely the process in verbal communications. For the purpose of confidentiality, names of persons and places have been changed. The group of children to whom we are indebted exceeds the number of single cases described. Without their openness and willingness for reciprocal exchange and communication this work would not have been possible.

14 June 1990   Paulina F. Kernberg, M.D.
White Plains, New York   Saralea E. Chazan, Ph.D.

INTRODUCTION: A TRIO
OF THERAPIES

Bob   *(eleven years old) has been suspended from school. Today his teacher called and said she will not permit him to return to class until we come in to speak with the principal. It seems he took another child's homework and said it was his own. I know he's been fresh before, but now he's lying. We've tried everything—threats, punishments—but nothing seems to work. Can you help us?*

Andy   *(six years old) is entirely unpredictable. I can never tell when he will be all right and when he will burst out with his horrible temper, yelling, screaming, even hitting me. Why does he do these things? At other times, he is docile, fun . . . even loving.*

David   *(eight years old) just can't sit still; he seems to be a moving target. Yes, he'll sit for hours playing with his baseball cards, but in the classroom he's always restless. Whenever there are rules, he simply cannot follow them. Sometimes it seems as if he deliberately sets out to do everything wrong. Naturally, his friends lose patience with him after a while. It seems impossible for him to behave. What will become of him?*

ALL of these children meet the criteria for mild-to-moderate conduct disorders and/or oppositional defiant disorders (DSM-III-R, pp. 53–58). The children about whom this book is written include those with oppositional defiant disorders and those with mild-to-moderate conduct disorders, who exhibit a capac-

1

ity for guilt. Such children have a diversity of behavioral problems and are often impulsive, expressing themselves more through action than through words. We will offer a trio of therapies adapted specifically to the needs of this group of children. Based on ego psychology/object relations theory, our approach stresses the importance of the development of representational thought. Categories of play and language are carefully articulated as the means and measure of therapeutic progress.

Disruptive behavior is common among children, especially boys, who are more likely to display conduct disorders than girls (DSM-III-R 1987). One estimate places the incidence of conduct disorders at 74 percent among a clinic population of primary school children (Wolff 1971). Another study (Rutter et al. 1976) concludes that conduct disorders occur in 4 percent of a general population of children ten and eleven years old. These children are all at serious risk for the development of adult psychopathology: 37 percent to 71 percent of them will be diagnosed antisocial as adults (Annesley 1961; Morris et al. 1956; O'Neal and Robins 1958; Pritchard and Graham 1966; and Robins 1970). Other common adult diagnoses include psychoses, nonaggressive personality disorders, and anxiety disorders. This book is intended as a contribution to the amelioration not only of conduct disorders and their impact on the family but of the negative prognosis the disorder implies.

Let us take a closer look at the subjective experience of children with conduct disorders. We stress that these children express themselves through action, rather than words; they prefer not to use language to communicate, to share experiences, or to express feelings. In their own view of events they tend not to perceive the connections between motive, action, and consequence. Memory, attention, and reflective thought are not reliably available to them. Authority figures, including parents and teachers, are frequently experienced as interfering and unfairly punitive. Adults are generally perceived as unhelpful. These children relate to the therapist both positively, as a resource and tool in play, and negatively, as a critic or obstacle, to be acknowledged or avoided.

Within this group of children with conduct disorders, two subtypes can be discerned: aggressive-socialized and aggressive-nonsocialized (Wells and Forehand, in press). Aggressive-socialized children manifest some capacity for peer relationships, social attachments, guilt, shame, and remorse, whereas aggressive-nonsocialized children are characterized by overt antisocial behavior and an inability to understand rules or the feelings of others. Although the current diagnostic manual of the American Psychiatric Association (1987) has deleted this distinction, we believe that the two categories refer to different clusters of disorders and require different interventions. The aggressive-socialized category tends to occur among latency and early adolescent age groups, while the delinquent category, also detectable in latency, is diagnosed more frequently in adolescence. The two groups are differentiated from each other by their social ties as well as by their sequelae in adulthood. For example, socialized delinquents were remanded fewer times to training school and were more responsible on parole than were those in undersocialized groups (Henn, Bardwell, and Jenkins 1980). The aggressive-unsocialized group were arrested as adults for violent crime, including assault, rape, and murder.

This book is written for use with children who do manifest social bonding, even though it may be accompanied by disruptive behavior. Children are considered socialized if they exhibit at least two of the following characteristics: sustaining peer-group friendships for at least six months; extending self for others; feeling a minimal sense of guilt; being loyal to companions; and showing some concern for others' welfare. When these conduct disorder children become aware that they have done something wrong, they try to cover it up. They worry about being caught, exposed, blamed, or punished rather than about being wrong. Although they may possess a capacity to feel bad about what they have done when it is pointed out to them, they are not driven by an internal sense of guilt. Instead of holding themselves responsible for the negative consequences of their behavior, they generally blame circumstances and other people. Their self-esteem is low, because they do not value the outcome of their efforts. Their play tends to be concrete, repetitive, unimaginative, and aggressive. These children show a narrow range of expressed feelings and hardly ever express happiness and enjoyment. Their mood is predominantly sad, with a sense of hopelessness and signs of overt depression (Edelbrock and Achenbach 1980; Puig-Antich 1982).

Other problems that commonly occur in conjunction with conduct disorders include attention deficit disorder (associated with a prevalence of 75 percent) (Safer and Allen 1976); reading disabilities (associated with a prevalence of 33 percent) (Rutter, Tizard et al. 1976); social skill deficits (associated with a prevalence of 72 percent) (Lorber and Patterson 1981). In addition to disruptive behavior, these children experience several possibly related difficulties in learning and in forming relationships. Not surprisingly, a review of several studies indicates that conduct disorder children account for one-third to three-quarters of the children referred to outpatient clinics for professional intervention (Wells and Forehand, in press).

Theoretical Perspectives

This book draws upon several different theoretical perspectives in concep-
tualizing the processes whereby conduct disorder behavior develops and
persists despite its negative implications for the child, his family, and his
friends. The major framework that will integrate the various perspectives
is a psychoanalytic model based on ego psychology and object relations
theory. Our approach draws from the contributions of Anna Freud (1965),
Heinz Hartmann (1958), René Spitz (1957, 1958), Margaret Mahler
(Mahler et al. 1975), Edith Jacobson (1964), D. W. Winnicott (1965, 1971),
Joseph Sandler (1960), and Otto Kernberg (1977).

According to ego psychology, conduct disorder children experience difficulties within their internal world owing to its structural deficiencies. In
psychoanalytic theory these structures have been defined by Sigmund
Freud as the *ego,* the *superego,* and the *id:* The id is the domain of impulses;
the superego, the voice of conscience and self-control. The ego is the
executive agent that acts in coordination with the other structures to effect
self-regulation and adaptation to the environment. It is the ego that maintains responsibility for reality testing and validation of thoughts and impulses.

Otto Kernberg (1977) describes object relations theory as focusing on

the buildup of dyadic or bipolar intrapsychic representations (self- and object-
images) as reflections of the original infant-mother relationship and its later
development into dyadic, triangular and multiple internal and external interpersonal relationships. This . . . definition of object-relations theory stresses
the simultaneous buildup of the "self" (a composite structure derived from the
integration of multiple self-images) and of object-representations (or "internal
objects" derived from the integration of multiple object-images into more
comprehensive representations of others). . . . what is important is the essentially dyadic or bipolar nature of the internalization within which each unit
of self- and object-image is established in a particular affective context. In this
conceptualization, the self-object-affect "units" are primary determinants of
the overall structures of the mind (id, ego and superego). (P. 57)

As viewed under this umbrella of psychoanalytic concepts drawn from
ego psychology and object relations theory, the child with a conduct disorder is understood to manifest major developmental impairments. Psychoanalytic thinking affords the framework within which to view these
conduct disorder children, revealing them as deficient in the basic personality structures and relationships that lead to healthy integration.
Throughout their development, children with conduct disorders tend to

internalize negative parental images associated with negative feelings. Rage, hostility, anxiety, and concomitant negative self-images accrue to form a negative self-concept with low self-esteem and dysphoria. The conduct disorder perpetuates itself, because these introjected negative representations of self and others tend to be projected onto the outside world. Thus, the children come to perceive others as they have been perceived themselves. Identification with good feelings and helpful people is severely hampered as the children's perception of other people (parents, teachers, friends) is distorted by their projection of aggression and also by the aggression they induce in others as a secondary reaction. In response to provocative behaviors by these children, the adults around them, often unaware of the projections, assume the role of the aggressor. For instance, a parent may begin to command, criticize, or be directly negativistic, thus enacting for the child his own self-criticism, while the child feels himself to be the victim of misunderstanding and blame.

In structural psychoanalytic terms, conduct disorder children have ego deficits in the following areas: cognitive functioning, attention, impulse control, judgment, modulation of affects, language, and tolerance for anxiety and frustration. In the domain of the id, aggression predominates at the expense of integration of impulses with libidinal or affectionate feelings. Finally, although impulses break through the frail equilibrium of the superego, some capacity for remorse, guilt, and more frequently, shame remains, permitting these children to be accessible to therapy.

In their relationships, conduct disorder children are often encumbered by primitive organizational principles that govern their perceptions of themselves and others. They find it difficult to understand that peers have motivations, characteristics, and preferences different from their own, tending instead to attribute to others their own feelings and thoughts. They frequently lack the necessary, age-appropriate social skills for peer interaction. When their need to control their environment is thwarted, they act out, unable to contain their feelings of frustration.

Conduct disorder children share a core feeling of being unloved and uncared for. Although this perception may have no grounding in reality, nonetheless their subjective representational world is constructed around the premise of rejection and abandonment. When they are responded to in a way that is attuned to their needs, they are certain that their low self-esteem and sense of worthlessness will be perceived by others as their true qualities (Willock 1986, 1987). Therefore, to terminate this tension, they may strive to bring down on themselves what they consider inevitable rejection, often provoking others to be furious at them. Although this negative behavior fills a void and causes others to attend to them, it further alienates them from the love and concern they need.

Moreover, these children expect to see reruns of the dreaded interactions between the rejecting parent and the disregarded self and to induce and repeat endlessly these unrewarding, frustrating interactions. This expectation permeates their relationship to the therapist. The chronic worry of these children is that someone else will suddenly replace them, destroying whatever importance they held in their therapist's eyes and leaving them totally in the cold. This fantasy, taken as absolute truth, represents the core of their self-image and their representational world. It is a fantasy near the surface, and therefore it is enacted. Because of the child's deficiencies in organizational structure, there are no defensive layers to be penetrated. In fact, the child does not experience his or her fear as a fantasy at all, but as a straightforward perception of reality and of the therapist's true feelings. The child's behavior reflects his or her acceptance of the rejection fantasy as real; he or she experiences no distance from it and no awareness of its origins or its pervasive effects (Donnellan 1989). It is the deepening of experience to permit new perceptions of self and others to emerge that becomes the essence of treatment.

To understand the development of conduct disorder behavior, we will trace the earliest manifestations of aggression in the life of a child. The youngest of human beings arrives on the scene not as a *tabula rasa* but as an active agent interacting with his animate and inanimate environment in various ways designed for survival. Interacting with him are those caregivers responsible for providing the aliments, both psychological and physical, required for his adaptation to his new surroundings.

Earliest aggression is not negative in its intentions. It is neutralized aggression, or assertiveness, that is part of the organism's program to survive (Hartmann 1958). It manifests itself as a part of the mobilization of energy in the face of a barrier or obstacle (Parens 1979; Prelinger 1989). Everyone has seen an infant try to force his way past an obstacle to get at a toy he wants to play with. Similarly, a child will grab at a baseball card held by someone else, exert determination and strength to climb to the jungle gym's highest rung, or require restraint not to knock the child in front of him off the slide pond. This added push, or shove, to get through a barrier is a major source of aggressive behavior.

Another commonplace but more extreme early form of aggression is the rage reaction, which is seen, for example, in the infant's urgent crying and screaming, face and body taut and red, thrashing about. This state communicates panic, extreme discomfort, and what seems like intense resentment. We recognize this state as akin to the stress of extreme provocation. At this moment the entire world seems like a "zero barrier" (Prelinger 1989), as if there were nothing in the world that could relieve the discomfort. The barrier being imposed can be conceptualized as existing on three levels: (1) the concrete, physical world; (2) the interpersonal world of human relationships; and (3) the intrapsychic world of one's inner thoughts and feelings.

In the examples cited at the beginning of the Introduction, in which three children demonstrate conduct disorders, all three levels are present in each case. Bob seems most upset by a reality barrier, not having the homework that he wants and that another child possesses. On an interpersonal level, we can wonder about his peer relationships and feelings of envy. On an intrapsychic level, we can intuit Bob's feelings of inadequacy and failure that obstruct more positive experiences of self-esteem. Andy, on the other hand, seems to be propelled by primarily internal factors, perhaps temperament, which have not yet been deciphered. It is the sense of unpredictability experienced by his mother that cues us to the apparent lack of an external clue to the disorder. Although Andy's omnipotence allows him to exert control over others, it impinges on his interpersonal relationships and compels him to risk his safety with the physical environment. David's difficulty following rules clearly raises issues regarding all three barriers to adaptation and also raises questions about parental management of frustration and gratification. Not following rules would generate a constant barrage of external difficulties with things as well as people in the environment, with resultant ill effects for the development of David's internal life.

We are saying that these children's manifest conduct disorder behavior is the final common pathway for a variety of experiences in their efforts to cope with frustration and to cope with ubiquitous aggressive feelings. These efforts fail because they have not been integrated within a context that could contain them and permit their expression in a manner that is both communicative and safe. An undue sense of frustration and failures of attunement, consistency, and empathy have caused their aggression to take a deviant path and be counterproductive, rather than to be enlisted toward surmounting the difficulty—what we have referred to as overcoming a barrier. It is because of this failure in integration between positive and negative states, or synthesis, that these children exhibit a lack of connectedness between cause and effect and a lack of continuity in their relationships with other people.

In their play behavior, conduct disorder children are bound to one-dimensional, concrete interaction with objects. Within the context of a therapeutic play relationship, however, symbolic meanings emerge, and imagination is used creatively to communicate. Similarly, a line is discernible in the use of language, from words that name and describe action to words that communicate and share experience. Through integration, these children's actions become connected to their thoughts, ideas, and feelings.

Thus, the behavior of each child no longer exists in isolation but becomes part of the totality of the child's individuality and his or her unique adaptation to reality.

A second perspective to shed light on the understanding of conduct disorders is attachment theory, which helps to provide a basis for understanding the etiology and development of deviant models of relationship. Characteristic of children with conduct disorders is an underlying pattern of insecure attachment to the significant persons who are responsible for their care. Negative and resistant behaviors maintain their maladaptive responses, which may under extreme stress result in acting-out behavior.

Attachment theory also draws on concepts of object relations as well as concepts of development and dynamic interaction. Through continual transactions with the world of persons and objects, the child constructs increasingly complex internal working models of the world and significant persons in it (Bowlby 1969, 1973, 1980; Bretherton 1985). These models appraise and guide the child's experience and behavior. Dyadic interaction patterns form the basis for representation within a working model (Emde 1983; Emde and Sorce 1983). Once an internal working model is formed, it tends to be resistant to change and to operate outside awareness (Emde 1989; Sroufe 1988). This formulation complements that of object and self-representation. Joy Osofsky (1988) suggests that this developmental aspect of working models parallels the psychoanalytic notion of peeling layers of an onion, the earlier internal working models being more resistant to change than those that develop later. Thus continuation of conduct disorder behavior patterns would indicate ongoing distortions in the internal working models of children as well as longstanding difficulties in relationships with significant persons in their lives.

A third theoretical perspective drawn upon in this book is that of temperament theory (Thomas, Chess, and Birch 1968). Temperament denotes innate characteristics of a child. This viewpoint stresses the importance of the child as contributor and/or initiator in continuing patterns of interaction. We focus particularly upon the characteristics of the difficult child (Turecki and Tonner 1985) and the effect that these characteristics have upon parent-child relationships. Noted also are parental characteristics that might contribute toward a problem of "fit" or mismatch within the dyad.

A fourth theoretical perspective that lends its concepts to our approach to conduct disorders is that of learning theory. In our discussion of both etiology and intervention, the principles of modeling, reinforcement, extinction, and coercive interaction are central to our proposals. The emphasis upon learned patterns of behavior helps to clarify how object relations and internal working models are acquired through life experience and how they can be altered through therapeutic intervention. The learning principles enable us to structure and operationalize in concrete and specific terms the interactional behaviors we are observing (Patterson 1982; Wells and Forehand 1981), thus facilitating the reorganization of intrapsychic structures, either object relations or working models.

We have reviewed briefly how four complementary theoretical perspectives contribute to our understanding of conduct disorder behavior in childhood. Although psychoanalytic object relations theory and ego psychology offer an integrating model, no one perspective is sufficient to account for the diversity of constitutional, familial, intrapsychic, interpersonal, and cultural factors that produce and perpetuate this disorder. Bob, Andy, and David can be viewed from various perspectives, each theory adding to our understanding of their individuality.

Organization of the Book

This book offers the child therapist three different approaches to be used specifically for the treatment of elementary school-age children within the diagnostic group of conduct disorders. These three approaches are as follows: individual supportive-expressive play psychotherapy, parent training, and play group psychotherapy. We put the three treatment modalities in this order because parent training is relevant to both individual treatment and treatment of the parents of the children in play group. Described individually, with specific treatment techniques for each, the three approaches can be used separately or in combination, at the discretion of the therapist. It is our intention that this careful delineation of methodology will serve both clinicians and researchers. For the clinician, this book offers the opportunity to refine treatment techniques and expand the variety of treatment approaches. For the researcher, this book provides a means of assessing the outcome of child psychotherapy through the use of well-defined treatment modalities. In all three approaches, the treatment is divided into beginning, middle, and end phases. In individual therapy, explicit recommendations are made about play in each phase. Similarly, phase-specific treatment tasks are defined in parent training and play group psychotherapy. For individual therapy, group therapy, and parent training, the type of verbal interventions for both parent and child are described by the phase of treatment.

The choice of treatment approach is often pragmatic, determined largely by the staff and their particular skills, as well as by the facilities. In the best of circumstances, treatment choice can be determined by the child's

presenting problems. For example, if the main difficulty is with peer relations, then play group psychotherapy is indicated. If the child presents
with low self-esteem, depression, or impulsivity, then individual supportive-expressive play psychotherapy is indicated. If the disorder is mild and
clearly due to difficulties in parental management, then parent-training
procedures are indicated. Frequently, however, these problems present
themselves in different combinations and with varying intensities. In each
case the choice of modality, or combination of modalities, needs to be
individually determined. For training purposes, it is recommended that
each treatment approach be learned separately in order to develop in the
beginning clinician an in-depth knowledge of the issues tapped by the use
of a single modality.

Concepts and Techniques Common to the Three Approaches

The Importance of Social Relationships

The problems of the conduct disorder child unfold against a background
of disturbances both in interpersonal relationships and within the child's
internal representational world. All three therapeutic approaches outlined
in this book focus on interventions directed at social understandings and
experience of the child within his or her family, school, and peer relationships. It is assumed that because of these deficits, aggressive impulses are
not sufficiently processed through inner structures, and the child's direct
actions upon those around him or her result in negative feedback, leading
to an image of himself or herself as rejected and unloved. All three treatment approaches emphasize the need to restructure the life experience of
the child, as well as the inner representational structures that underlie his
or her behavior.

The Context of Play

Play provides a context within which the relationship between the child
patient and the therapist unfolds. Children with conduct disorders frequently demonstrate an impaired capacity to use play for interacting and
sharing with others, or for problem solving. Instead, their play serves
primarily to discharge aggression. The task of the therapist is therefore to
facilitate sublimatory play activity, whereby the child comes to express his
or her assertive initiative in constructive ways.

The form of play changes during the course of treatment: gross motor play, in the early phase of treatment, is often followed by structured games and then by creative fantasy. A major goal of treatment is to have play increasingly fulfill the needs of gratification and communication of all personal concerns, including traumas. Thus, the process of play becomes free from repetitive, tense, impulsive actions. By staying within the metaphor of play with the child, the therapist encourages the expression of feelings with a protective distance. Play is carefully monitored to allow gradually increasing access to material that heretofore had not been perceived and experienced. Throughout the treatment the therapist supports, encourages, and tactfully suggests play activities and expands whenever possible the length and scope and understanding of play interactions. In parent training the therapist guides the parents toward appropriate playful interactions with their child through education.

Verbal Interventions by the Therapist

The therapist communicates to the child in various ways, using both verbal and nonverbal means of expression. A major focus of this book will be on the therapist's verbal interventions. This emphasis may seem surprising, as conduct disorder children are not usually verbal. Because of their inability to contain affective experience within the psychological realm, the words describing feelings or painful events may take on a reality that is as painful as the feelings or events themselves. Thus, language can have a magical, powerful meaning. The increased ability to tolerate affects through the use of words in place of action is another major goal of treatment. The symbolic function of language emerges as a corollary of the therapist's tact and attunement to the child's inner world and as a result of the child's identification with the therapist's use of words instead of actions.

The therapist's statements are one indication of the level at which the treatment is being conducted. Our guiding assumption is that a hierarchy and sequence of interventions exist, ranging from those involved with conscious awareness, to those directed at preconscious awareness, to depth interventions aimed at unconscious experience within the patient. Where in this hierarchy the therapist is operating varies with the phase of treatment the patient is in, with the child's level of cognitive and emotional functioning at any given moment, and with the therapist's purpose at the time. In parent training the hierarchy of verbal interventions will be applied in a general way. Although the parents are defined as the patients in parent training, their relationship to the therapist differs from the patient-therapist relationship that unfolds in individual treatment. In the context of this counseling relationship, the hierarchy of verbal interventions will be applied less rigorously.

The Hierarchy of Verbal Interventions

A schema was developed to operationalize the conceptualization of a hierarchy of verbal interventions, which range from ordinary social behavior, such as greeting and leave-taking, to supportive and facilitative interventions, to interpretations about defenses, motives, and the implications of past experience of which the child is unaware. Since these interventions are organized into a hierarchy, the ascending categories subsume the characteristics of categories under them. For instance, an interpretive statement contains supportive and facilitative components and should be identified as belonging to the highest category whose criteria it meets (P.F. Kernberg et al. 1986a, 1986b). In addition to being assigned a position in the hierarchy of verbal interventions, a statement by the therapist can also be categorized in terms of mode:

→   *Direct:*   The therapist refers directly to the child's behaviors, thoughts, feelings, or descriptions of other people or things.

                  You look upset today.

←   *Therapist-*   The therapist refers to the child's view of the therapist.
     related:
                  You're feeling upset about me right now.

(→) *Indirect:*   The therapist refers indirectly to the child's behavior, thoughts, and feelings by using play, role taking, fantasy, or the child's perceived or imagined responses of other people or things.

                  The rabbit doesn't like to be alone.

A fourth mode of verbal intervention, which occurs when the therapist verbalizes his own feelings, thoughts, and behaviors to the child or group, introduces the child, or children, to another person's perspective. When these statements occur in the treatment, they will be indicated by an asterisk (*). These interventions cannot be planned for conduct disorder children but often make the impact of an intervention more vivid. These statements are potentially supportive and facilitative in communicating to the child the therapist's intimate understanding of the child's experience. If these statements occur frequently, they might indicate a problem in the countertransference. In our approach to the treatment of conduct disorder children, the preference is for interpretation in terms of the child's experience, rather than that of the therapist.

What follows is an outline of the hierarchy of verbal interventions by the therapist, with examples of the different modes in which the interventions are made.

1. Ordinary social behavior

Aim   To engage the child in a neutral interaction that communicates "I'm not dangerous; everything is okay." Greetings and normal etiquette are reassuring and help to diminish the child's apprehension.

Content   Appropriate, conventional expressions of greeting, leave-taking, and politeness

→   Hi, Jason!
→   Thank you.
→   Good-bye, Matthew.

2. Statements relating to the treatment

Aim   To support ego functioning by making the unknown known. These statements invite a special type of communication and feeling between therapist and child. The child's anxiety is allayed through orientation and anticipation. The beginning of a therapeutic alliance is facilitated. The child's anxiety may become focused on the treatment setting, where it is more accessible to mediation by the therapist.

Content   The boundaries, the rules, and the work of therapy. Statements may concern the structure of therapy sessions, behavioral limits on the child within sessions, or the process of therapy and the therapist's role.

→   We will meet here every Tuesday at this time for the next few weeks.
→   You can't destroy the furniture in here.
→   Here we talk and play about any kind of feelings and ideas.

3. Requests for factual information

Aim   To elicit information that the therapist needs in order to conduct the therapy and at the same time to increase communication with the child. Requests for information allow the child to clarify certain things about himself, so that he feels he is an important source of information and interest.

Content   Objective information

→   Was that when you were in third grade or fourth grade?

4. Supportive interventions

Aim   To allay the child's anxiety and increase his or her sense of mastery and self-esteem through the use of education, suggestion, encouragement, and empathy.

Content   Education: Factual information, or correction of misinformation, on matters other than therapy, or teaching of new skills.

→   It would take you more than an hour to walk that far.
←   I'll have to keep the cast on my arm for two weeks for it to heal well.
(→)   It is dangerous for the princess to climb on the castle roof.

Suggestion: At the therapist's initiative, introduction of ideas, alternatives, or courses of action to the child. (This category does not include setting behavioral limits within sessions.)

→   Do you want to see the new toys?
←*   If they called me names, I'd pretend I didn't hear.
(→)   Maybe if Rabbit asked Bear what games he likes to play, it would make Bear more comfortable.

Encouragement, reassurance, and empathy: Approval of actions or resonating with thoughts or feelings of the child by labeling or echoing the child's perceived affect.

→   Look how well that turned out. And you thought you couldn't do it.
←*   I'm very glad you noticed I felt sad last time.
(→)   The princess is so happy to marry the prince.

5. Facilitative interventions

Aim   To initiate, enhance, or maintain the exchange with the child through invitations to continue or review statements.

Content   Invitations to continue: Responses that normally convey ongoing attention, interest, and comprehension. Statements may quote or repeat what the child has said or done. The invitation to continue may be open-ended or may pick up a theme from what the child has said.

→*   Oh. Mm-hm. Yes . . . I see (other than affirmation).
→   What are you thinking about?

←   What else were you thinking? (following a reference to the therapist)

(→)   The rabbit is dying to hear more.

→   What pops into your thoughts when you think of that dream?

←   What about my new baby?

(→)   Is Rabbit angry?

Review Statements: Paraphrases, summaries, or integrations of what the child has said or done, currently or in the past.

→   So, in class today you learned how to write four different letters in script?

←   So you've just been telling me about all the things I do wrong.

(→)   Now we know all the things the rabbit has been doing to prepare for his trip.

6. Directing attention

Aim   To focus the child's attention on events, affects, behaviors, and issues, and to imply the possibility of new meanings and connections through preparatory statements—"look-at . . . " statements (in the present), "look-at . . . " statements (in the past), and "see-the-pattern . . . " statements.

Content   Preparatory statements: Statements alerting the child to the possibility of new meanings in his or her affects, behavior, play, or ideas.

→   We'll have to notice more times like that and maybe get some ideas about what makes that happen.

←*   I think you have some ideas about me.

(→)   That daddy doll seems up to something. We need to figure it out.

"Look-at" statements (in the present): Statements that identify and direct the child's attention to affects, behaviors, play, or ideas that occur entirely within the present session.

→   It seems to me you look uneasy right now.

←   You just gave me that "are-you-angry-at-me?" look.

(→)   Did you notice that the rabbit went to the bathroom four times this session?

"Look-at" statements (in the past): Statements identifying and directing the child's attention to affects, behaviors, or ideas that have taken place earlier.

→   You were sad last week.
←   When you started treatment, you often asked me if I was angry with
    you.
(→) Remember when Rabbit always played baby?

"Look-at" statements (in the future): Statements identifying and directing the child's attention to affects, behaviors, or ideas that will take
place in the future.

→   You seem happy; next week will be the beginning of summer vacation.
←   If you keep trying to hit me, I will have to restrain you.
(→) The mouse wants to steal the cheese—that way he will have food for
    tomorrow.

"See-the-pattern" statements (in either the past or the present) identify
patterns and/or sequences in events, affects, behaviors, or ideas to
indicate significant connections for the child.

→   Have you noticed that your stomachaches almost never happen on
    weekends?
←   Whenever I give you————, you want something different.
(→) No matter how many gifts the Dolly gets, she's always unhappy.

7. Interpretations

Aim   To help the child to see links between behaviors, feelings, and ideas of
             which he or she is aware and attitudes, assumptions, and beliefs of
             which he or she is unaware. These links refer to defenses, wishes, or
             past experiences.

Content   Defenses: Explanations of the maneuvers by which the child protects
             himself or herself from unacceptable thoughts and feelings.

→   You wish you could be king of the world, because then you would be
    the boss of everybody and no one could do anything that would hurt
    you.
←   You expect me to yell at you, because actually you are mad at me and
    feel like yelling at me.
(→) The horse tries to scare the other horses so that they won't guess he's
    scared of them.

Motives: Explanations of unrecognized emotions underlying the child's
behavior.

→   When you get scared you'll never have enough—that's when you eat
    up all the cookies.

←   You wish you were my baby because you think then you could stay here with me.

(→)   The little calf wished her mother would take a trip so she and Daddy could stay home together, just the two of them.

Past experiences: Explanations of the possible influences of the child's past experiences on his present functioning.

←*   When you keep playing the "falling-off-the-table" game, I think you are playing what you think happened to Mommy when she got hurt.

←   You've been afraid that your mean wishes may come true ever since your baby brother died.

(→)   When the mommy and daddy doll had that new baby, the girl doll thought that she wasn't enough for them and now she has the same idea whenever she thinks she's disappointed them. It started back then.

Generally speaking, the therapist's verbal interventions should follow an orderly sequence to avoid the suggestion of a confusing and confused therapeutic process. Not all levels need be represented in any single session. In fact, they rarely are. Depending upon the phase of treatment and the type of treatment approach, different categories will predominate. In the discussions of the three treatment modalities in Parts I, II, and III, illustrations will be given of the categories related to particular phases in the treatment process.

The Process of Change

All three treatment approaches have as their goals a decrease in the child's pattern of ongoing disruptive behavior and an increase of adaptive functioning. Each approach uses different means to reach these ends.

Individual supportive-expressive play psychotherapy addresses these goals by strengthening the child's ego through the relationship with an adult who does not react to his provocations with criticism and hostility. Instead, the therapist's consistent empathy and realistic hopefulness help the child to become increasingly aware of his distorted perceptions. The child becomes aware first of his misperceptions of the therapist and then gradually of his misperceptions of others. The ability to make these new differentiations results from ongoing opportunities to express fantasies, feelings, and experiences in relationship to the therapist. The therapist, in turn, clarifies, confronts, and interprets the child's experiences in the sessions. The child is thereby enabled to expand his capacity for play and to channel acting-out behaviors into the realm of symbols and words.

The supports to the ego of the child stem from the experience of being empathized with, approved of, and encouraged by an adult. Via therapist-related interventions, called transference interpretations, the adult becomes increasingly detached from the negative projected self- and object representations of the child. In place of the internalization of bad images and identifications with the aggressor, we can now see a modification of good and bad images contributing toward the formation of an integrated superego. The child becomes capable of monitoring, correcting, and rewarding her own behavior in a manner consistent with socially regulated reality. Self-esteem improves, and impulse control increases. Both of these achievements enable the child to improve her relations with the external world, offering her the chance to proceed with identification in depth, to enrich her internal world, and to increase or improve her social skills and sublimatory activities (play, language, sports, and other creative endeavors). The dialogue and interaction with the therapist act to repair her attention, concentration, memory, anticipation, and planning. All of these improved ego functions enhance and promote cognitive activity.

Parent-training paradigms focus first upon the practice and attainment of synchrony within the parent-child dyad. Attunement and empathic understanding are also the hallmark of the relationship between the therapist and the main focus of the training—the parents. One aspect of this relationship is that the therapist serves as a model of parenting behavior for the parents. It is through these therapeutic links between parent and child and between therapist and parent that increased mastery of the parental role is experienced and the way is paved for further development. By being emotionally available, the therapist supports the parents and provides a secure base, enabling the parents to share thoughts freely, pointing out relevant patterns of experience, teaching and demonstrating new skills, providing feedback, and validating the parents' experience.

As a secure relationship between the therapist and the parents is formed, the therapist directly affects earlier patterns of deviant interaction internalized by the parents. Like a good parent, the therapist is available, consistent, and responsive, intervening judiciously when the parents appear in need of assistance. With the growth of the reciprocity and sharing of emotions between therapist and parent, an improved level of parental understanding emerges that directly affects their child. John Bowlby (1969) assumes intergenerational continuity in the quality of parental behavior. Selma Fraiberg (Fraiberg et al. 1975) describes the ghosts from the parents' earlier experience that impinge upon parent-child relationships. These internalized and deviant parental models are the inheritance from their own parents and are the ultimate targets of the therapist's interventions in parent-training paradigms. By effectively counseling the parents, the therapist assures the process of change, forging new links between the past and a positive future.

Play group psychotherapy operates from the perspective of peer interaction to provide opportunities for projection and introjection of interactions that have been clarified by the therapist. The child's perception of the group as maternal matrix, and of the group therapists as symbolic parents, provides the substrate for identifications. Facilitation of play contributes to a growing sense of mastery, competence, and self-esteem. The children's perceptual distortions of self and object are experientially corrected, allowing for a progressive clarification and correction of negative perceptions. In this way, the interruption of negative cycles of interaction permits modification of the child's sense of self, autonomy, and conscience.

We now have a map of the course we will follow, the main milestones along the path and the goals we wish to pursue. What remains is the detailed description of each treatment modality and its individual applications. It is to this venture that we now turn our attention, beginning with individual supportive-expressive play psychotherapy, proceeding on to parent-training paradigms, and ending with a consideration of play group psychotherapy.

PART I

SUPPORTIVE-EXPRESSIVE PLAY PSYCHOTHERAPY

PAULINA F. KERNBERG, M.D.
SARALEA E. CHAZAN, PH.D.
ROBERT S. KRUGER, PH.D.
ALICE KROSS FRANKEL, M.D.
HANNAH H. SCHOLL, PH.D.
PATRICIA S. SAUNDERS, PH.D.

1

Overview

THE concept of a "supportive-expressive" parameter along which to classify types of psychoanalytic psychotherapy was originated by Lester Luborsky (1984). The supportive components of treatment are those that strengthen the ego, such as a specific kind of relationship with a particular therapist or interventions by the therapist that facilitate ego development. The ego functions targeted for intervention include impulse control; tolerance for frustration, anxiety, or depression; capacity for anticipation and reflective thought; and sublimation and communication through play or language. The expressive component refers to the therapist's efforts to address the patient's unconscious conflicts and maladaptive coping mechanisms, so as to render them conscious and therefore within ego control.

We include *play* in our nomenclature for this therapy because we consider it to be an essential, developmentally appropriate component of supportive-expressive psychotherapy with children. Thus, we use the term *supportive-expressive play psychotherapy* (SEPP) to refer to the method of, and approach to, individual treatment described in this book. Therapeutic play can provide support to the ego through exploration, manipulation of objects, problem solving, anticipation, thinking, practicing, and mastery and can shed light on hidden meanings with which the child is struggling. For the troubled, beleaguered child, play also provides a safe haven in which reality can be suspended temporarily and new possibilities explored with-

23

out fear of retaliation. Thus, play contributes to the supportive and expressive goals of therapy in a developmentally significant and appropriate way.

Who Can Be Helped by SEPP?

In this book our focus is on supportive-expressive play psychotherapy for a particular kind of patient: the school-aged child who meets the criteria for oppositional defiant disorders and mild or moderately severe conduct disorders (DSM-III-R). There are, however, important qualifications. First, the child must demonstrate some capacity for genuine guilt, remorse, or shame about his stealing, lying, or hurting others. Further, he must manifest during the diagnostic evaluation some potential for engaging in a therapeutic alliance; the therapist can best make this judgment by reflecting on the child's willingness to come and interact with her at some level, albeit a negative one. Finally, parental and school cooperation with the treatment plan should be available. We have conceptualized SEPP for children in the spectrum of conduct disorders. This specific approach has not been tried systematically with other patient populations.

The SEPP mode of treatment is contraindicated for children with moderate to severe mental retardation or with psychosis and for those conduct disorder children who are incapable of guilt, remorse, and shame. Similarly, it is not indicated if the child is unwilling to cooperate even minimally with the therapist or if environmental support for treatment is missing.

Initial Assessment Procedures

It is assumed that prior to the referral the child has been appropriately assessed, either in a team clinic or by a skilled clinician, and has fulfilled the diagnostic criteria. These records should then be available to the mental health worker who is considering the child as a candidate for SEPP. In meeting with the parents, the therapist reviews the family and developmental history, eliciting a full description of the problem behaviors and the way the parents respond to these behaviors. Early developmental data should be reviewed to uncover indications of significant temperament components, such as "difficult baby," "irritable baby," or irregular patterns of sleeping, eating, attention, bowel discharge, or hypersensitivities. Early parental perceptions of the baby should be elicited, with attention to any a-priori bias toward viewing the child as "good" or "bad."

Family interactions can be inquired into as well as observed. The family may be invited in for a family play session, and interactions can be observed around structured and unstructured tasks. Special attention should to be given to activity and engagement around clean-up tasks and academic tasks. Within this context, the therapist will be able to observe the ongoing tension and frustration between the child and his parents. Other observations might reveal a lack of mutuality, a difficulty in setting limits, the anger-provoking behaviors of the child, and a pervasive hopelessness. The parents' own emotional adjustment should be assessed. Is there indication of parental depression, anxiety, or conduct disorder? Is there any indication of potential abuse on the part of the parent to the child?

Information from parents and teachers about such areas as the child's difficulties in compliance and disruptive behaviors can be elicited not only in the history review but more systematically through clinical data-gathering instruments—especially the Conners Teacher Rating Scale (1969), the Conners Parent Rating Scale, and the Achenbach Behavior Check List (1978). School records of academic achievement, the Peabody Individual Achievement Test Revised (1989), and the Wide Range Achievement Test Revised (1984) provide useful indicators of academic standing and progress. Because the Wide Range Achievement Test Revised is only a test of word recognition, we recommend the use of supplementary tests of reading comprehension. A full-scale neuropsychological battery may be indicated if there appear to be specific academic deficits or a significant gap between academic potential and achievement.

Assessment of peer interactions may be acquired via report by the child, parents, or teachers or by direct observation of the child in a diagnostic play group. Perceptions of friends and peer relationships may be ascertained through the child interview, such as the structured Cornell Index of Perception of Friends and Peer Relationships (1985). Self-esteem in areas including social, cognitive, and physical functioning can be measured through the use of the Harter Scales (1982), which include parallel forms for parents, teachers, and child.

These instruments are adjuncts to the skills of the clinician in making recommendations about the appropriateness of SEPP for a particular child. SEPP is indicated when assessment reveals an impaired capacity to play and to interact in a rewarding manner with parents and peers. This serious interference with social-emotional development is seen in the pouting, whining, sulking, low frustration tolerance, and poor modulation of her own aggression, anxiety, and impulsivity that accompany conduct disorders. Constitutional, biological, and genetic components are also implicated. The therapist must consider each of these factors in order to understand their impact on family interactions, and their impact on the attribution of blame in fantasies of punishment.

In sum, the assessment picture reveals that children with socialized conduct disorders experience an ongoing sense of failure and frustration in their interactions with others (adults and peers) and concerning their own competence. Indeed, because of their impulsiveness, their aggressiveness, their lack of social skills, and their associated learning problems, these children find themselves unable to master their school situations and family interactions. They become angrily despondent and act out their conflicts in ways that are often socially unacceptable. Because the child induces frustration and anger around him, his fantasies that he is unloved, misunderstood, and uncared for can become actualized. The eventual bond with the therapist will be formed around the child's efforts to understand why he is this way and why others respond to him the way they do. It is the clinician's judgment of the child's capacity to form an alliance with her for treatment, based on her own interactions with the child and on collected data, that will determine the decision for treatment using SEPP.

The Ego–Object Relations Psychoanalytic Framework

The ego-psychoanalytic framework is the major theoretical basis used in SEPP to understand conduct disordered children. It is a theory that examines distortions both in personality structure, including superego formation, and in interpersonal relationships.

According to psychoanalytic theory, the ego is a complex structure that mediates between the internal and the external world of the child. It is a structure that attends to the functions of attention, perception, memory, anticipation, integration of functions, and adaptation of the self to changing internal and external circumstances. The ego also discharges impulses in sublimated, or socially approved, ways. *Sublimation* is the process by which unacceptable primitive impulses are transformed into socially acceptable actions through words, fantasy, or play. SEPP focuses on the changes in language and play and on the fantasies that underlie these activities during treatment. These ego functions are monitored by the superego, a personality structure that according to psychoanalytic theory is the voice of conscience. It rewards the ego with approval, raising self-esteem, or punishes the ego with disapproval, resulting in shame, remorse, guilt, and lower self-esteem.

Through the treatment procedures of SEPP, the aggressive behavior of children with socialized conduct disorders can be attenuated and integrated adaptively, because the treatment increases the effectiveness of ego and superego functioning. The therapist supports ego functions through both verbal and nonverbal means. She also increases the effectiveness of the child's superego by providing a relationship in which the child can become aware that his perceptions of others are partial and/or distorted by his cognitive limitations or that he externalizes his aggression—that is, perceives it as stemming from others (teachers, parents, peers, therapist). Through many interactions with a consistent, empathic therapist, the child may internalize the therapist's functions of monitoring, approving, and disapproving, and may gain in ego and superego function through identification. Thus, the child's disorder may be seen in part as a disorder of identification that is repaired through the therapeutic interaction with the therapist.

It is important to understand that these failures of identification vary in their severity. In the more severely conduct disordered child, the personality structure is distorted or deficient. The ego has relied upon primitive defenses against anxiety, such as denial, projection, and splitting, which interfere with ego and superego development. In these cases, the structure does not permit observation of oneself. The child has little capacity to observe his or her own behavior and relies upon the therapist to provide supports that will eventually lead to a greater differentiation in his or her perception of self and others. It is against this background of gradually emerging new perceptions and understandings that the therapeutic work takes place.

Initially, support is essential as the therapist communicates to the child an attunement to, and an understanding of, his or her feelings. As the feelings are shared in this open and nonthreatening way, an arena of safety emerges within which the child is free to explore, in play and in words, feelings, wishes, and behaviors he or she had heretofore hidden not only from others but from his or her self-awareness as well. Thus, the expressive aspects of SEPP become clearer as the child becomes increasingly open to deeper understandings of his or her wishes, motives, and thoughts. It is important to stress that the supportive element of SEPP is always present; it is the extent to which deeper feelings are observed and are permitted expression that changes with treatment. In some instances, the expressive component may emerge only minimally, and the main locus of treatment will be supportive. The extent to which deeper feelings can be shared and examined varies from child to child. What does remain constant is not only the therapist's steady tolerance for negative and adverse feelings and wishes but for the child's autonomy. This therapeutic stance allows the child to discover his or her own self and to explore his or her range of adaptive behaviors within the safety of appropriate limits. Thus, the therapist does not impose her values and remains supportive of the child's initiative and positive self-assertion.

The therapist-child relationship is aimed at correcting specific ego-deficiencies and superego deficits, at first through play and increasingly through verbal interaction. Cognitive functions are facilitated, developed, and practiced through education, encouragement, and empathy. Attention, anticipation, and integration are enhanced through the therapist's and the child's observations. Self-esteem improves as a sense of acceptance and mastery develops. Clarifications of behaviors and experiences within the sessions and with the therapist increase the child's effectiveness in social skills. The child becomes more knowledgeable about his or her styles of responding and, in turn, of contributing to his or her problems.

Phases of Treatment

The therapy generally proceeds predictably through beginning, middle, and end stages. All of these phases share three common goals: the first is to reduce problem behavior; the second is to improve adaptation within the family, in school, and with peers; and the third is to improve self-esteem.

In addition, each phase has its characteristic goals. The goal of the initial phase is to establish a therapeutic alliance in a secure and predictable environment that permits the child to unfold her concerns. In the middle phase, the goal is for the child to expand her spectrum of coping techniques, to increase her capacity to play and talk, and to become aware of her behavior and its meaning in the sessions as well as in her experiences outside the sessions. In the termination phase, consolidating and strengthening prior gains are the major goals. The child establishes a clearer sense of internal control and increased autonomy, decreasing her reliance on the therapist.

Duration of the treatment is not predetermined (Luborsky 1984). Ideally, the participants decide on the ending of treatment as goals are achieved. Treatment may therefore last from a few months to two or three years. The sessions may be held either once or twice weekly, but we believe twice a week to be preferable.

Modes of Interaction

As the child and the therapist encounter each other on a regular basis and in the same setting, a relationship develops and a process unfolds between them that includes verbal and nonverbal interactions. We recognize and discuss the importance of play, but we believe that it is with the enhanced understanding and communication through language—within play, along-side the play, or without play—that consolidation of progress occurs. The child's use of play and of verbal language ultimately provides the keys to her organizing her world into modes of understanding that, on the one hand, are unique to her experience and, on the other hand, relate to mutu-ally validated categories of experience. Play and verbal language, then, are our indicators, the litmus paper, of underlying emotional processes and therapeutic progress.

Play

Conduct disorder children play aggressively and destructively with the therapist in an attempt to express without words why they are the way they are and to see if the therapist will respond to them as others have done in the past. In fact, they do not know how to play in any other way. Their aggressive behavior is often an unconscious effort to ward off the aware-ness of feelings of being disregarded and devalued. These children demon-strate an impaired capacity to play in a truly reciprocal manner or for problem solving; instead, they use play to control others. The therapist may be confronted with aloofness or a barrage of aggression. These behav-iors are the children's attempts to distance themselves from painful feel-ings that they find extremely difficult to tolerate. The fantasy of being rejected by others restricts the children's play to concrete, repetitive themes. The therapist's task is to facilitate the unfolding of sublimatory play activity.

This process of unfolding play activity follows a predictable progression. The dominant theme at the beginning of treatment is "I am (I have) everything. You are (you offer) nothing." This is a narcissistic defense. It becomes a playful theme as it is elaborated and shared with the therapist in a nonthreatening way. Another theme is a familiar counterpoint: "To be grandiose versus to be small, dependent, and helpless." The therapist assumes the role of small, dependent, and helpless in various ways that combine joyful play with the devalued self-representations of the child or with their alternate side in grandiosity until the negative, rejected self-representations become tempered by a new sense of shared reality. The child identifies with the therapist's capacity to tolerate the negative self-representations that he or she projects on her and feels safe within clear limits set on acting out his or her feelings.

It is the attitude, most often expressed nonverbally, of playfulness that permits the intertwining of reality and illusion. The therapist and the therapy become identified as sources of comfort and safety, where dangerous impulses and wishes can be explored and understood. The therapist does not seek to reassure the child or to disavow her experience. Rather, through play the therapist becomes familiar with the troubling themes that have dominated the child's life and strives to know them intimately. It is important that the therapist not try to wrench away these troubling thoughts and feelings; they are the child's inheritance from those she has depended upon for her security—her parents and other caregivers in her life.

Gradually, by participating in the metaphors of the child, the therapist is able to put them within a new framework constructed together with her child patient. Since this framework allows for joy, laughter, flexibility, and adaptability, it more closely approximates the world of shared reality.

The form of play varies. During the course of treatment gross motor play is likely to be succeeded by structured games and later by creative fantasy play. The therapist must be attuned to the changing levels of play from sensorimotor efforts to establish contact (ball playing, dart games), to symbolic play (war games), which increasingly serve the purpose of communication, to structured games with consensually shared rules, to role-playing in creative fantasy play.

Play materials should be adaptable to aid in expressing aggression but not to encourage destruction. Spongeballs, guns with soft-tip darts, soldiers, and one or two structured games are useful as organizers. Board games such as checkers and Monopoly require thinking, ordering, exchange, and planning. With increased control of aggression, more capacity for the expression of fantasy develops, and unstructured materials such as paints, play dough, paper, and crayons can facilitate symbolic fantasy play. As treatment progresses, role-playing materials, including puppets, can also promote make-believe activities.

Several excerpts from therapy play sessions will allow us to follow the therapist's support of the child's growing capacity to use play for fun and self-understanding. We will be using a split column to indicate the flow of therapeutic intervention.

Zachary, seven and three-quarters years old, is a brown-haired, dark-eyed boy with a thin, tense frame. His demeanor is that of a negativistic youngster who is restless and fidgety and who blames every problem at school on his teachers. He cannot be trusted with even a simple chore, since he challenges authority as a matter of principle. Because of his aggression, he has problems with self-esteem and with making friends. He is seen in treatment twice a week. The following interaction occurs during his second visit:

ZACHARY: What are we going to do today?	
THERAPIST: Let's wait and see if your mind comes up with something.	→ Supportive intervention: Suggestion
ZACHARY: Nothing. It's boring here. What is there to do?	
THERAPIST: Let's wait a little bit longer.	→ Supportive intervention: Suggestion
ZACHARY: Let's play with the chairs. [He rearranges the furniture, plays musical chairs with the therapist, and enjoys himself. The therapist follows his lead.]	

The next session begins with a familiar refrain:

ZACHARY: What are we going to do?	
THERAPIST: Last time you came up with something. Why not today too? [Zachary plays with a dart gun, having the dart stick on a glass surface of a picture hanging on the wall.]	→ Supportive intervention: Encouragement
THERAPIST: Look how long it sticks! [with admiration] How did you do that?	→ Supportive intervention: Encouragement → Directing attention: "Look-at" statement (in the present)

Zachary orders the therapist to pick up the darts as if wanting to be in control.

THERAPIST: You like to feel like the boss here . . . I notice you want me to be the only one to pick up the darts.	⇄ Interpretation: Motives: The interpretation recognizes the omnipotent wish of the child to dominate the therapist.

A month later as the session begins, Zachary has found a small set of cars, which he arranges in different configurations and distributes between himself and the therapist. For the entire session the play consists of pushing the cars along the melamine surface of a table. The cars clash against each other, sometimes tipping over the edge and landing on the floor right side up, to the glee of the patient.

THERAPIST: Now you are ready.	→ Directing attention: "Look-at" statement (in the present)
ZACHARY: Yup!	
THERAPIST: Wait. How many cars do you have?	→ Supportive intervention: Suggestion → Directing attention: "Look-at" statement (in the present)
ZACHARY: Bronco, Fiery, police car, racer.	
THERAPIST: Hmm . . . it looks like I am going to have a rough time, as I have only two cars.	← Directing attention: "Look-at" statement (in the present)
ZACHARY: Let's start. [Impatient, he propels his cars with full force.]	
THERAPIST: Wow! How did you do that? [He points to car that is tipped over on the very edge of the table.]	→ Supportive intervention: Encouragement → Directing attention: "Look-at" statement (in the present)
ZACHARY: Well, I just did! [looks happy at the compliment]	
THERAPIST: This time I'll be tougher on your cars. [Zachary pushes his car and wins again.]	←* Directing attention: Preparatory statement
THERAPIST: You see, these guys thought they were big shots, and they are not.	(→) Directing attention: "Look-at" statement (in the present)

Zachary gives the therapist a relatively large bus.

THERAPIST: Now, this is going to be like Goliath and David.	(→) Directing attention: Preparatory statement

ZACHARY: Look! [rolls all his cars and eventually tips the big bus so it is standing on its rear wheels.] [in a mocking tone] So, you were going to win, huh?

THERAPIST: [with surprise] Well, Zachary, how did you know the little cars could really get at the big bus?   (→) Supportive intervention: Encouragement

Feeling great, Zachary jumps around the room.

In these vignettes, we have seen the therapist join Zachary in his oppositional stance, set limits for his aggression by channeling it into the play, and recognize his need to win against big people. Rather than being a threatening figure, however, the therapist is seen as a helpful participant who joins in and augments the fun. She also demonstrates she can tolerate feeling weak and losing the battle. In doing so, she provides a model for identification to the patient, who tends to deny his vulnerability. Playful affect is the key to designating this interaction as somehow the same in aggressive content (in theme), but somehow different (in playfulness and fun). It is this new flexibility of playful response that will widen the child's constricted illusion and transform it into shared adaptive activity.

Verbal Interventions

The theoretical assumptions that form the basis for SEPP stress the functioning of the child as an active agent—active in simultaneously facilitating and derailing treatment. It is the child's alliance with the therapist and his increasing identification with her that enables him to represent himself to himself in all his aspects. The unloved and unlovable child discovers he can also be loved and lovable and, moreover, that these two aspects of himself are integrated parts of a whole and subject to his own initiative. Thus, the child comes to experience himself as capable of reflection and making choices.

As we have noted, our basic assumption is the need to strengthen the child's ego functions in the context of a specific relationship to the therapist. The therapist therefore uses every opportunity to enhance the child's impulse control by helping him to transform action into words and play; to improve the child's social skills by developing his awareness of his own behavior and clarifying his interaction with the therapist and others; and to improve the child's self-esteem, which will grow as he becomes more competent in play, receives direct support and approval from the therapist, and begins to identify with the therapist's role of monitoring and disapproving of maladaptive behaviors while praising adaptive ones. The therapist's verbal interventions therefore reflect patterns of organized ego activity that the child then integrates into his own repertoire of relationships.

We have noted earlier the emphasis given to the child's use of language as an indicator of therapeutic progress. In this book the Introduction detailed how verbal interventions by the therapist can also be analyzed and organized into a hierarchy of statements, ranging from superficial social greetings to the interpretation of underlying meaning in a child's play and behavior.

At the superficial level, verbal statements address the child's conscious experience of emotions and of events. Less available to the child are preconscious experiences. These are thoughts, feelings, and behaviors that when focused upon by the child, with the therapist's assistance, become more readily available to him. This category of preconscious material, then, lies beneath the level of conscious awareness but becomes retrievable. At a deeper level exist unconscious experiences (thoughts, feelings, and behaviors) of which the child is completely unaware. These experiences influence the child's life indirectly and covertly, but they have not yet been connected into the network of experience that the child can retrieve at will. To uncover them requires a joint effort by therapist and child. In order to work at this level, the child must possess sufficient internal structure to understand that he is an active agent in structuring his experiential world.

Where in the hierarchy of verbal interventions the therapist is operating will vary. The level of operation depends on many different factors, including the phase of treatment and the child's cognitive and emotional functioning at the moment. Verbal interventions are usually best when they are brief, to the point, and appropriate to the child's cognitive level and style.

The categories of interventions that predominate vary according to the phase of treatment. Similarly, the prevalence of different modes—direct, indirect, and therapist-related—will change with the progress of treatment. Each phase of treatment has a unique profile of interventions.

In the beginning phase, the indirect mode, communication through play or metaphor, is usually dominant. Children at this phase of treatment do not rely on verbal communication and do not perceive the therapist as a separate individual. Instead, they anticipate that the therapist will understand their metaphor and personal understanding of life and events as it exists from within their own perspective. The therapist's verbal interventions include ordinary social behavior—statements and questions that relate to treatment and that elicit biographical data. In order to enhance the therapeutic alliance, reduce initial anxieties, and facilitate early interactions, as well as to foster the child's self-esteem and sense of competence, the therapist offers support in the form of education, suggestion, encouragement, reassurance, and empathy. We note that all these activities by the therapist contribute to the building of structure and the child's understanding of his or her sense of individuality.

As part of the ongoing therapeutic process, children need reminders that the therapist is present and attentive to them at all times. The therapist therefore promotes the therapeutic dialogue by inviting the child to continue his or her communications and summarizes in review statements what the child has conveyed verbally and nonverbally. These interventions facilitate verbalization by the child and begin to expand and maximize the child's self-awareness. In this way, therapist and child attain a consensual validation, a shared understanding of the child's way of experiencing his or her world both in the sessions and outside treatment.

The next step is further expansion of the child's awareness, as the therapist's interventions convey the possibility of new meanings and new information. It is as though the therapist says to the child, "If you look carefully and frequently enough at your own behaviors, feelings, and ideas—those you have now or those you have had in the past—you will learn much more about yourself." Given opportunities to scrutinize these experiences, the child gradually gains more self-control. The feeling of being understood and supported, along with the ability to recognize and control problem behaviors or feelings, opens the path to more adaptive and creative solutions.

By the middle stage of treatment, the children increasingly use words to communicate with their therapist, and interventions in the direct mode often rise as a new capacity begins to emerge. Therapists can apprise these children of sequences or patterns of experiences of which they have been unaware, and they can now recognize them as valid. Reaching this deeper awareness is a significant step for them, particularly because these children tend to focus more on external than internal events. The children's awareness of their patterns of behaving and thinking gives them a new perspective, and they begin to experience themselves as the agent of their circumstances, not their victim. Furthermore, they now know that they can influence their surroundings by autonomously choosing alternative adaptive responses. In some instances, therapists can then guide them to a deeper level of understanding and awareness, which is the domain of defenses, motives, and wishes about these previously unconscious patterns. In essence, the therapists now help the children to understand why and how they respond as they do. Not every child can reach this level of understanding, but those who attain it are able to integrate within their concept of themselves a broader picture of their own capacities and relationships. Throughout the middle phase of treatment, dialogue between the therapist and child may take place either within the metaphor of play or in more direct conversation.

The ending phase of treatment is characterized by increasingly direct dialogue between child and therapist, in which therapist-related interventions are growing. The child is better able to accept who he is and the reality of the therapist as a separate individual with her own feelings, thoughts, and ideas. As the child's competence and confidence develop, he is able to speak directly with the therapist about their relationship and about his hopes and aspirations. Therapy grows to a close as the child's adaptations improve and as issues of the outside world begin to take precedence over previously pressing therapeutic concerns.

At this point, the child has gained the capacity to acknowledge and interact with the therapist as a meaningful person. In turn, the child is willing and able to look at his behaviors, ideas, and feelings in more detail and with less defensiveness as the therapist uses "look-at" statements to encourage this self-observation. Although play is still used, the child is more active in initiating and choosing the play activity, and the therapist can give the child a new perspective by commenting on the relevance of the play to the child's experiences.

During this ending phase of treatment, review statements are typically used to synthesize and anchor the overall therapeutic experience of the child, including the history of the events of the treatment. Consequently, review statements can encompass longer periods of time. In contrast, "see-the-pattern" statements are less necessary by this time, because few new explorations are made. Toward the end of this phase, the content of therapy centers around expanding the child's communications about his life outside the sessions in order to prepare him for the transition to life without treatment. The therapist also addresses the child's reactions to the impending loss of the therapist and the treatment.

The following three chapters deal individually with successive phases in treatment with supportive-expressive play psychotherapy. Each chapter illustrates with case examples the process of treatment within a particular phase. In addition, each phase of treatment is described in terms of specific verbal interventions appropriate to that phase. Our intention is to acquaint the reader with the flow of treatment as well as with separate instances of the therapist's interventions.

The Roles of Therapist, Supervisor, and Parents

The Therapist

Crucial to the success of SEPP are the training and commitment of the therapist. Of primary importance is the therapist's willingness to work with interest and enthusiasm with the conduct disordered child. Beyond this basic prerequisite, we propose a specific profile of attributes and attitudes that we believe to be optimal for a therapist treating this kind of child. Our formulation derives from several sources: descriptions from the book *Interpersonal Therapy for Depressed Patients* (Weissmann and Klerman 1984), a survey of child psychiatry training directors, and the clinical consensus of members of our research group, coming from our experience both as therapists and supervisors. For convenience, in this book we will often use feminine pronouns to refer to the generalized therapist.

The qualities that make an optimal therapist for these children include personality attributes as well as expertise. The therapist should convey calm and authoritative competence. She should demonstrate a warm, positive acceptance of the patient as a person, communicating a recognition of and a sensitivity to the patient's experiences and feelings. Flexibility in approaching issues in various ways and from different perspectives is desirable, but predictability and consistency of the therapist's overall attitude is vital. She should be open to clarification and new information, showing concern and respect for these patients and taking their communications seriously. Essential to the therapist's work is an attitude of realistic hopefulness, communicating an objective optimism about achieving the treatment goals and a willingness to continue to try to achieve them. She must show tolerance of the patients' aggression and explosive affects by preserving her equanimity and concern for the patients while acknowledging the presence of those intense feelings.

The therapist maintains her therapeutic role by avoiding excessive familiarity, criticism, or permissiveness and by not using the child to gratify her personal needs. She must have technical skills such as the ability to put the child's concerns, thoughts, and behaviors into words for the child; skill in maintaining therapeutic momentum by conducting the process actively and purposively; and a good sense of timing that enables her to intervene at optimum points without interrupting the flow of the session. Tactfulness in respecting the patient's self-esteem when intervening is also important.

Throughout the process, the therapist must demonstrate a willingness to deal with other professionals. Because of the externalizing characteristics of conduct disordered children, involvement with those people responsible for the child is crucial in coordinating strategic approaches for daily management. (See the discussion of the therapist's role in dealing with the school later in this chapter.)

The Parents

The parents' role is essential to maintaining treatment and to bringing about its positive outcome. The therapist establishes a collaborative alliance with the parents (Mahler, personal communication, 1975) in which the parents support their child's treatment by regularly bringing him on time, by providing necessary, ongoing information about their child's functioning at home and at school, and by working with the therapist to achieve an empathic understanding of their child's developmental stage, personality traits, and personal issues facing him. The parents must also work with the therapist to clarify distorted expectations about the therapist and the therapy in order to facilitate the treatment. For instance, they may have unrealistic, magical expectations of the therapist, or they may fear that the therapist will regard them negatively, blaming them for their child's difficulties.

Finally, the therapist aids the parents in management issues as they learn to meet their child's needs for consistent limit setting in a firm but nonaggressive way. Many of the techniques of working with parents and maintaining the collaborative alliance are described in detail in Part II, Parent Training, and are applicable to parents with children in SEPP. The population of parents in SEPP, however, is different from that of parents who are candidates for parent-training paradigms. First, their children present with more severe difficulties and require individual attention by a skilled professional. Second, the parents require the additional support of a therapist who will work directly with their child, not as a parental substitute but rather as a more potent agent of intervention for the more seriously problematic children on the spectrum of socialized conduct disorders. Third, for personal reasons, the parents may feel more secure with the direct intervention of a therapist with their child on an individual basis, rather than as a member of a group.

The Supervisor

The main goal of the supervisor is to support the therapist by helping her maintain an attitude of realistic hopefulness and develop maximum flexibility in using a range of therapeutic modes and interventions. Through the use of written process notes as well as videotaped sessions of the therapy, the supervisor also helps the therapist refine her skills of observation, especially of nonverbal behaviors, thereby enhancing the therapist's empathy with the child.

The supervisor also monitors specific verbal interventions to assure that the therapist's statements do not seem haphazard to the child. Premature verbal interventions are incomprehensible to the child and indicate that the therapist is confused about the nature and the course of therapy. They cause the therapeutic process to unfold in an erratic manner, which bewilders the child.

The supervisor also explores with the therapist countertransference issues, such as anger at the child and inappropriate responses to aggression, including excessive kindness, criticism, withdrawal, boredom, and impatience—all common countertransference reactions evoked by conduct disorder children. The supervisor clarifies these interactions and helps the therapist to become aware of how they can interfere with optimal functioning. If these countertransference problems do not respond to supervisory help, the supervisor may tactfully suggest the advisability of the therapist's seeking therapy for herself.

Special Issues

Several elements that go beyond actual contact with the child and involvement with the parents can potentially interfere with treatment and are therefore of concern to the therapist.

The Involvement of the School

Contact with the school has a conceptual basis similar to that of work with the parents. The therapist tries to create a collaborative alliance with the teacher and other school authorities, such as the school psychologist or principal. We recommend that at the beginning of treatment the therapist, with the permission of the parents, take the initiative in enlisting the cooperation of the teacher and in establishing a bridge between them. Only then can the teacher's questions and concerns about the child be understood and addressed in the therapist's initial efforts with the child. The bridge serves the needs of both teacher and therapist; the teacher has the opportunity to discuss problems regarding management of the child and provides the therapist with a significant source of information.

In the middle phase of treatment, as the therapist gets to know the child in more depth, the therapist can share this understanding with the teacher to increase her empathy with the child and to encourage her to act in specific ways that help the child. For example, the therapist can suggest the teacher prepare a structure to contain a child's difficulties—for instance, provide expectations for the child that are commensurate with his abilities and thus increase his sense of mastery, and recommend associations with certain children, or even younger children, in order to facilitate social skills.

> It is hard for Johnny even to understand what other kids his own age are about. It might work quite well to have him spend some time with a kindergarten group and be the "big brother" there. As he gains self-esteem because he's bigger and older and knows more, he can also learn the social skills he has skipped.

Expressions of empathy with the teacher, such as acknowledging how difficult things are for her, with twenty or more children to handle at a time, convey that the therapist understands and appreciates the time the teacher gives for these additional contacts with herself and the child.

In the last stages of the treatment, it is important to include the teacher in the plans for termination, both to inform her and to give her the opportunity to agree or disagree with such plans on the basis of her observations of the child in the school setting.

We have recommended that the therapist communicate with the teacher regularly, in person or by telephone at least once a month. Unfortunately, parents often refuse to allow the therapist to have any direct contact with the school staff. In these cases, it is important to explore the parents' reluctance. The source of this resistance is often due to the parents' feelings of shame or mistrust of the school authorities' reactions to the child in treatment. When parents are not yet ready to consent to direct contact, the therapist can discuss with them the same issues that would be presented to the teacher to allow the parents to assume the responsibility of communicating with the teacher. In their meetings with the therapist, the parents then report their discussion with the teacher.

Parents often have questions regarding school placement, as well as placement with one kind of teacher rather than another. It is generally advisable for conduct disorder youngsters to have a teacher who is authoritative, clear, and firm—one who can provide an understandable and predictable structure to the child to avoid situations of anger and punishment.

Behavioral Crises

Perhaps the most frequent crisis is an aggressive outburst that leads to physical fighting, hurting others, or destroying property and results in suspension from school. Clear, prompt response to injury to another child or damage to property should be instituted, in accordance with school policies. The parents, in turn, should follow the same disciplinary measures that they have employed on other occasions, making them commensurate with the seriousness of the crisis and the child's developmental capacities. If the child has sufficient superego functioning, the therapist can encourage the child to suggest an appropriate punishment for his misbehavior. Alternative ways of handling situations can be rehearsed with the parents ahead of time or at the time of the crisis.

Other important crises are truancy and stealing. The same courses of action should be taken in response to these two behaviors. Working with the child should include highlighting in great detail the disadvantages of lying, in terms of spoiling relationships with friends and parents.

> Johnny, if you do not tell the truth, nobody will trust you and nobody will want to do anything for you, like lending you toys or exchanging cards, because everybody will feel that if you cheat once, you may cheat all the time. It will be very hard to keep friends.

It is not uncommon for therapists to have reactions that can interfere with the treatment. Provocative and action-oriented, conduct disorder youngsters test the therapists' capacity to maintain realistic hopefulness and fondness for them. Time must be allowed for developing the therapeutic alliance at the beginning of treatment. Meanwhile, the therapists may experience boredom, hopelessness, and even anger and impatience with these children. Therapists who do not have the flexibility to interact with youngsters at the motoric and action level may find these mood states particularly stressful and may disengage and even terminate their treatment.

The use of supervision and/or consultation may open some alternative views on the child's behavior and help to relieve the therapist's sense of hopelessness, which often echoes the child's desperation and loss of self-esteem. The therapist's own therapy might contribute even more effectively in providing insight into these reactions to the patient and even into the therapist's suitability to working with this type of child.

2

The Initial Phase of Treatment

THE priorities in the initial phase of SEPP are to establish a collaborative alliance with the parent and to create a therapeutic alliance with the child. Although the structure and goals of these two sets of relationships differ, they share a common theme: with both the parents and the child patient, the therapist works to communicate and maintain a consistent, realistic, and hopeful attitude. This positive orientation is the underlying affective tone of treatment and is vital to holding the treatment to a steady course through many episodic ups and downs. For both parents and child, this calm attitude of experienced optimism and openness to events communicates the message that problems can be worked through and storms endured without losing the continuity of treatment.

Working with the Parents

The parents initiate the request for treatment, often at the behest of school authorities or at the suggestion of friends, relatives, or their pediatrician. We therefore begin with a discussion of parent meetings. Parents need to be introduced to SEPP. From the beginning, the therapist explains to the parents that they will play an important role in the treatment process. They

42

will provide information about the child's progress at home and in school, and they will share their observations about interactions in the family. We encourage parents to raise questions about the treatment, including fee scale, frequency of meetings, and length of treatment. Nearly everyone approaches psychotherapy with a bias and a set of presuppositions. These doubts and worries must be discussed. The therapist listens to parents' concerns and, when possible, attempts to allay their anxieties by describing the process and structure of SEPP. In addition, the therapist tries to pinpoint specific issues to be addressed in treatment with their child.

The process of introducing parents to therapy is well illustrated in the following excerpt from a case we will trace through the three phases of treatment. When Dr. Smith meets for the first time with Mr. and Mrs. Howser, their son, Mark, is a cherubic nine-year-old with curly blonde hair and light blue eyes. Most adults who meet him for the first time remark that his disposition matches his appearance, sunny and exuberant. In school he is generally a delight. Teachers find him to be articulate and curious. Although they occasionally remark on his tendency to be impulsive and quick-tempered, they usually minimize these characteristics as part of his generally energetic nature. At home, however, Mark's behavior is another story. It is so distressing that his mother, Joan, a diminutive woman in her late thirties, has sought professional psychological help for Mark from Dr. Smith.

Mrs. Howser likes Dr. Smith from their first meeting and trusts her immediately, perhaps because Dr. Smith is a woman about her own age. She finds herself wondering whether Dr. Smith has children and how she would cope with a child like Mark.

For the first meeting, Dr. Smith has asked Mrs. Howser to attend without Mark but with her husband, George. While Mrs. Howser thinks she understands the point of this arrangement, she does not see how it will change Mark. George is rarely around, she thinks, and even when he is, he spends little time with Mark or with Sarah, their daughter. He seems to prefer reading the newspaper, watching TV, or doing paperwork for the office. Of course, once in a great while he takes the children to one of their after-school activities, and sometimes the family goes out as a group to dinner or to the beach, for example.

In their first session with Dr. Smith, both Mr. and Mrs. Howser notice the many questions Dr. Smith asks. Her opening question—"Well, how can I help you?"—is addressed to neither parent specifically. After a slightly uncomfortable silence, Mrs. Howser begins.

Mrs. Howser: It's our son, Mark. Everyone says what a nice kid he is and all, but at home he's a holy terror. I'm close to my limit with him. I was afraid that if I didn't do something soon, I might hurt him one of these days.

Mrs. Howser sits back, appearing relieved that she had been able to express these bitter and angry feelings. Her expression of feelings is noted by Dr. Smith.

DR. SMITH: It certainly looks as though Mark can be a trial for you. Can you tell me more specifically what he does that's so upsetting?

MRS. HOWSER: Apart from being constantly rude, obnoxious, and disrespectful to me, he picks on his sister without mercy.

DR. SMITH: Tell me a little more about Mark and his sister. What is her name, by the way, and how old is she?

MRS. HOWSER: She's Sarah and she's five. Well, Mark just finds every opportunity to bully her, call her names, push, hit, kick, destroy her toys and so on. . . . And Sarah, of course, is no angel either. If she knows I'm around, she'll deliberately provoke Mark so I'll hear him and yell at him.

DR. SMITH: How does Sarah seem to feel when Mark gets yelled at?

MRS. HOWSER: Oh, she loves it. Of course, by this time, I can't say that I blame her. He's been so hard on her that she must absolutely hate him by now.

DR. SMITH: How long has this conflict between Mark and Sarah been going on?

MRS. HOWSER: Well . . . Mark has never been overjoyed with Sarah, but I would say that the situation has become much worse in about the last two and a half years.

DR. SMITH: What about the rest of Mark's behavior that now troubles you? Did that begin then, too?

At this point Mr. Howser joined in the conversation with his memories of Mark.

MR. HOWSER: As I recall, Mark has always been a handful. Even as a toddler he was full of energy and high-spirited, always into everything. You had to watch him constantly. He always had a big mouth and said exactly what he was thinking.

DR. SMITH: What was he like as an infant?

MRS. HOWSER: Squirmy. He was hard to hold for any length of time, almost as though he didn't want to be held. He also didn't need that much sleep. At times I felt he didn't want to be close to me, as though he wanted to be left alone. I know that's silly, but he often pushed me away when I'd go to pick him up. Of course, as he got older, he changed.

DR. SMITH: How so?

MR. HOWSER: He became very much more affectionate—clingy at times. But we always had a hard time getting him to mind. It seemed as if we had to tell him things a dozen times. Sometimes I wondered if he could hear me or not, and I guess I'd yell a little louder. He was always short-tempered. And if he didn't get his way, look out!

DR. SMITH: What would happen?

MRS. HOWSER: He'd have a temper tantrum—scream, pound the floor, bang his head, turn blue—the whole bit!

DR. SMITH: Is Mark experiencing difficulty outside the home?

MR. HOWSER: He wasn't until recently. In fact, Joan and I used to joke about it. We'd call him our secret monster. In school he'd do well. Teachers would adore him; he was so smart up until recently. Now he's stopped doing his homework, and the teachers feel he is not learning the way he should. This last report card he got only fair grades, with a poor rating for effort. The teachers are beginning to wonder if there is a learning problem.

DR. SMITH: How is he doing with other children his own age?

MR. HOWSER: Well . . . he has a bad temper that sometimes gets him into trouble and he fights with the other kids. He'll shout his mouth off in the playground, and they'll want to exclude him from a game. But this doesn't usually last. He's very athletic, and the kids want him to play on their team. He also doesn't hold grudges—just blows up and then it's over.

DR. SMITH: Does he have any close friends?

MRS. HOWSER: Well, maybe one. There's a little boy, Jason, who lives down the street. He and Mark are a lot alike and they spend a lot of time together. Mark's temper seems to keep the other kids away.

Dr. Smith has made a good start at forming a collaborative alliance with Mark's parents. She has expressed empathy, encouragement, and support while asking them to look at their interactions with their child. These shared observations will serve as a base for future interventions with Mark. She has elicited from them considerable information about the home atmosphere and their difficulties with parenting. She has begun to formulate some working hypotheses regarding the factors that contribute to family dynamics. There is still much information she will need before she can understand the situation fully, but she does not rush to collect this information or set herself up to be the "all-knowing" expert. Rather, she has attuned to the parents and registered their degree of frustration and despair. She contains these parental feelings and conveys an attitude of respect for the parents and a willingness to work together with them. It is particularly gratifying for Dr. Smith to note that both parents seem able and willing to join in a collaborative effort. Indeed, they apparently value their son, who seems to hold a special meaning to their relationship as a couple, signaled in Mr. Howser's expression—"our own little monster." What this meaning will turn out to be, however, is still unknown.

As part of the initial interview, the therapist explains to the parents the framework for the structure of the treatment process. The issues of fees, frequency of visits, duration of treatment, parent participation, confidentiality, and collateral contacts, such as with teachers, must be discussed. Any questions pertaining to treatment and any parental anxieties and concerns are relevant at this juncture. The therapist and parents must also settle what the child should be told about the treatment and who should inform him. These decisions, among the first to be made in consultation with the therapist, should be considered a significant part of the total therapeutic engagement. Becoming acquainted with therapy may seem a forthright process to someone who is experienced as a patient or therapist, but for many parents the issues are new, and the demands of treatment can seem overwhelming. This sense is often imparted during practical considerations, such as bill payments and transportation problems. The therapist must be attuned to these signals of distress and proceed slowly, reassuring the parents that these issues are always up for review and discussion. For the therapeutic relationship to begin, however, some basic guidelines must be adhered to. The following are some concrete illustrations of how to deal with issues of technical arrangements. These examples are designed to convey the therapist's attitude as well as to suggest specific content in introducing parents to therapy.

Overall Process:	I want to tell you a little about how I will be working with Joey. I'll be doing what we call play psychotherapy with him. I'll be using many different ways of relating: playing with him, talking with him, and pretending with him to try to help him gain control of his behavior and feel better about himself. I hope to gain some understanding of his behavior so he can get to understand it as well.
Purpose:	Right now, Joey doesn't have any sense of his part in his own difficulties, nor does he feel that he can control in any way what happens to him. This kind of therapy can help him function with a clear sense of control and can improve his self-esteem and his ability to deal with friends, siblings, and parents. It is my hope that he will learn to see how what he does contributes to his problems.

Specific　　As we discussed, just telling your child to change the way he is
Methods:　　behaving does not work. You've tried it yourselves. In his
sessions, Joey will be learning and practicing ways to control
his aggressive behaviors, becoming more aware of other people and improving his ability to make and keep friends and
to deal with authority. You and I will meet once or twice a
month to find out about how you and he are managing things.
I'll try to help you gain his collaboration through listening to
him, helping him put his ideas into words, helping him play
and get along better with others, and helping him feel better
about himself. It is important to clarify what issues he is
trying to deal with in his stage of development. It will also be
an opportunity for you to share your thoughts and feelings
about the treatment.

Whatever I learn about how to help Joey in these areas, I will
share with you in our meetings without betraying the confidentiality of the sessions with him. One of the crucial elements, not always easy for parents, is the question of confidentiality. I will not be able to tell you specifically what's
going on in his sessions, though if he chooses to talk about his
sessions with you, that's fine with me. However, I will be able
to talk with you about how things are going in general terms.
For instance, Joey may have been playing at throwing the
baby doll into the crocodile's mouth. In a general communication to you, this would be translated as Joey's struggle with
his feelings of competition and aggression with his sister, and
how he is trying to work them out. I want you to understand
that such confidentiality does not apply in the same way to
our sessions. I might find it useful to share with Joey what we
have discussed here.

One of the ways in which you will be important contributors
to therapy for Joey will be by keeping me informed about
what's going on, so I can decide where my focus should be.
We'll explore together the problems with which both of you
have been struggling and work out ways to deal with them
more effectively.

As you recall, we worked hard together to find times that
would be mutually convenient for us. It is very important for
the success of the treatment that each of us make every effort

to be reliable and consistent, not to miss appointments and to change as few as possible.

I will be going over with Joey the arrangements we have made and will let him know how I will be working with you.

In the initial phase, a major part of the therapist's activity consists of gathering factual information. In addition, the therapist is already setting up a supportive framework within which the collaborative alliance will take form. She gives information regarding the process and course of treatment, makes explicit what parental responsibilities are involved and how critical the parents' participation in the process will be, and offers encouragement, reassurance, and empathy. As the work with the parents progresses, the therapist must be attuned to the possible need for another category of verbal interventions, addressing the parents' displaced, often negative feelings related to the treatment. Displacement can take many forms. It may appear as metaphor, as generalizations, or as references to other authority figures that can be understood as indirect references to the therapist. The therapist's verbal interventions might remain within the metaphor, or indirect mode, of the parent. This disguised communication is experienced by the patient as safe, and exploration within the indirect modality affords the parents an opportunity to express their feelings, ideas, and experiences.

Let us return to Dr. Smith and the Howsers to see how the initial phase of SEPP proceeds beyond the information-gathering phase and leads into the middle phase of treatment. At the close of the first interview, Dr. Smith discusses with Mr. and Mrs. Howser what to tell Mark about his initial visit to her. She suggests being honest with Mark and telling him together that they are concerned about his fighting with his sister and his problems at school. They should go on to tell him that they have discussed the problem with their pediatrician, Dr. Holmes, and that he has recommended they consult Dr. Smith. They should emphasize that they have seen Dr. Smith together and that now Dr. Smith wants to talk with him. It would be helpful to add that Dr. Holmes has recommended Dr. Smith because she's the kind of doctor who helps kids with their problems and worries, that she has no needles or medicines, and that in fact she has toys and does most of her work with children by playing. After making an appointment for Mark in a week's time and arranging a session for themselves the following week, the Howsers leave.

Over the next several meetings with the Howsers, Dr. Smith finds out more about the family and discovers that Mark was an unplanned baby (although not unwanted) and that he was quite ill with pneumonia when he was three, just before Mrs. Howser became pregnant with Sarah. More-over, the Howsers were married for six years before having children and were undecided about whether they wanted any when Mrs. Howser became pregnant with Mark. Mrs. Howser's older brother lives in the next state and is, according to her, similar to Mark in temperament. He was also a trial for his mother, but he was not the quality student that Mark is. Mr. Howser is an only child, and his parents, who live some distance away, visit with the family on holidays. In turn, the Howsers make an annual visit to their home at Christmas. Mr. Howser, a successful attorney, is a partner in a large firm. Mrs. Howser was a kindergarten teacher before Mark was born, but she has remained at home since his birth. Mrs. Howser sought psychotherapy for depression from a school counselor while in college. A combination of therapy and antidepressants resolved the depression. The couple acknowledge that they have talked recently about seeking marital therapy because they seem "at odds" with each other, especially regarding the management of Mark. They are now going to delay this action, however, to see what effect Mark's treatment will have on the family.

Dr. Smith taps into Mark's effect on the marital relationship by asking, "Does Mark react differently to the two of you?" Both parents nod.

MR. HOWSER: I think I have more control over him. I also don't yell and scream the way Joan does. I think Mark responds better to the quiet approach.

MRS. HOWSER: I agree that he listens better to George. But I think that's because George is never around. I think Mark's afraid to disobey him.

DR. SMITH: Why would Mark feel like that, do you think?

MRS. HOWSER: Well, George goes away so much on business, I think that Mark thinks if he misbehaves with his dad, George will just leave.

DR. SMITH: You mean you think Mark worries about keeping his dad's affection more than he thinks about keeping yours?

MRS. HOWSER: That's one way of putting it.

The work with the Howsers goes well as the parents feel more and more at ease with Dr. Smith. One meeting, about the fourth session, Mrs. Howser comes in very troubled, wanting to talk about Mark's new teacher.

MRS. HOWSER: I don't like to say this . . . but, I feel Mark's new teacher is a real "busybody." She asked us to meet with her and talk with her first, before she fills out those forms (Conners Rating Scale; Harter Teacher Rating Scale) you sent her. She says she will be very firm with Mark and make clear to him what her expectations are. She will be calling us each month to tell us how he is doing. I guess I was annoyed with her because I felt she had an "attitude" problem. She seemed to "know it all," and I felt like such a "dummy." I remember Mrs. Davis, Mark's teacher last year. She was so sweet and never made demands on us.

DR. SMITH: Tell me more about Mark's teacher and how she makes you feel dumb.

MRS. HOWSER: I guess I feel this way whenever I have to work with someone who knows more than I do.

MR. HOWSER: That's how it is, Dr. Smith. Whenever my wife feels someone "knows it all," she stays away from them. It reminds me of my wife's older sister. My wife always felt dumb around her.

MRS. HOWSER: Yes. I always had trouble getting along with my older sister Susan. When she finally moved out of our home, I remember feeling very relieved. But I also felt very guilty. I never let anyone know I wanted her to leave—and then it just happened. From then on, I only work with people I like, not those who make me feel dumb.

DR. SMITH: Thank you for telling me about those feelings. I can certainly understand better your feeling about Mark's teacher now that you've explained them. Do those feelings get in the way of your coming to treatment? There might be times you feel I seem to be "bossy."

MRS. HOWSER: Oh, no. I've never felt that way about you.

MR. HOWSER: Now, Judy, don't you remember when we left our first meeting with Dr. Smith? What did you say to me?

MRS. HOWSER: I said—I said I felt shy about speaking up around a professional like Dr. Smith.

DR. SMITH: It is hard to talk about your private feelings and thoughts with a stranger. That is what makes therapy difficult; you need to talk about things you usually try to avoid discussing. However, I wonder if it doesn't bring up the old issue for you of feeling like a "dummy" with someone who "knows it all." Somehow the situation in school with Mark's new teacher seems like a repeat of the situation with Mrs. Howser's sister Susan. [Mr. and Mrs. Howser smile in assent and recognition. There is a moment's release in tension for all three persons in the room. Dr. Smith continues.] Does this idea seem to make sense to you?

MR. AND MRS. HOWSER: [in unison] Yes it does!

MRS. HOWSER: I never thought of it that way, but I guess it makes a lot of sense. I wouldn't want to hurt your feelings, Dr. Smith. I really want to work with you to help Mark.

DR. SMITH: But, isn't it important for us all to understand these feelings. Then, it will be possible for us to work together.

MRS. HOWSER: [sighs] It is really good to be working with someone who can understand.

This vignette clearly illustrates an instance of displacement, in which the parents defend against feelings by displacing them onto someone else. The therapist must be alert to the use of displacement and work though these feelings by urging the parents to express them fully while respecting the metaphor. Although in this example a direct connection was made between feelings for the sibling, teacher, and therapist, it is not necessary to interpret the full meaning of the displacement. Simply staying within the metaphor used by the parents and limiting exploration to this level can be extremely useful. Whether a more in-depth interpretation is timely is a judgment that the therapist must make in each situation. In some instances, making the in-depth interpretation would only enhance the already frightening magical powers the parent is attributing to the therapist. The therapist must assess the rapport within the parent-therapist relationship and the forces of resistance, or the need by the parent to remain in disguise. The alliance can be greatly strengthened and important new data gathered without full disclosure. The empathic response of the therapist to the parental feelings can have a positive effect, even when the target of these feelings remains hidden from the parents' conscious awareness. The Howsers' capacity to work through these feelings indicates a readiness to proceed.

Working with the Child

Getting Started

After the assessment is completed and the decision has been made to proceed with SEPP, the child is informed about the rules, limits, structure, and process of therapy. Here are some examples of ways the therapist might talk to the child in introducing him to therapy.

Purpose: What you and I are going to do together is to try to figure out ways to get your parents off your back, to get your teacher and your principal off your back, and maybe to figure out ways to keep from getting into so many fights with kids you want to be friends with.

In this example the child's externalization of his difficulty is respected, and the therapist presents the issues from the child's perspective.

You're getting into so much trouble at home, in school, and with other kids. People get angry with you, and you get mad at them. You don't understand why that's happening, and you need to learn how to change that. You need help figuring that out. You are having a lot of trouble, and I'm going to help you figure out how to change that.

Specific   We will have different ways to help you with these troubles.
Methods: The ways can be by talking, or by playing, or by thinking about your troubles.

There's something else I want to be sure you know. The things we talk about, play about, and think about are all private, and nobody is going to know about them except you and me. Even when I talk with your parents, I won't be telling them what's going on here with you and me. Of course, if you want to tell them things, you can.

Setting: You and I will meet for 45 minutes every Tuesday and Thursday afternoon right here in this office. That will be our special working time together, and we'll do everything we can to have that time just for us. We'll try not to change that time. We'll try never to miss any of our working times together. And when I see your parents, it won't take the place of our working times.

To illustrate the initial phase of SEPP with the child, we will continue with our observation of the Howsers as Mark is brought by his mother to his first session with Dr. Smith. Some of the difficulty of which his parents have spoken is immediately apparent in the waiting room. When Dr. Smith comes in, she sees that Mark has taken the magazines off the coffee table and piled them on the floor. He is repeatedly jumping off the pile as though he were an athlete in competition. Dr. Smith hears Mrs. Howser say feebly, "Stop that, Mark . . . please . . . stop that," but Mark continues despite the availability of many other toys in the room. He does not acknowledge his mother's request and seems to treat her as if she were part of the furniture.

As Dr. Smith enters, Mark looks up in her direction with curious eyes and a half-smile, as though he wonders how she will handle this situation. She simply says in a friendly way, "This must be Mark" and holds out her hand. He stops jumping, takes her hand, and replies quite unexpectedly, "This must be Dr. Smith." Dr. Smith then comments, "It looks like you are inventing a new athletic event. Before we go into my office, would you mind putting the magazines back?" In a semihumorous tone, Mark answers, "Well, I would mind, but I'll do it anyway." And he did.

Having arranged the magazines neatly in their original spot, Mark looks expectantly at Dr. Smith. "The office is this way," she says, leading the way through a door and down a short hall. As they are departing, Dr. Smith sees that Mrs. Howser looks uncertain as to whether she should accompany them. Dr. Smith tells her, "Mark and I will spend this session together, and we'll be about 45 minutes."

As they enter Dr. Smith's office, Mark inspects the various toys and games.

MARK: Oh, you have "Trouble."	
DR. SMITH: Yes, would you like to play?	→ Supportive intervention: Suggestion
MARK: That would be okay.	
DR. SMITH: Before we do that, Mark, I'd like to talk with you. Please sit down.	←* Supportive intervention: Suggestion
MARK: Okay.	
DR. SMITH: Did your parents talk to you about coming to see me?	→ Request for factual information
MARK: Yeah, a little.	
DR. SMITH: What did they tell you?	→ Request for factual information
MARK: They said I was coming to you to find out why I was bad so much.	
DR. SMITH: Do you think you are bad at home?	→ Directing attention: "Look-at" statement (in the present)
MARK: Yeah—sometimes. But I just do that because Mom's such a nag. She bugs me all the time.	
DR. SMITH: When you're "bad," does she stop bugging you?	→ Directing attention: "Look-at" statement (in the present)
MARK: Sometimes.	

*In the following pages, asterisks indicate the therapist's verbal interventions that express his or her feelings, thoughts, and patterns of behavior to the child or group. These statements introduce the child to another person's perspective (for full discussion, see p. 12).

DR. SMITH: Well, I think you may sometimes provoke your mom because she's bugging you. But I also think you often don't know why you do things that upset your parents. One reason to come to see me is that I'm the kind of doctor who helps kids understand what they feel. Usually, what you feel has a lot to do with how you act. So I'm going to try, with your help, to understand and help you understand what you feel and why you act the way you do.

→ Directing attention: "See-the-pattern" statement about the treatment

MARK: What good will that do?

DR. SMITH: Well, if we can understand that, maybe we can figure out different ways of acting when you feel like doing something to upset your parents. If you can act differently, they won't get upset, and then, I'm guessing, you'll be happier too.

→ Directing attention: Preparatory statement

MARK: But I don't care if they get upset.

DR. SMITH: Not at all?

→ Facilitative intervention: Invitation to continue

MARK: Well, sometimes I don't like it when they punish me.

DR. SMITH: I guess it would be nicer if it didn't happen.

→ Supportive intervention: Empathy

MARK: But how're you going to find out what I'm feeling when I'm at home?

DR. SMITH: That's a good question, Mark. One way is to talk with you as we are now and for you to tell me what you remember feeling. Another way is for us to spend more time playing together.

→ Supportive intervention: Reassurance

→ Statement relating to the treatment

MARK: Playing? Why?

DR. SMITH: Because sometimes when kids play, they relax and it's easier to understand what's troubling you. Also, the way we play together may tell us a bit about how you feel and what matters to you.

→ Statement relating to the treatment

MARK: Can we play anything?

DR. SMITH: Anything, as long as no one gets hurt and nothing gets broken or is dangerous. As you can see, I have a lot of toys and games. I also have paper, crayons, magic markers, and clay. So there are lots of things for us to do.

→ Statement relating to the treatment

MARK: Can I bring some of my toys if I don't like yours?

DR. SMITH: Sure, as long as they are not dangerous.

→ Supportive intervention: Encouragement

→ Statement relating to the treatment

MARK: How often do we have to do this?

DR. SMITH: We'll start off by meeting twice a week for 45 minutes each time.

→ Statement relating to the treatment

MARK: Wow, that's a lot!

DR. SMITH: How do you feel about coming that much?

→ Directing attention: "Look-at" statement (in the present)

MARK: It'd be okay, I guess. Could we start by playing "Trouble"?

DR. SMITH: Sure.   → Supportive intervention:
                                        Reassurance

Dr. Smith's treatment of Mark begins with her observations in the waiting room. She notes that Mrs. Howser seems ineffective in limit setting and that Mark seems interested in testing limits. Mrs. Howser's behavior in the waiting room is characteristic of "nattering," or "nagging," parents as described by Patterson (1982). Such parents tend to cope with their children's inappropriate or aggressive behavior by persistently complaining but without taking any firm, decisive action. The result is that the child's behavior continues or escalates until a confrontation is precipitated between the child and the parent. These confrontations often lead to violence, but they need not.

By contrast, Dr. Smith's actions demonstrate how an adult can take charge of a situation in which a child is testing the limits and obtain compliance with rules in short order. Note that Mark responds quickly to the clarity of Dr. Smith's command and the firmness of her voice. Vocal tonality, or voice control, is a powerful tool with most children when used appropriately. Many parents of aggressive youngsters have not learned how to modulate their voices to convey commands effectively. In asking Mark to stop his provocative behavior and enter the office with her, Dr. Smith is assessing how responsive he is likely to be to her direction. Clearly, the results are quite positive and encouraging. Dr. Smith then goes on to inquire what Mark believes are the reasons for his coming to see her. This is a standard opening question in a variety of child psychotherapy approaches. Mark's responses to her questions are direct and well formulated and reveal, not disorganization, but rather a wariness and a desire to take control of the unfamiliar situation, as seen in his repeated request to play. Having ascertained Mark's perception of her role, Dr. Smith is in a position to correct his distortions and provide accurate information about the process of treatment. Mark's response ("Wow, that's a lot!") suggests that he is impressed with the degree of interest and attention to be devoted to him by a concerned adult other than his parents. Dr. Smith's initial approach to Mark is designed to facilitate his awareness of her as a warm, yet firm authority, who can set limits but who allows for the gratification of some wishes, such as playing games of his choice.

In subsequent sessions, Dr. Smith adopts an approach of minimal intervention, allowing Mark to decide what activities to pursue and how to pursue them. Her purpose is to maximize opportunities for Mark to demonstrate how he behaves in an unstructured situation and his usual ways of relating to people, as well as the ways in which he tests a new situation.

She assumes that given this freedom, his problem behaviors will gradually emerge, as they do in a game of "Trouble."

MARK: Let's see . . . that's 5. I get to move . . . 1-2-3-4-5.	
DR. SMITH: You actually moved six.	→ Directing attention: "Look-at" statement (in the present)
MARK: No, I didn't!	
DR. SMITH: Look. Let's count: 1-2-3-4-5. See?	→ Directing attention: "Look-at" statement (in the present)
MARK: Okay. It's my turn again?	
DR. SMITH: No. Remember, you said you get an extra turn when you get a 6? You got 5, so now it's my turn.	→ Facilitative intervention: Review statement → Supportive intervention: Education
MARK: You got a 4.	
DR. SMITH: That's right, 1-2-3-4.	→ Supportive intervention: Encouragement
MARK: A 6! Now I get to go again! I'll take this guy out.	
DR. SMITH: All right. But you can't move him six spaces too.	→ Supportive intervention: Encouragement, Education
MARK: But I got a 6.	
DR. SMITH: But you know the rules. When you get a 6, you can either take a man out or move six spaces, but not both. You believe that to break the rules is really the way to play.	→ Supportive intervention: Education, Empathy
MARK: Yeah.	
DR. SMITH: You want to take all of my markers. When you play by the rules, a Mr. Greedy is saying that's not the right way.	(→) Directing attention: "Look-at" statement (in the present)
MARK: [Grins, but as it registers that Mr. Greedy is part of him, he yawns.] Go on, go on, play.	

DR. SMITH: Well, I see it is very   (→) Interpretation:
important for Mr. Greedy to   Motive and Defense
win, and that's why he wants to   Facilitative statement:
break all the rules. Shall I play   Invitation to continue
with Mr. Greedy now, or with
Mark?

MARK: [mumbling] Shut up,
with me, of course.

Tactfully, Dr. Smith allows Mark to determine the game to be played, but not the way in which to play it. As often as he attempts to stretch limits and break rules, she gently but firmly reasserts the rules and the limits to his rule breaking. It is important to note that she does this without being punitive or critical. If she had assessed that Mark was not ready for direct limit setting, she might have spoken less directly, adopting the voice of a puppet, for instance. Or she might simply have observed what he was doing and its consequences, letting the game proceed according to Mark's innovations and then commenting on the outcome. In this case she would be assuming the role of an observing ego, narrating the proceedings without rendering judgment.

Regardless of her tactfulness, at some point Mark will inevitably register some frustration at not being able to gratify his infantile wishes to play according to his own rules, thereby assuring himself of control and success. This attempt to control the play and impose rules favorable to themselves is typical of children with a conduct disorder. Much of their desire to control the behavior of others stems from a need to preserve a frail sense of self-esteem. In their world the law of all or nothing prevails; one is either a winner and all-powerful or a nothing, a loser. Therefore, these children need to flaunt their victories, further alienating potential playmates.

At this point in their relationship, Mark assumes that Dr. Smith perceives situations as he does. He wants to win to avoid Dr. Smith's flaunting her victory to him. Note that Mark does not yet confide in Dr. Smith or perceive her to be a helpful ally. Moreover, all information about events outside the treatment—at home, in school, or with friends—is still coming from the parents. At home, Mark has begun to complain to his parents of headaches and of being "no good."

We will rejoin Mark and Dr. Smith in the middle phase of treatment. At this juncture we will summarize the initial phase of SEPP with the child, with a focus on the activities and interventions of the therapist.

Play in the Initial Phase

In this early phase, play is used mainly to help the child become comfortable with the therapy and the therapist. The therapist actively facilitates the play to establish the child's acceptance of her through nonverbal interaction. The play most often consists of games and gross motor play. The kinds of materials the therapist supplies for play are dart games, basketball, toy animals and people, board games, and army toys. In the choice of play materials, the therapist tries to follow the child's lead. The child may request supplies she does not find in the room. It is often helpful to provide a box with the child's name on it to contain supplies specifically for that child. A file cabinet can be used to contain items the child produces and wishes to keep in the room, retrievable at her initiative.

If necessary, the therapist offers the child suggestions on playing the game, learning its rules, and keeping score. This game play may last for several weeks. The therapist should be patient and wait until the child is ready on his own to branch out to more creative and symbolic fantasy play. Themes of play may fluctuate rather than proceed in succession. Sensorimotor play may take on an often repeated theme that gradually becomes symbolic. Examples of this type of activity are ball playing and potion making. For instance, mixing vinegar and baking soda is first enjoyed for its explosive quality and is later integrated into a larger fantasy by the child as a volcano. Magical power may then be attributed either to the mixture or to the potion-maker himself. The therapist is active in supplying materials, making suggestions when necessary, participating, and observing as the child's play unfolds.

Verbal Interventions in the Initial Phase

Five types of verbal interventions are characteristic of the initial phase of SEPP.

Ordinary social behavior

Greetings, leave taking, and everyday courtesies are part of a basic socially appropriate relationship. Greetings are reassuring. The therapist who acts naturally communicates that she is not intimidated or put off by the child's behavior. The view of the therapist we wish the child to have is of a friendly, tolerant, approachable, and nonjudgmental person.

→   Hi, Johnny!

→   Please hand me the hammer.

→   See you next week!

Statements relating to the treatment

Because communications about SEPP are of special significance, we have made them a separate category. The therapist's purposes in talking to the child about treatment are (1) to allay the child's anticipatory anxieties and fears about treatment by providing a predictable setting and clear framework, thus making the unknown known; (2) to invite a special kind of partnership at the child's pace and in accordance with his or her agenda; and (3) to foster the development of patience or tolerance for frustration. To accomplish these goals the therapist delineates the boundaries, rules, domains, and work of therapy, specifying the structure of sessions, the behavioral limits during the sessions, the process of therapy, the child's role, and the roles of the therapist and the parents. The therapist explains session arrangements such as time, place, frequency, and duration. She talks about play activities and the use of toys and materials. Statements or questions relating to the treatment should be concrete in order to be clearly understood.

> We will meet in this room every Tuesday and Thursday at 4:00. I am going to close the door so nobody can hear us.

→   Our time is up for today.

→   You can't break furniture in here.

⇄   I will not let you hurt yourself or me.

⇄   This matter is between you and me.

Requests for factual information

The primary purpose of these verbal interventions is to gain useful information in order to fill gaps in the therapist's knowledge of the child's history and everyday life. In addition, the therapist specifically inquires about the child's perspective, to obtain insight into his individual circumstances and point of view. These inquiries facilitate the therapist's conduct of the treatment and enhance communication by conveying to the child that he can be a reliable source of information. Furthermore, they give the child the opportunity to clarify issues about himself and his experience with others.

→   Was that when you were in third or fourth grade?

→   Who is the boy you were fighting with?

→   How many cousins do you have?

The therapist must exercise tact and sensitivity by not inquiring into areas the child may not yet be able to share. The purpose of these interventions is to begin to weave the fabric of a life story, but not all the threads may yet be available.

Supportive interventions

We define three subgroups of supportive statements: (1) education; (2) suggestion; and (3) encouragement, reassurance, and empathy. Although all three modes of verbal intervention—direct, indirect, and therapist-related—may be used, in these initial stages the indirect is employed most often.

Education serves to supply factual information, to correct misinformation on matters other than treatment or to teach new skills.

→   You can build a fort bigger and bigger if you put the blocks this way.

(→)   It is dangerous for the princess to climb on the castle rock.

←   Yes, I always wear glasses.

Suggestion refers to the therapist's introduction, at her own initiative, of ideas, alternatives, or courses of action that the child might take. Suggestions serve to broaden the child's awareness of alternatives and possibilities for problem solving and provide opportunities to break old patterns. They encourage cooperation, thereby promoting the working alliance and fostering a positive attitude toward adult authority.

→   Let's see the new toy soldiers.

(→)   Maybe if Lion smiled in a really friendly way, Bear wouldn't feel so scared.

⇄*   You know what I do? I don't hit back if somebody hits me. I tell them to stop it. What about trying that?

Encouragement implies the suggestion to repeat an approved action. Reassurance refers to the therapist's recognition and expressed approval of the child's thoughts and actions. It confirms the child's own inclinations, relieves his uncertainties, and reinforces his own suggestions to himself. Empathy refers to the way the therapist resonates with the child's thoughts and feelings by labeling or echoing the child's affect, as the therapist perceives it. Encouragement, reassurance, and empathy frequently appear together in the therapeutic process, hence we have considered them as one category.

$\rightarrow$ Look how well that turned out, and you thought you couldn't do it.

$\rightarrow$ You really felt grossed out!

$(\rightarrow)$ It was okay for the frog to cry when his best friend Rabbit died.

$\leftarrow$ Gee, it was really great that you noticed I had a cold.

$\rightleftarrows$*   I feel sad, too, just like you.

Facilitative interventions

The overall goal of these statements is to foster and maintain a flow of interactions between the therapist and the patient. The therapist initiates, enhances, or maintains the exchange with the child through (1) invitations to continue and (2) review statements.

Invitations to continue convey the therapist's ongoing interest and encourage talking rather than acting. They also provide continuity within and between sessions. The therapist may verbally initiate play activity or conversation or instruct the child to go on, without giving specific directions. Another way of inviting the child to continue is to request expansion or additional information on a specific topic after it has been introduced or discussed by the child.

$\rightarrow$ Oh, hmmm . . . I see.

$\rightarrow$ What are you thinking about?

$\rightarrow$ And then?

$\leftarrow$ Tell me more!

$(\rightarrow)$ The frog really wants to hear more.

$\leftarrow$ What about my broken eyeglasses?

$\leftarrow$ What else are you thinking about me?

Review statements support the synthetic function of the ego and model sequential, logical thinking. In her review statements, the therapist paraphrases, summarizes, or integrates what the child has said or done.

→   So, in class today it was hard to learn the times table.

(→*) Now I know all the things that made Bear start a fight.

←   So you've been telling me the things I do wrong. I butt in and I talk too much.

These five major categories of verbal interventions by the therapist also appear in the middle and termination stages of treatment, but in the initial stage they are in the foreground. In the middle and termination phases, they form the background for other interventions that are characteristic of the later phases, which are described in chapters 3 and 4.

3

The Middle Phase of Treatment

T HE transition to the middle phase occurs in different ways with different children and at different rates, depending upon the nature of the developing therapeutic relationship. In general, however, the indications that the middle phase has been reached are clear.

Perhaps the most important sign of progress to the middle phase is that the child communicates in some way that he has established an alliance with the therapist in the pursuit of treatment. This alliance between therapist and child does not mean that every session runs smoothly. Rather, it becomes clear from the child's demeanor and actions in the therapist's presence that he is coming to view the therapeutic process as worthwhile and the therapist as a valued person. The therapist, in turn, has come to know her patient and has developed a regard for him as an individual. This growing attachment between therapist and child implies that a therapeutic structure is emerging that will promote further exploration and creative activity. This attachment structure is facilitated by the stabilization of parental support and the child's progressive confidence in the reliability of the therapeutic setting. The physical factors that contribute to this feeling of constancy include a regular schedule and a consistent time and place for the sessions. The psychological factors that remain invariant include the therapist's attitudes and conduct in the treatment.

As this bond between therapist and child patient is strengthened, the child begins to respond more actively to the therapist's interventions. The form of their relationship acquires the constancy and resilience of an ongoing structure, in which both members are joined in an alliance toward therapeutic progress.

When the middle phase has been reached, the therapist can begin to work toward expanding the child's awareness of his behavior, feelings, and thoughts—facilitating his capacity to play and to express himself in fantasy. By developing his capacity to verbalize, the child improves his ability to express his feelings in a more adaptive and modulated way. This work is referred to as *working through the issues of treatment.*

The following session with Dr. Smith and Mark clearly signals the onset of the middle phase of treatment. To prepare Mark for ending the session and returning at the next appointment time, Dr. Smith mentions to him that their time together for that day is growing short.

DR. SMITH: We have about ten minutes left, Mark, and then we will have to stop for today.	→ Statement relating to the treatment
MARK: Why?	
DR. SMITH: Well, you remember, we meet twice a week for 45 minutes each time. [Mark nods.]	→ Statement relating to the treatment
DR. SMITH: Well, our 45 minutes is almost over for today.	→ Statement relating to the treatment
MARK: Do you have other kids you see?	
DR. SMITH: Do you mean, do I play with other children as I've been playing with you?	← Supportive intervention: Suggestion
MARK: Yeah.	
DR. SMITH: Well, I'll be glad to answer that if you can help me out by telling me what makes you curious about that.	⇄* Facilitative intervention: Invitation to continue
MARK: I don't know. . . . I just thought of it.	

DR. SMITH: I wonder if you asked   ← Interpretation:
that because you thought I was   Motive
going to see someone else after
you left and that's why we had
to stop?

MARK: Yeah, I did think that.

DR. SMITH: Did you also imagine   ← Interpretation:
that if I weren't going to see   Motive
someone else, maybe you could
stay longer and we could play
some more?

MARK: [eagerly] Could we?

DR. SMITH: No, I'm afraid we   → Statement about the treatment
couldn't. Even if I were not see-
ing someone else soon, and even
though we would be having
fun, we would have to stop.

MARK: [puzzled] But, why?

DR. SMITH: Because doctors like   → Statement about the treatment
myself, Mark, who try to help
children with their worries,
have found that we can be most
helpful if we make sure that visits occur regularly for a set
amount of time. So we don't let
the visits go on a lot longer, and
we also don't end them sooner
than the set time. Even if we
were not having a good time
and you were upset with me for
some reason, I'd want us to have
our full 45 minutes.

MARK: How come?

DR. SMITH: Because I would know there was something upsetting you and it would be important for us to talk about it. You see, Mark, we play here, but we also talk. Talking helps because it helps us to understand what's upsetting you and what we can do about it. If we talk and understand it better, I can help you find some ways of feeling better without doing something that gets you into trouble.

→ Statement about the treatment

MARK: You mean like hitting my sister when I'm mad at her?

DR. SMITH: Exactly! That's just what I mean. So when you come back again, maybe we can talk about what kinds of things do bother you. Right now we have to pick up the toys because it is time to stop.

→ Supportive intervention: Encouragement
→ Statement about the treatment

In this segment, Dr. Smith readdresses the issues of limits and the purpose of treatment. It is clear that Mark is growing attached to her and has concerns regarding exclusivity as well as separation. Dr. Smith attempts to explore these themes, but because time is short and Mark is not yet able to articulate his thoughts about these feelings, she focuses on one aspect of his feelings—his wish to remain in her presence. She knows that if this wish were indulged, it would violate the defined boundaries of treatment. Dr. Smith alerts Mark to the presence of this wish, but at this juncture she does not delve into the more primitive aspects of Mark's thinking and feeling for her. To interpret his deeper wish to be with her all the time to the exclusion of others would overwhelm him and would unsettle the therapeutic process at this moment. Instead, Dr. Smith draws Mark's attention to his wish and notes to herself the absorption this child has with attachments and separation. She wonders how these issues will continue to manifest themselves in play and language as the treatment progresses.

Dr. Smith gives Mark an opportunity to describe and amplify his reasons for asking about other children at that particular time. She does so by responding to Mark's question with another question, but not an open-ended one. His response is typical of impulsive children: "I don't know. . . . I just thought of it." Dr. Smith then offers him a plausible explanation for acting as he did, touching on his wish for exclusivity but not divulging the more unconscious features of his wish. Mark finds it comfortable to acknowledge his desire to continue playing without feeling threatened by more disturbing competitive wishes related to his growing attachment for Dr. Smith and a wish to have her all to himself. These wishes will be expressed in their own time as it becomes clear to Mark that other people (especially other children) constitute a barrier to his fulfilling his wish for exclusivity. This wish will be expressed within the transference relationship; its origins will be traced to relationships within Mark's family.

Working with the Child

Play

Erik Erikson (1950) described latency—the school-age period—as an age of industry. The child is engaged in play that is also his work. Play and work meld as the child becomes the producer of various products and the performer of tasks that are essential for survival within a given society. To the extent that the child is sufficiently free of more primitive impulses and feelings, he is able to invest his energies into these relatively neutral, conflict-free tasks (Hartmann 1958). In the middle phase of SEPP, play comes increasingly to approximate the age-appropriate play expected of the latency-aged child (Sarnoff 1976).

In the middle phase of treatment, the therapist facilitates a shift in the child's play from structured materials such as board games to materials that provide more opportunity for the child to express his thoughts and feelings and to elaborate fantasy themes. For example, the therapist initiates and participates in play activities that do not have set form and rules but involve imaginary play. Toy cars, prehistoric animals, clay, and paper and crayons are used to create possibilities for imaginary events, such as accidents, family trips, and traffic jams. As the child begins to develop his own imaginative use of these materials, the therapist guides him and adapts to him.

During this phase, the child in treatment is beginning to free himself of his egocentric stance and to understand the ideas and feelings of others. Developmental psychology, based on naturalistic observations (Dunn 1988), affords us a framework for the facilitation and emergence of these new capacities in treatment (Fonagy 1989). The child proceeds along a developmental line (A. Freud 1965) from egocentricity to socialization as he acquires the following abilities: (1) understanding others' feelings (Stern 1985; Katan 1961; Bretherton et al. 1981; A. Freud and Burlingham 1944; Radke-Yarrow et al. 1983); (2) understanding others' intentions (Dunn 1988; Kennedy at al. 1985); (3) understanding rules and conventions (Kagan 1981, 1984); and (4) understanding that others have minds and can think thoughts and experience feelings independently (Dunn 1988). This final acquisition, the awareness of mental states as separate from physical realities, has been suggested as the prerequisite for pretend play. George S. Moran (1987) has defined playfulness in terms of the child's pleasure at intentionally blurring the boundary between fantasy and shared reality.

The child patient thus comes to a full realization of his capacity to play, to change and express his feelings within the context of an "as-if" world of which he is the primary creator. His co-producer is the therapist, who charts his progress, mirrors his mental states, and actively participates in the play when invited, while at all times keeping the play setting as a secure and safe place to be.

Verbal Interventions

Ordinary social behavior

Certainly, this behavior continues as in the initial phase of treatment. Greetings to the child and other social interchanges remain essentially unchanged.

Statements related to treatment

In the middle phase, this intervention is expected to decrease significantly. Continuing interventions relating to the treatment might, however, be needed to complete or clarify prior information or to fill in omissions. Statements or replies related to the treatment may be responses to the child's having forgotten the explanation given in the initial phase. This forgetfulness might be an expression of the child's wishes to control the therapist or his opposition to the limits implicit in the therapeutic setting.

Requests for factual information

By the middle phase of therapy, the therapist's inquiries about the biographical aspects of the child's life have significantly decreased, to be replaced by inquiries about what is now happening in the child's experiences outside the therapy sessions. Thus, although the frequency of these inquiries may be unchanged, their content shifts to current concerns relevant to the therapist's treatment focus. For example, the therapist would need to know the specific details of a shoplifting episode in order to work on it with the child in the sessions.

Supportive interventions

Statements that provide education, suggestion, encouragement, reassurance, and empathy continue from the initial phase of treatment. Again, however, their content shifts as treatment themes expand, ranging from dealing with friends, to sexual or masturbatory activities, to using computers or electronic toys. The therapist is often in a role similar to that of a teacher-coach as she makes supportive interventions.

⇄*   You know why I think you've been having trouble sleeping and have a hard time going to the bathroom at night? I think it's because when you touch your penis at night, it gets hard. Then you have to wait till your penis gets back to its regular size to go to the bathroom. This happens to all boys.

→   What about trying to show this other kid your own collection of baseball cards? You could suggest a trade so he could see your collection and you could see his collection. That's a way you could get started with him.

⇄*   (After the same child reports that he was able to trade a few cards with the boy sitting next to him at school.) You see you could do it, and I think you did it very well. I'm very glad that you did it, and I bet it will be even easier next time.

Facilitative interventions

Because they serve both to convey concretely the therapist's ongoing interest and to enhance the child's ability to talk about himself, invitations to continue and review statements increase in frequency in the middle phase. Now that the therapist has become better acquainted with the child's problems and has developed a relationship with the child, she can use facilitative statements extensively to expand the child's awareness of the themes involved.

→   Tell me more about how you felt when you weren't invited to Johnny's last birthday party.

Invitations to continue are often mixed with suggestions and encouragement.

→ Let's think about what you can do so maybe it won't happen again this year.

Review statements are often followed by suggestions. In the following example, the therapist might suggest looking for alternatives.

→ You've been telling me today that you don't want to talk about it; that I should shut up; that you don't want to think about it and you want to do something else; and that you try to forget about it.

Directing attention

These interventions are aimed at readying the child for later interpretations. They are perhaps the most characteristic interventions of the middle phase.

Preparatory statements alert the child to an interpretation to follow and are designed to enhance the child's self-observation and his interest in discovering that his thoughts, actions, and feelings are potentially meaningful.

←* Would you like to know my idea about why you get into so many fights?

"Look-at" statements are aimed at enhancing the child's awareness of aspects of his behavior and helping him focus his attention on particular types of behaviors, feelings, or thoughts. They may refer to immediate behavior taking place in the session or to behavior outside the session, either in the child's current experience or in the past.

⇄ While you were talking to me, did you notice that you were kicking the chair very hard?

→ Did you notice that when your mother came to pick you up last time, you didn't feel like going with her right away?

"See-the-pattern" statements take the child's attention a step further, showing him meaningful aspects of his behaviors. These statements may focus also on the present or the past, on the session itself, or on experiences outside the session.

(→) Have you noticed that each time you start playing Cowboys and Indians, you suddenly have to go to the bathroom?

←   Each time you say that you're winning, you think I'm going to be
     very mad at you and spoil your victory.

Here-and-now interpretations

The prior interventions, particularly the last, have been setting the stage
for interpretations. In this mode of therapy, the focus of interpretations is
most frequently on the relationship and interaction with the therapist in
the sessions, especially negative interactions that interfere with the work.
These kinds of interpretations, commonly called here-and-now interpretations, are most likely to occur late in the middle phase of treatment. With
conduct disordered children, the use of interpretations is generally limited
because these children have difficulty seeing themselves as contributing to
their problems, and instead, tend to externalize the source of the difficulty.
Interpretations are aimed at solving internal sources of problem behavior
and require some minimal capacity for introspection and seeing oneself in
perspective.

   Different levels of verbal interventions occur during the middle phase,
depending on a specific child's individual needs. Because interpretive
statements can best be understood in context, larger excerpts will be
used as examples. The first example is drawn from the first year of
treatment with a child seen once a week. Michael, nine years old, has
stolen $200 from his mother's purse. His older brother informs the ther-
apist that Michael has not told his parents about the theft, although
three weeks have elapsed. The therapist's goals involve building up Michael's superego.

MICHAEL: I told my parents, but
   they didn't listen. I don't want
   to talk about that. Now can we
   play? [pushes older brother out
   the door]
THERAPIST: This is so serious, I   → Directing attention:
   don't feel I can play with you   "Look-at" statement (in the
   until we can solve this problem.   present)
MICHAEL: I took the money. I'll
   give it back now.
THERAPIST: How?   → Facilitative intervention:
                                               Invitation to continue

MICHAEL: [hesitates] My parents
   don't care. They will forget
   about it [not entirely untrue].

THERAPIST: Let's follow that idea and put it in writing. When you stole the money—

→ Facilitative intervention: Invitation to continue

MICHAEL: [corrects therapist] Took the money.

THERAPIST: If you took the money without the person knowing, that's stealing.

→ Supportive intervention: Education

MICHAEL: [proceeds to write] "Dear Mother, I stole $200 from your wallet on April 19 . . ."

THERAPIST: How are you going to repay it?

→ Directing attention: "Look-at" statement (in the present)

MICHAEL: From my allowance. No, from doing chores.

THERAPIST: What chores? How much a week?

→ Directing attention: "Look-at" statement (in the present)

MICHAEL: Taking the garbage out, walking the dog, washing laundry . . . [impatiently] I can't think of anything else.

THERAPIST: Let's write it down.

→ Supportive intervention: Suggestion

During the last fifteen minutes of the session, Michael plays "Bad Guy," who is followed by the police. The therapist and patient then exchange roles, with the therapist being the thief and the child playing the police.

THERAPIST: Michael, you are more of the "Bad Guy" when you steal, but you also know the "police" so well. If you could just ask the "police" part of your mind to watch out for the "thief" part, you would feel much better inside.

(→) Directing attention: "Look-at" statement (in the present)

(→) Supportive intervention: Suggestion Encouragement

MICHAEL: [listens] I like to come here. I haven't been here for a while.

In the second example we rejoin Mark and Dr. Smith in the middle phase of treatment. In these segments we will follow the therapist's use of facilitative statements as well as statements directing the child's attention to aspects of his behavior and their possible meaning.

DR. SMITH: I notice that you've decided to draw again. It seems as if whenever we play a game and I won't play according to your rules, you start to draw. [Mark does not answer.] Perhaps today you would like to play a drawing game with me?	→ Directing attention: "See-the-pattern"
	← Supportive intervention: Suggestion
MARK: [looks up from drawing] Maybe . . . What's it like?	

This "maybe" is a notable departure from Mark's usually unqualified refusal.

DR. SMITH: It's like this: once I make a squiggle, you have to turn it into something. You can make it whatever you like, and then you tell me something about it. When it's my turn, you make a squiggle and I have to turn it into something and tell you about it. Okay? [Mark nods.]	→ Supportive intervention: Education Suggestion

One of the significant aspects of Winnicott's squiggle technique (1971) is its reciprocity. The child is an active participant in the process, giving the therapist ample opportunity to reflect on his own unconscious associations to the interaction.

DR. SMITH: Good. Let's start. I'll make one first.	→ Supportive intervention: Encouragement Suggestion
MARK: Can I turn it around?	
DR. SMITH: Sure. Any way you would like.	→ Supportive intervention: Encouragement Reassurance

MARK: [after a pause, during which he examines the squiggle from several different angles] It's a boot, and it's about to kick somebody.

DR. SMITH: What makes it want to do that?

(→) Directing attention: "Look-at" statement (in the present)

MARK: It's trying to walk somewhere, and somebody got in its way.

DR. SMITH: Where was it going?

(→) Directing attention: "Look-at" statement (in the present)

MARK: Up a mountain—to the top.

DR. SMITH: That was good, Mark. Now you make one.

→ Supportive intervention: Encouragement Suggestion

MARK: [draws a dark, heavy squiggle] Let's see you make something out of that [sounds triumphant].

DR. SMITH: It sounds as if you're hoping I won't be able to. Do you feel that way?

← Directing attention: Preparatory statement
→ Facilitative intervention: Invitation to continue

MARK: I don't know.

DR. SMITH: Maybe you hope it will be hard for me and your drawing will be better than mine?

← Directing attention:
→ Preparatory statement

MARK: Yep.

DR. SMITH: I guess you're thinking of this game as one you can win?

→ Supportive intervention: Empathy

MARK: Well, if you can't draw anything, mine is better.

DR. SMITH: Not really, Mark. The idea of the game is to use our imaginations. There is no winner. But let's see what I could do with that. [draws] It's a hand reaching out.

→ Supportive intervention: Education
←* Directing attention:
(→) "Look-at" statement (in the present)

MARK: Is it going to grab someone?

DR. SMITH: What do you think?

→ Facilitative intervention: Invitation to continue

MARK: Yeah, and then it's going to squeeze them.

DR. SMITH: Why would it want to do that?

(→) Facilitative intervention: Invitation to continue

MARK: To stop them from doing it to them first.

DR. SMITH: Sounds like you think it's worried about being attacked.

(→) Supportive intervention: Empathy

MARK: Yeah.

DR. SMITH: Well, I thought about it a little differently. I thought the hand was trying to help someone get up because they had fallen down.

←* Supportive intervention: Suggestion
←* Directing attention:
(→) "Look-at" statement (in the present)

MARK: Oh . . .

DR. SMITH: Do you think that is possible?

(→) Facilitative intervention: Invitation to continue

MARK: Maybe . . . let's do another. [Dr. Smith draws a squiggle.] That's easy [draws quickly]. It's a gun like policemen wear.

DR. SMITH: Why do police wear guns, do you think?

→ Facilitative intervention: Invitation to continue

MARK: To protect themselves, silly!

DR. SMITH: Not to hurt people?

→ Facilitative intervention: Invitation to continue

MARK: Well, not mostly . . . [seems uncertain]. Sometimes they hurt people, but only if somebody tries to hurt them, or doesn't listen to them. Mainly it's to protect them from bad guys.

DR. SMITH: You know, Mark, I have an idea that these squiggles tell a bit about you.

←* Directing attention: (→) Preparatory statement

MARK: What do you mean?

DR. SMITH: Well, I think sometimes you feel very angry when you can't do what you want, and maybe you feel so angry at me when I won't play with you when you cheat, you feel like kicking me because I won't let you come out on top.

⇄* Directing attention: "See-the-pattern"
← Interpretation: Motive, Defense

MARK: You mean like the boot?

DR. SMITH: Exactly! Did you notice yourself feeling that way, a little while ago?

→ Supportive intervention: Reassurance
→ Directing attention: "Look-at" statement (in the present)

MARK: Oh, I always feel that way when you won't let me win. That's why I draw.

DR. SMITH: Why is that?

→ Facilitative intervention: Invitation to continue

MARK: [with anger] Because you can't mess it up and tell me I am wrong.

DR. SMITH: Is that why you haven't wanted to draw what I've suggested and won't answer any questions when I ask you about your drawings?

← Interpretation: Defense, Motive

MARK: That's right.

DR. SMITH: But you agreed to play squiggles today.

→ Directing attention: "Look-at" statement (in the present)

DR. SMITH: How come?   → Facilitative intervention:
                                           Invitation to continue

MARK: I don't know. . . . I guess
I wasn't as mad as before.
DR. SMITH: I think that's right. I   ←* Supportive intervention:
think also that maybe you felt it   Reassurance
was okay to play with me today.   ⇄* Directing attention:
                                            "Look-at" statement (in the
                                            present)

MARK: Yeah, I did.
DR. SMITH: But maybe you   ← Directing attention:
weren't so sure it was all right to   "Look-at" statement (in the
trust me?   present)
MARK: Why do you think that?
DR. SMITH: Because you thought   (→) Interpretation: Motive
that the hand was going to grab   ← Directing attention:
and hurt someone, not help   "Look-at" statement (in the
them. Then you told me that the   present)
gun was like a policeman's and
he needs that to protect himself.
Maybe, sometimes, I seem like a
policeman, because I tell you
what the rules are here. Maybe
you were feeling a little nervous
about playing this game with me.
MARK: Well, I didn't know what
you were going to do.
DR. SMITH: What did you imag-   → Facilitative intervention:
ine I might do?   Invitation to continue
MARK: I don't know . . . maybe
stab me with the pencil.
DR. SMITH: Did you think I   ← Directing attention:
wanted to hurt you?   "Look-at" statement (in the
                                            present)

MARK: No . . . but you could
have.
DR. SMITH: Have you ever felt   ← Directing attention:
that way toward me?   "Look-at" statement (in the past)

MARK: Oh, sure. But I don't do it.
I draw instead.

Dr. Smith: Yes, you do. And that's a very good way to keep yourself from acting angry and hurtful to me. Maybe you thought when I wanted to do a drawing game with you that I felt the way you do when you draw, and that I wanted to hurt you?

Mark: Yeah, I did.

→ Supportive intervention: Reassurance

← Interpretation: Defense Motive

In this session the therapist helps Mark to verbalize feelings that heretofore have been inaccessible to shared communication. Moreover, the use of "look-at" statements facilitates the reciprocal interaction between therapist and child and enhances the growth of mutual trust. Clearly, considerable therapeutic groundwork, carefully laid, has preceded these gains and made them possible.

Our third example of the use of interpretation in the middle phase of treatment involves a nine-year-old child who is both disruptive and driven to activity. He has a history of impulsive behavior and distractibility, which began in the middle of his second year, the rapprochement period (Mahler et al. 1975). We have chosen this child to illustrate the use of SEPP with a relatively nonverbal child. The treatment depends heavily upon the therapist's empathic attunement and resonance with the child. The child assimilates the therapist's verbal interpretations but gives feedback primarily through nonverbal cues, such as expressive body movements and facial gestures.

Jeremy, a student in the fourth grade, is in his third year of psychotherapy. The frequency of sessions, twice a week during the first year, was increased to three times a week in the second year when aggressive behavior at school and at home became unacceptable. Jeremy, the eldest of three children, all boys, was referred for treatment when the youngest child was seven months old. Reportedly, his uncontrollable outbursts increased at the time of the youngest child's birth, and they continued to worsen throughout the first year of treatment. At the time of this session, Jeremy is exhibiting better control in the classroom and has begun to make several friends, who admire him for his athletic abilities and knowledge of sports.

Jeremy experiences deep-seated feelings of deprivation. He has never felt he receives enough nurturance, and he is very attached to concrete objects and adamant about winning games, particularly chess. His anxiety about receiving adequate love is linked to a fear of loss. Not only does he need to hold on to things because of low emotional supplies, but he also fears losing what he has acquired and therefore needs to "keep score" of his acquisitions. The week before this session, Jeremy suffered the loss of his beloved grandfather, and the day before, he attended the funeral. It was a poignant session filled with intense feeling.

THERAPIST: How are you, Jeremy? [Jeremy nods and sits down, with a sad expression on his face.]	→ Ordinary social behavior
I wanted to speak with you about Grandpa. If we could talk, it might be better.	⇄* Supportive intervention: Suggestion Encouragement
JEREMY: I don't think about him all the time, only now and then.	
THERAPIST: Can you tell me how he died?	→ Directing attention: "Look-at" statement (in the past)
JEREMY: He couldn't breathe. Can a body move after it is dead? Maybe it could a little, like fish in water. It wouldn't have helped to put in an artificial heart.	
THERAPIST: What could his body do?	→ Directing attention: "Look-at" statement (in the past)
JEREMY: He couldn't think. He'd just be a . . .	
THERAPIST: When something is dead, it cannot move by itself. It cannot talk.	→ Supportive intervention: Education
JEREMY: Not at all.	
THERAPIST: That's why it is so scary—it does not respond. The person does not need his body anymore. It is dead. Did you see the body?	→ Supportive intervention: Education → Direction attention: "Look-at" statement (in the past)
JEREMY: No, it was . . . I don't like to say the word . . .	
THERAPIST: Cremated?	→ Supportive intervention: Education
JEREMY: My Grandma has the . . .	
THERAPIST: Ashes . . .	→ Supportive intervention: Education

JEREMY: In a little box. They are deciding what to do with it.

THERAPIST: It is sad that Grandpa has died, and all there are left are ashes. Do you have memories, too?

→ Supportive intervention: Empathy

→ Directing attention: "Look-at" statement (in the present)

JEREMY: I remember when I was very little, three or four; my preschool was across the street from his apartment. I rode horses by his house. They have a good bakery there.

THERAPIST: What else do you remember now about Grandpa?

→ Directing attention: "Look-at" statement (in the present)

JEREMY: He smoked a pipe. He used to like the Cardinals. We sometimes watched baseball together. He taught me to play solitaire.

THERAPIST: You shared many things, and now you have those memories.

→ Directing attention: "See-the-pattern" statement (in the past and present)

JEREMY: [takes nerf ball and starts to shoot baskets] Yea. I also have another Grandpa. He is eighty-two. He had better live until my graduation, or I'll . . . [continues to shoot baskets].

THERAPIST: You stopped because you are afraid of how angry you could be if he died before your graduation. [Jeremy grins as if in recognition.] It seems as if you are so angry with your other Grandpa for dying. It is almost as if he went away and you got so angry about his leaving you that you began to think your anger might have killed him.

→ Interpretation: Defense Motive

JEREMY: Well, [softly] it is hard missing him. All those people were crying. All I could think of was how much I missed him.

THERAPIST: He was really important in your life. There is so much you will miss.
→ Direction attention: "Look-at" statement (in the past and future)

JEREMY: But . . . my other Grandpa . . . I hope he will live to be a hundred. Maybe he could live to be a hundred.

THERAPIST: You want your other Grandpa to be with you for a long, long time.
→ Supportive intervention: Empathy

JEREMY: [Jeremy picks up a puzzle and starts to put it together.] This is hard.

THERAPIST: Perhaps you would like to draw. [Jeremy draws a picture of many flowers.] All of those flowers look like many memories. They are not just one memory, but many memories. [Jeremy becomes teary-eyed and sits closer to the therapist.] Memories of eating chicken soup, of watching baseball, of pipes smoking [a faint smile from Jeremy], of playing cards, and much more.
→ Supportive intervention: Suggestion
(→) Interpretation: Motive
Facilitative intervention: Review statement

JEREMY: I can't remember.

THERAPIST: It will take time. You are very, very sad. Maybe later on you will have more memories.
→ Supportive intervention: Education, Empathy, Suggestion

JEREMY: I want to draw another picture.

THERAPIST: Then it will be time to leave.
→ Statement about the treatment

JEREMY: [draws quickly] This is a picture of a champion—a Cardinal champion—that is my Grandpa! See you.

In this clinical segment, the therapist is able to give the child active support as he searches for words to verbalize his grief. By connecting with the child in this way, she helps him control impulsive expression and gives him access to ideation by providing information and labeling experience. The therapist also facilitates the child's recall and his formation of associations between thoughts and events. Words are linked with feelings when the therapist points out to the child his underlying anger as well as his sadness, which are his immediate reactions to the loss of a loved one. It is important to note that Jeremy is beginning to deal with issues of loss that will prepare him to cope with ending the treatment. Jeremy's dealing with his intense feelings with the therapist and his openness to the interpretation of his feelings are indications of work in the late middle phase of treatment. What remains is to consolidate these therapeutic gains before the process of termination can begin.

Working with the Parents

Strengthening the Collaborative Alliance

By the middle phase of treatment, through direct explanations, but more important, through the example of how the therapist has been working with them, the parents come increasingly to feel like part of the team working to help their child.

The following clinical excerpt demonstrates the emergence of parental trust in the therapist in the middle phase of SEPP.

Dr. Smith has been meeting with Mark's parents twice a month for three months to conduct parental counseling sessions, which parallel their son's individual treatment. As we join them, Dr. Smith is continuing to explore specific events within the family that occurred at the outbreak of Mark's disruptive behavior.

DR. SMITH: Did anything happen to anyone in the family two to three years ago?
MRS. HOWSER: [looking reflective but puzzled] Hmmm . . .
MR. HOWSER: [who has been silent] How can you have forgotten?

MRS. HOWSER: [irritably] Forgotten what? Oh, my mother died about
. . . oh, almost three years ago. Well, maybe not three years, maybe two
years and nine months. [She looks shaken, and her lower lip quivered.]
It is . . . [slightly tearful]. I was very close to my mother. She helped me
a good deal.

DR. SMITH: When you say that she helped you, did she help you taking
care of your children?

MRS. HOWSER: Oh, yes! She was a big help, especially with Mark. And he
was very fond of her.

DR. SMITH: So, it must have been very upsetting for all of you when she
died.

MR. HOWSER: It was more than upsetting to my wife, Dr. Smith. She was
bonded like glue to her mother, who was a tireless person. Her mother
was always ready to help out at a moment's notice. She lived very close
to us and was at the house very often. It was a blow to all of us when
she died; it happened so suddenly.

DR. SMITH: It was a terrible loss for all of you.

MRS. HOWSER: I was overwhelmed.

MR. HOWSER: That is putting it mildly. It was as if Joan was stricken with
a disease. She could barely get out of bed. She cried all the time . . . had
no energy . . . and absolutely couldn't cope with the children. They, of
course, were impossible. The little one didn't really know what was
going on, but Mark did. He was very close to his grandmother, and so
it was hard for him to understand what had happened. But . . . more than
that, it seemed as if his mother now wanted nothing to do with him.

MRS. HOWSER: I think he was hurt and upset by my reaction to Mom's
death. I was so tired and preoccupied with my own thoughts.

DR. SMITH: How soon after your mother's death did you notice that the
children were beginning to fight?

MR. HOWSER: Well, they had always fought, but it got worse. It was as if
they were trying to get my attention.

DR. SMITH: How did you react to that?

MRS. HOWSER: I generally tried to ignore it.

MR. HOWSER: But if your mother was over, it was a different story.

DR. SMITH: What was different?

MR. HOWSER: Well, Mom, she tended to . . . indulge Mark. He was her first
grandchild, and if he was being difficult, for instance, she'd say to him
in that way of hers, "Oh, Markey. What's the matter?" And he'd usually
relent and tell her.

MRS. HOWSER: Then, she'd usually give in to him—give him what he asked
for. I'd say to her, "Mom, that's not the way to teach him discipline."
But she'd ignore me. She'd say, "One little cookie. Is that so terrible?

And it makes him so happy." There was no arguing with her once she had made up her mind.

DR. SMITH: She sounds a bit like Mark in that regard.

MRS. HOWSER: In that way, yes. But it got so that Mark would listen only to her, not to me.

DR. SMITH: So when she died suddenly, it must have been hard for Mark.

MRS. HOWSER: Yes, I guess it was.

In this clinical material we can clearly see that Dr. Smith has gained the trust of the parents. She is working with them in a collaborative alliance to understand the factors that led up to Mark's current difficulties. As the parents begin to understand the underlying issues, they become better equipped to deal with the changes that are needed. It is of note that a major issue in Mark's case, as well as in Jeremy's, is the death of a loved one. In Mark's case, the loss was an important etiological factor. In Jeremy's case, it was an event that occurred during treatment and acted to illuminate current therapeutic process.

Although we are dealing here with losses of important persons, losses can also occur in the form of loss of expectations about a loved one, loss of personal competencies or expectations about the self, or loss in the physical surround, such as a move to a new home and neighborhood. In each instance, what is involved is the child's perceptions of the important persons in his life and the nature of his attachment to them. These continuities and discontinuities in the life of the child are the focus of the middle phase of treatment. In the parallel process of parent counseling, the parents work through the issues that concern the child and confront them in a way they were unable to do previously without professional guidance.

Maintaining Support for the Treatment

In all phases of treatment, the first priority of work with the parents is to maintain the collaborative alliance. In the middle phase of treatment, the alliance can be threatened in two opposite ways. On the one hand, treatment forces self-awareness that can be difficult to accept. As the child becomes uncomfortable, he may well protest, try to avoid sessions, voice antagonism toward the therapist, and raise other objections to therapy. The therapist must help the parents to tolerate this negativism and understand what is causing it. Often it is helpful to alert the parents to this possibility before it happens. Having a warning helps them to perceive the resistance as something anticipated and expectable, rather than as an untoward problem.

An opposite challenge to the parents' support of treatment is not uncommon when the child's behavior begins to improve. Parents frequently view this improvement as a sign that successful therapy has been accomplished and expect that therapy will end or at least diminish in frequency of sessions. Helping them to understand the gradual and uneven nature of behavioral change and the need for consolidation of new patterns is an often recurring aspect of work in the middle phase of treatment.

Keeping Informed

Another reason to meet with parents regularly is to keep the therapist informed. Even children who are more verbal and self-observing than these action-oriented children characteristically do not tend to keep their therapists informed about their daily lives. The parents are vital informants, though often they need to be educated about what information is important. They readily report problems and crises, but they may not recognize events such as the father's taking a business trip or a grandparent's sudden hospitalization as relevant.

Teaching Parenting Skills

The other dominant focus in this phase of treatment is on enhancing the parents' ability to parent. Many of the suggestions and procedures described in Part II, Parent Training, are relevant to this work with the parents. The techniques used vary, depending on the parents' capacities, style, and pathology. They range from concrete suggestions and strategies to teaching the parents attunement to their own and their child's feelings. Here the therapist uses her general knowledge of child development. The parents are not dealt with as patients in psychotherapy, but as their relationship with, and trust in, the therapist grows, it is not uncommon for the personal and marital concerns that color their relationship with their child to emerge.

Usually the therapist works with the parents in an array of educative efforts and facilitative interventions, and only rarely with interpretive interventions. Interpretive statements might well be used, however, if parents become disillusioned or discouraged with the therapy and begin to express their dissatisfaction in ways that interfere with the treatment, such as bringing the child to appointments late or missing appointments altogether. In such circumstances, tactful interpretation is necessary and frequently helpful. For example, the therapist might comment:

It is understandable that as you feel under stress because of your job and your husband's problems, you might in part feel that Johnny is getting all the attention and yet is not getting better as fast as you would wish.

As the parents' skills in parenting improve, a major shift occurs: the parents become increasingly active in initiating and designing strategies. The frequency with which the therapist initiates and designs new strategies decreases as the parents become more confident and have a clearer understanding of the importance of consistency, clarity, and nonpunitive authoritativeness. The most common themes of the work with the parents involve providing a more secure structure and consistency in daily family activities and living patterns, maintaining clarity in verbal messages, being firm but nonpunitive in limit setting, and providing emotional rewards, praise, and empathy for good behavior. In most cases, the parents of conduct disorder children have been focusing almost exclusively on misbehavior. When the child starts being good, they are so relieved that they unwittingly ignore him.

As both parents and child continue to make and consolidate their gains, the therapy proceeds into the ending phase of treatment described in chapter 4.

4

The Ending Phase of Treatment

HE entire process of treatment may be conceptualized as planning and preparing for an ending that is agreed upon by therapist, child, and parents. Throughout the course of treatment, weekend interruptions, vacations, and absences due to illness have all presented opportunities to explore attenuations of this more definitive separation. The ending phase of treatment should give the child a chance to examine issues of separation and loss, to draw connections with past experiences of separation, and to prepare for future ones. The ending phase of SEPP can have long-range benefits for the child if full opportunity is given to explore these issues, in all of their past and current aspects, with a therapist who is emotionally close yet who is an objective observer.

The ending phase of SEPP is more than a summation of a series of therapeutic sessions; it implies the acquisition of a structure internalized within the intrapsychic life of the child and the interpersonal life of her family. Physical separation occurs when the child ceases to attend regular sessions with her therapist. Because the therapist has always shared with the parents the role of responsibility for the care and nurturance of the child, however, the separation is in some ways a partial one. The parents are returned to the position they held prior to treatment as the sole caregivers of the child and agree to assume the full burden of responsibility.

Criteria for Ending

The criteria for ending treatment are essentially the same as the overall goals of SEPP. For the children, these include improved impulse control, enhanced self-esteem, and improved peer interactions. They show greater capacity to use their adaptive resources with their families and in school. The children are better able to play and engage in playful activity, to make more use of words instead of actions to express their emotions, and to externalize their problems less. There are also criteria for the parents. They should demonstrate an increased capacity to deal with their children's aggressive and demanding behavior, to maintain their role as adults despite the manifold stressors of parenting, and to enjoy their children and engage in pleasurable activity with them.

The achievement of these goals both for the children and for the parents is relative to the children's psychological profile of symptoms and strengths as well as to the family matrix within which each child lives. It indicates a repair in the maladaptive interactions that led to disruptive behavior. What has changed within the internal life of these children are the negative and positive representations of themselves and others. Formerly, these internal representational schemas were skewed in negative perceptions that led to destructive and disruptive actions. The basis for these negative representations could be traced historically to negative patterns of relationships, or attachments, internalized early in the lives of these children and maintained within the interactions of their families.

Working with the Child

As the child approaches the end of her treatment, the same issues that brought her to therapy once again come to the fore: (1) Do they (the parents) care? (2) Does the therapist care? (3) Do I care for you (the therapist)? (4) Do I care for them (the parents)? (5) Can I care for myself? (6) Will you remember me? (7) Will I remember you? All these questions emerge in one form or another during the ending phase of treatment, and the therapist must attend to them carefully, exploring connections with past feelings and experiences as well as anticipations of the future.

Underlying these questions are the self- and object representations, or internalized relationships, described in the Introduction and chapter 1 of this book. The therapist and the child explore the child's memories of treatment together and determine whether sufficient integration has occurred to enable the child to tolerate intense states of ambivalence. Specifically, does the child possess an autonomous sense of herself, separate from areas of conflict, that will support a sense of inner security? Can the child tolerate frustration and conflict without loss of control? Is she able to forgive, so that she shows less need for revenge and rage?

With respect to the child's capacity to care for herself and others, the therapist and the child need to assess together the child's ability to accept limits as helpful and her tolerance for delayed gratification. With the recognition of the impending ending, these issues take on a new intensity. Indeed, some resurgence of the old symptoms may appear as one last test of the child's achievements, although overt signs that she will miss the therapist might not be evident in many cases.

Significant Developments in the Therapy Sessions

Within the sessions themselves, clear signs of change and improvement, indicating a readiness for ending, can be seen in a number of areas.

Statements about the therapist

As the ending approaches, the child may directly acknowledge the therapist's role. For example, the child may comment on a sense of being listened to or helped to find connections. The child may use humor in the presence of the therapist or make observations that indicate an awareness of the realistic aspects of the therapist's personality. The child's sense of individuation within the context of a trusting relationship is illustrated by his ability to talk about the therapist's traits and to use his observing ego. The child may begin to anticipate comments by the therapist or to make statements reflecting an identification with the therapist or the therapist's role.

The therapist's interventions

Verbal interventions shift to an increased focus on review statements and statements directing the child's attention to connections between past and present events and patterns of feelings and behavior that emerge. With some children it is possible to offer interpretations about their defenses and motives and their relationship to past experiences.

Perceptions of treatment

The child's investment in the treatment will increasingly be countered by interest in school and after-school activities. A clear sign of this shift is the child's bringing in more material from current reality. In addition, the child may begin to anticipate what it would be like not to be in treatment. An important change in the child's perception of the treatment is a beginning sense of the passage of time within the therapy, a sense of history. The patient may spontaneously reminisce about past events in the therapy, showing a sense of relationship with the past and a continuity in self-concept. This sense of time may also project into the future with the child investigating how he would keep in contact with the therapist should the need arise.

Quality of communications

Although conflicts may remain, their resolution proceeds at a faster pace and requires less verbal intervention by the therapist. The quantity of the child's verbalization may increase, and reflectiveness in general may be more apparent.

Play

As treatment comes to an end, play is used as a vehicle to express fantasies and resolve conflicts. There is no disruption of play, but instead an increased absorption and pleasure in play.

Affects

Affects become modulated and have a more appropriate range, intensity, and content. Shifts in affects fit the situation, and the child is more inclined to talk spontaneously about what he is feeling. Expressions of gratitude and concern are indications of readiness to end. These high-level affective responses imply a deepening of object relations with a toning down of aggressive components.

Sublimatory behavior

Within the session, sublimatory behavior can be seen in the child's taking the initiative to share new interests, including toys, games, or reports of achievements in the arts or sports.

Defenses

The child's ability to assume responsibility for himself and his actions indicates the diminution of externalization. Related to this development is his acceptance of rules and norms of self-control. Another sign of growth is the child's tendency to apply the therapist's remarks to other areas of his life. In place of impulsivity, reflection and observation become a means of reacting to a situation with thought rather than action.

Appearance and behavior

Age-appropriate behavior should be predominant, indicating an age-appropriate sense of identity. Body posture and manner of dress may provide further clues to an objective self-image and positive self-esteem.

A number of these changes can be seen in a session between Dr. Smith and Mark. At this point, Dr. Smith has been meeting with Mark twice a week for over a year. Mark's aggressive, destructive behavior at home has diminished significantly, and his parents have begun to question the need for continued treatment.

MARK: [Going over to the puppets and taking them off the bookshelf, he puts on the male puppet.] Today the little boy's gonna be bad. You be the mommy. [He gives Dr. Smith the adult female puppet.]

DR. SMITH: Okay. What's the little boy doing to be bad?
→ Supportive intervention: Reassurance
(→) Directing attention: "Look-at" statement (in the present)

MARK: He's hitting his sister. [takes female child puppet and puts it on his other hand and speaks in role as sister] No, don't! Mommy, he's hitting me! Ha! Ha! That's mine, and you can't have it!

DR. SMITH: [in role as mother] What's going on here?
(→) Facilitative intervention: Invitation to continue

MARK: [as sister] He hit me . . . hard.

DR. SMITH: What's this all about, Mark?
(→) Directing attention: "Look-at" statement (in the present)

MARK: [as brother] She took my transformer.

DR. SMITH: Did you ask for it back?
(→) Directing attention: "Look-at" statement (in the present)

MARK: [as sister] I only wanted to look at it. [as brother] No, you didn't. You were going to keep it!

DR. SMITH: What happened when you asked your sister to give back your transformer?

(→) Directing attention: "Look-at" statement (in the present)

MARK: [as sister] He didn't ask. He just grabbed and hit me. [as brother] You didn't need it anyway! And besides, you wouldn't let me play with your toys!

DR. SMITH: Did you want to play with anything particular, Mark?

(→) Directing attention: "Look-at" statement (in the present)

MARK: [loudly and very immersed in role] You shut up, Mom!! You always take her side! And you don't care about me anyway!

DR. SMITH: [as herself] It sounds as if Mark is pretty angry.

(→) Directing attention: "Look-at" statement (in the present)

MARK: [continuing in role as puppet] I am! My mom always gives my sister what she wants. But when I ask for something— oh, boy! Do I get it? No! [*sotto voce,* mimicking mother] You can't have that, Mark; you have enough already. [out of role, as himself] My mom's a jerk!

DR. SMITH: It also sounds as if Mark feels very sad that his mom won't help him or give him something when he needs it.

(→) Interpretation: Motive

MARK: Well, I am. [looks sad]

DR. SMITH: I know, it certainly seems to you, Mark, as though your mom doesn't care enough about you at times. What do you usually do when you feel that way?

→ Directing attention: "Look-at" statement (in the past)

MARK: Yap! I get mad.

DR. SMITH: And what do you do when you're mad at Mom?

→ Directing attention: "Look-at" statement (in the present)

MARK: Well, I used to hit and throw things and not listen.

DR. SMITH: And sometimes try to get Mom's attention by bugging her?

→ Interpretation: Motive

MARK: Yeah, that a lot.

DR. SMITH: What about now?

→ Directing attention: "Look-at" statement (in the present)

MARK: Well, she still doesn't pay a lot of attention to me.

DR. SMITH: You've been letting me know lately that you feel very angry at your mom. How about telling her she makes you angry when she doesn't seem interested in you?

→ Facilitative intervention: Review statement
→ Supportive intervention: Suggestion

MARK: [eyes downcast] I don't know.

DR. SMITH: What do you think keeps you from telling her?

→ Directing attention: "Look-at" statement (in the present)

MARK: I don't know.

DR. SMITH: Well, we know that when you say "I don't know," it's usually a question you don't want to think about or answer. What makes it hard to answer this one?

→ Interpretation: Defense, Motive
→ Directing attention: "Look-at" statement (in the present)

MARK: I don't want to tell Mom.

DR. SMITH: Why?

→ Facilitative intervention: Invitation to continue

MARK: She doesn't care.

DR. SMITH: You feel she doesn't care?
→ Facilitative intervention: Review statement

MARK: Ya. Sometimes.

DR. SMITH: I guess that makes you feel very angry when you think that?
→ Interpretation: Motive

MARK: Yeah, it does.

DR. SMITH: I think it might help your mom to understand why you act up if you told her it made you angry when you felt she wasn't interested in you.
→ Supportive intervention: Suggestion

MARK: But my mom just doesn't care.

DR. SMITH: What makes you think that?
→ Directing attention: "Look-at" statement (in the present)

MARK: She is always busy, and she only sees when I do something bad.

DR. SMITH: I guess it certainly seems that way at times.
→ Supportive intervention: Empathy

MARK: [angry] It's true!

DR. SMITH: Well, I think it's possible that your mom does have a lot on her mind. That's all the more reason to tell her how you feel.
→ Directing attention: "Look-at" statement (in the present)
→ Supportive intervention: Suggestion

Of note in this session is the transition from fantasy play to reflection about emotions. The affective themes expressed are characteristic of the underlying issues in school-age children with conduct disorder behavior—that is, deficits in parental attachment and responsiveness coupled with the child's anxiety. This shift toward verbalization of feelings and reflectiveness represents a significant change from Mark's earlier aggressive, impulsive style. Thanks to the therapist's active and persistent search for clarification, "look-at" statements, and "see-the-pattern" statements, the affects can emerge and suggestions on how to deal with them can be given. Also, Mark is able to articulate feelings of sadness and anger that heretofore he had directly expressed in action.

Yet, despite this progress and decrease in behavioral symptoms, Mark remains angry and distressed about a situation over which he feels he has little control. Clearly, further work is indicated. The ending phase of treatment may be a lengthy process. Mark needs to find satisfactory ways to express the feelings that trouble him and the problem situations that engender them.

At this juncture in treatment, it might be reasonable for Dr. Smith to involve the parents by communicating, with Mark's permission, the content of his anxiety. There are various ways a therapist might choose to handle this type of communication. One option, as Dr. Smith suggests, is to have a joint session with parents and child. Another alternative is a telephone conversation. Other therapists, however, might wait until they had several more sessions with Mark in order to give him the opportunity both to raise his issues directly with his mother and to talk further in treatment about the impact of this session's insights upon him. Dr. Smith has not committed herself to speaking with the parents at a specific time. Rather, she will probably want to explore further with Mark the significance of his belief that he cannot talk directly with his mother but must use her as an intermediary.

The child's wish to have the therapist talk to the parent for him is a common one. It often reflects both the child's perception that the parents are unreasonable (they won't listen) and the belief that therapists can somehow work magic, accomplishing with the parents what the child cannot do himself. Recognition of the child's concerns as legitimate is important. Rapprochement of parent and child through the child's willingness to express emotions, however, is an essential aspect of enhancing the positive attachment between parent and child. The child must resolve in an adaptive fashion the barriers the parents have erected to the gratification of his needs, without resorting to physical aggression.

Part of the task of SEPP's ending phase is to show the child how to substitute talk for aggression in pursuing his goals. The therapist is also concerned, however, with enabling the child to tolerate considerably more frustration than heretofore by finding satisfaction in the relationship with his parents. Thus the child comes to accept limits imposed by his parents as he comes to perceive them as caring. The parent-child relationship then provides the insulation needed against feelings of deprivation when particular wishes are thwarted. The child discovers that in the course of treatment the barriers to gaining the desired contact with his parents and other significant persons have been modified. These barriers no longer seem insurmountable and no longer require violent efforts to overcome them. Moreover, the meaning attributed to the frustration of the child's wishes has changed. Frustration is not represented by the child as rejection.

Rather, the child comes to appreciate that his parents can be loving precisely because they limit him.

Play

During the ending phase, play may continue to be in areas such as games and ball playing, but with a change in tone. Although the form of play may not have changed, the quality of play becomes relaxed. Increased enjoyment is derived from the activity itself and from the ability to play with another person, someone with whom the child can exchange impressions and reactions about the play without feeling threatened or crushed by defeat. In a smaller percentage of patients, play may begin to have symbolic meaning. Symbolic, or fantasy, play is a representational vehicle for the child to express his concerns and anxieties about ending his treatment.

For example, one child built a fortress made of chairs, forming an enclosure from which the therapist would be unable to escape. That done, the child-bandit could leave the premises feeling he could keep the therapist imprisoned. The therapist interpreted to the child his wish to keep her to himself in case he needed her again after the end of treatment. She also suggested that he might be leaving as a "bandit" because he felt the therapist was ending the treatment since he was still a "bad guy."

Verbal Interventions

Verbal interventions in this last stage of treatment again change in focus. For example, review statements increase as the therapist recapitulates for the child the events of his treatment. Also characteristic of the ending phase is a shift in mode, from the indirect mode of play and metaphor to a direct dialogue between the therapist and the child.

Ordinary social behavior

These interventions are unchanged during this phase of treatment.

Statements and questions relating to the treatment

These mostly concern the plans for ending: the date of the last session, the frequency of meetings until the end, and the possibility of seeing the therapist, if necessary, after treatment is over.

→   We are going to end on June 15th, but until then we are going to meet twice a week as usual.

←   Yes, I would be available to you, if you wish to see me.

Requests for factual information

Because most of the patient's biographical and personal circumstances are well known by this time, these interventions generally occur less frequently during the ending phase of the therapeutic work than during the other stages. Such an event as the family's moving or some unanticipated family stress might, however, increase their frequency.

Supportive interventions

Supportive statements continue to be important in the ending phase of treatment. Suggestions, encouragement, reassurance, and empathy are used to allay the child's anxieties regarding the permanence of his improvement beyond the ending of treatment. Here, the themes of mastery, competence, and self-esteem are focal. By supplying factual information, correcting misinformation, or commenting on the child's new-found skills, the therapist educates the child about his improved functioning.

→   You are less worried about grades, because you can study for a long time without getting sidetracked.

→   After we stop therapy, you can still contact me whenever you have a question or a problem you want to talk about.

⇄   You know, you have done a good job. We have a real good feeling that you've achieved so much in such a short period of time. You know how to stop yourself from getting into fights.

⇄ * Although we will stop seeing one another, I will always be interested in you.

Facilitative interventions

Invitations to continue remain unchanged as precursors of other interventions. Review statements become more prominent, crystallizing for the child the history of their relationship and highlighting changes.

⇄   Do you remember that when you first came here, you didn't even look at me, and you refused to do anything except shoot guns? Now you know how to work with me as a partner.

Directing attention

Verbal interventions in this group primarily focus on how the child is thinking and feeling about the impending separation from the therapist and its impact on his behavior. "Look-at" statements may concern only the present or may link the current experience to past experience.

→ I noticed that you're kicking the ball and looking very serious, as if you were expressing that you're feeling sad and angry when we talk about our last session, when we will be stopping.

→ It seems that now that we are about to stop our meetings, you're having similar reactions to when your father left home for the army.

"See-the-pattern" statements continue to link the past and the present.

→ It seems that each time we talk about your not coming here anymore, you change the subject and tell me how well you are feeling.

Interpretations

In the ending phase of treatment, interpretations occur more frequently in the therapist-related mode and specifically address the ending of the important relationship between the therapist and her child patient.

⇄ You want to show me that now you don't need me as much as you used to and that you can manage problems and worries on your own.

Dealing with Issues of Ending Treatment

The final sessions in the treatment mark the ending of regularly scheduled meetings between child and therapist. In the next transcript, a child is ending her treatment in a day hospital setting because she is being transferred to a school. Her psychotherapy is also ending because the student therapist is leaving the institution. This session is included to illustrate individual treatment within the context of a larger institutional program.

Ann is ten years old and diagnosed as having severe disruptive behavior. She is the child of a teenage mother and has been adopted by an elderly great-aunt. As the session begins, Ann and her therapist are crossing the campus to the gym at Ann's request.

ANN: Miss M. told me I was definitely going to George Washington and that I am going to leave Bradley House.

THERAPIST: It's true that you'll be leaving Bradley House this year, but whether or not you go to George Washington will be decided at the meeting today. How are you feeling about that?

→ Supportive intervention: Education

→ Directing attention: "Look-at" statement (in the present)

ANN: Are you going to say good things about me so that I can go? Do you think Mr. F. will say good things?

THERAPIST: I think you are ready to leave Bradley House, but I'm not sure what you think. How do you feel about leaving?

←* Supportive intervention: Giving encouragement

→ Directing attention: "Look-at" statement (in the present)

ANN: I do want to go to George Washington. Why wouldn't they take me?

THERAPIST: There will be a lot of people who will be at the meeting who want to make sure that they do what is best for you.

→ Supportive intervention: Education, Reassurance

Ann and the therapist arrived at the gym. Ann ran ahead and saw that although it was unusual for the gym to be in use, people were in there playing. Initially silent, Ann slowly became enraged as they walked back across the field. The therapist was feeling bad about having walked her over there only to disappoint her.

THERAPIST: You're very disappointed about the gym being used by the other kids.

→ Directing attention: "Look-at" statement (in the present)

ANN: [Her pace quickens until she is several strides ahead of the therapist.] [loudly] Why didn't you come and take me when you were supposed to? Now we have to go to the boring office. But nooo . . . you had to come late!!!

THERAPIST: We had agreed to change your session time because of the testing.

→ Directing attention: "Look-at" statement (in the past)

ANN: You could have taken me. Mr. F. let the boys go to level 5 club, that's no reason! I might as well go back to my classroom!!!

At this point she began to run and was unable and unwilling to listen further to the therapist. She got into Bradley House about 45 seconds before the therapist, who had no idea whether she was going to her classroom or where to find her. She gambled on her office and found Ann curled up in a chair with a coat over her like a blanket, her head in her hands. The therapist sat down in silence for about 30 seconds. Ann then picked up her head and glared at her.

ANN: Why couldn't you have called first instead of making us walk over there for nothing!

THERAPIST: [knowing of course, that Ann was right] You're feeling like you can't count on me to handle things the way I should.

→ Interpretation: Motive

ANN: That's right, and so now I'm angry, and then you go and tell me that you don't know if I'm gonna go to George Washington.

THERAPIST: You're upset about that because you felt sure of it when Miss M. said that to you, and then I made you feel unsure.

⇄ Directing attention: "Look-at" statement (in the present)

ANN: That's not what I'm mad about. I'm mad about the gym.

THERAPIST: It seems to me that you're angrier about the gym than you would be on another day. I wonder if it's because you're feeling a little scared about what's going to happen today.

→ Interpretation: Motive Defense

ANN: Hah! You're supposed to be the therapist, but you don't even understand; I'm mad about the gym, and you're saying it's something else!

THERAPIST: I know that you do feel angry about the gym, but I'm wondering why your feelings are so strong today?

←* Directing attention: "Look-at" statement (in the present)

ANN: Because of the gym! Don't you understand, or do you think I'm crazy and insane? They said I was crazy because I tried to jump out the window in the second grade and I bit the teacher and I hit people and I was out of control. Do you think I'm crazy? [She is very dramatic here but she has a somewhat frightened look on her face.]

THERAPIST: When you were a little girl it was hard for you to control your behavior. You had a lot of problems that you couldn't handle by yourself, but that's changed. You are a different person now.

→ Directing attention: "See-the-pattern" statement (in the past and present)

Ann got up and started pacing around the room. Her earring fell off, and she picked it up and rushed out of room. The therapist followed and found her in the bathroom in front of the mirror. She was annoyed with her attempts to put the earring back in.

ANN: [Staring at the mirror, she complains loudly.] My hole is too big!

THERAPIST: [offering to help her] Some earrings don't hold very well.
→ Supportive intervention: Education, Empathy

ANN: [shouting] I tell you it's my hole that's too big, and you say it's the earring. I tell you I'm mad about the gym and you say it's something else. You get me sick! [She rushes back to the office.]

THERAPIST: Nothing I say is making you feel better; it seems that you feel that today I just don't understand you.
← Directing attention: "Look-at" statement (in the present)
⇄ Supportive intervention: Empathy

ANN: I just feel like throwing everything off this shelf [looking at toy shelves].

THERAPIST: You're feeling so angry that you want to throw things.
→ Interpretation: Motive

She begins to take a plastic racquet and hits the tips of several magic markers, which splinter into pieces. She breaks three markers before the therapist intervenes.

THERAPIST: Ann, I can't allow you to destroy things from the unit.
→ Statement about the treatment

She mimics the therapist's saying this and picks up a paintbrush which she unsuccessfully attempts to smash.

ANN: How about if I take every toy off the shelf?

She begins to do this as she asks in a belligerent tone. She throws small objects up into the air and against the wall, her anger increasing as she does it.

THERAPIST: These are the kinds of behaviors that you were telling me about before, the things that made people think you were crazy.

→ Directing attention: "See-the-pattern" (in the past)

ANN: So I guess now you're going to tell the people at George Washington what I did; you're going to tell them how I destroyed the office.

THERAPIST: Maybe you're feeling so scared about going that you'd like to tell me to tell them that you don't feel ready. I can understand your being scared and sad about leaving this place.

⇄ Interpretation: Defense, Motive
←* Supportive intervention: Empathy, Reassurance

ANN: [still throwing things] Why do you have to change everything around? Can't you see that I'm mad at you. I bet you're not even gonna call me when I leave. [She is now smashing things against the wall; the desk and shelves are void of toys. The room looks like a hurricane hit it; there is now nothing left to throw.]

THERAPIST: There is nothing left but me and you.

⇄ Directing attention: "Look-at" statement (in the present)

ANN: I'd like to lock you in the cellar until you die. I never want to come in here again.

THERAPIST: You feel like you want to hurt me because I am leaving.

← Interpretation: Motive

ANN: I want to kill you. You're just like Miss D.; you'll just leave and never come back.

THERAPIST: It hurts when we have to leave someone we care for. ← Supportive intervention: Suggestion

ANN: [In more feigned anger, she begins to put things back into their crates and back on the shelves, watching the clock out of the corner of her eye as she slams the crates back into their place on the shelf. After everything is cleaned up, she says, as if to indicate she is not through being angry with the therapist.] And you won't even help me clean up! [She goes over to the telephone and lifts it up.] This is a toy I didn't throw yet.

THERAPIST: It is not a toy, and you cannot throw it. → Statement relating to the treatment

ANN: Yes, I can. What are you going to do about it?

THERAPIST: Ann, you cannot throw the phone. → Statement relating to the treatment

ANN: I want to call my grandmother.

THERAPIST: Go ahead. → Supportive intervention: Encouragement

Ann had difficulty getting an outside line, and the therapist offered to dial it for her. The therapist was surprised to hear Ann talking to her Uncle D. rather than to her great-aunt. Uncle D. and his wife are the planned adoptive parents for Ann, should anything happen to the elderly aunt. Ann spoke to her uncle for about three minutes, explaining that she was in school and was with her "individual" and had completed all her classwork that morning. She inquired at length about their puppy, asking why they had it outside in the rain and stating that they had better bring it in or they would get it from her this weekend. Her mood had totally shifted the moment she got on the phone. The therapist capitalized on this shift and asked her about the dog after Ann hung up. She talked about him briefly, looked up at the clock, and said it was time to go. She put her arms around the therapist's waist, hugged her, and left. It was exactly 11:45 A.M., the time that her session was scheduled to end.

This is a turbulent ending in the transition from a day treatment program to outpatient care. Despite Ann's anger and disappointment, which indicate the need for continued treatment, several elements of the ending phase of therapy are present. Ann is fully cognizant of the meaning of her role as patient and has clear expectations of the therapist's role as well. She identifies with the therapist's respect for limits, empathic attunement, and caring attitude. Perhaps because of the new school's possible rejection and the therapist's leaving, however, she is able to demonstrate her understanding only through a negative stance. She is aware of the history of her problem and taunts the therapist to repeat the experiences of rejection she has undergone in the past. The therapist is not seduced by this negative stance and interprets the meaning of Ann's disruptive behavior in terms of the ongoing events and her current level of understanding.

Ann shows us the intense ambivalence that underlies the acceptance of developmental growth and change. If the therapist had been uncertain in her attitude of understanding and acceptance or less firm in setting limits, Ann would indeed have been successful in tipping the outcome of events toward a negative resolution. It is the therapist's interventions that guide Ann's acceptance of her new status, and Ann's identification with the therapist is clearly seen in the displacement shown in her concern for her pet as well as in her affectionate leave taking. The transition had been successfully made, despite her history of trauma.

The case of Ann demonstrates the use of SEPP with a child with a severe and longstanding problem. Let us now turn to the case of a ten-year-old boy whose conduct disorder was more moderate. James had been seen for two years as an outpatient in once-a-week treatment sessions.

James comes in with a sober expression. The therapist told him the previous session they will stop meeting next month as he seems to have things under control. He is doing O.K. at school; he has begun making and keeping friends, instead of making enemies.

JAMES: [interrupting] Stop talking.

James looks around the room and picks up a dart gun. He shoots at the bull's-eye hanging on the wall. He then goes to the shelves, takes out a set of small cars, and throws them from the table over the edge, making accompanying noises of cars falling off a cliff and crashing to the bottom of an abyss.

THERAPIST: I wonder whether your play could be asking some questions about the future. Will you be hitting the bull's-eye and win? Or will you fall and hurt yourself, like the cars? Will there be anybody there to protect the cars?

→ Interpretation:
  Motive

James looks at the therapist, but says nothing. He quietly passes his hand along the border of the armchair and pauses.

THERAPIST: [softly] It'll be a change not to come to the sessions. A part of you will miss them; a part of you will be glad to have time for sports, friends, and just to relax. [James grins.]

→ Directing attention:
  Preparatory statement

At the next session, James looks restless. He picks up toys and scatters them, as in the initial phase of treatment.

THERAPIST: It seems as if you are doing the kinds of things you used to do when you started your sessions.

→ Directing attention:
  "See-the-pattern" statement (in the present and the past)

He picks up a piece of paper and tears it into little bits and blows them in all directions until the room begins to look as though a winter snow had fallen.

THERAPIST: What you're doing now reminds me also of the time you broke all the toys into pieces and of the feeling of sadness you gave me when you couldn't figure out how to play!

JAMES: [nods] Shut up! I have to make sure I have gone through everything.

⇄ * Facilitative intervention:
  Review statement

THERAPIST: It's like remembering the kinds of things you have done here since the beginning.

→ Facilitative intervention: Review statement

JAMES: Yup! [He opens a package he had brought with him. It is a plane he had assembled and called the "Explorer."] This is for you.

THERAPIST: Thank you! [grins] I wonder whether you wished I would give you something to remember me by—

→ Ordinary social behavior
← * Interpretation: Motive

JAMES: Shut up, silly! You have given me your friendship. When I grow up, I'll invite the kids in the neighborhood to drop into my house for some bull-sessions.

The quality of communications in these sessions is typical of the ending phase of treatment. Although some tensions remain, they are resolved more quickly than heretofore, and reflectiveness is more apparent. In addition, shifts in affect occur and are accompanied by the appropriate verbalization. James is able to talk spontaneously about what he is feeling. Finally, his expression of gratitude and concern for the therapist are high-level affective responses that imply a deepening of object relations with a toning down of aggression and that indicate a readiness for ending treatment. James's gratitude and concern reflect his capacity for deeper relationships with the family and for future investment in others.

Working with the Parents

In the ending phase of SEPP, interventions with the parents, like those with the child, revolve largely around issues of termination, including the plans, the final date, and the frequency of sessions until that time. As the actual conclusion of treatment approaches, reviewing the course of treatment and expressing appreciation of the parents' collaboration in the treatment are in order, as well as offering the availability of future consultation. As the parents and therapist begin to consider the feasibility of ending, the therapist elicits from the parents their view of the child's accomplishments and performance. The areas to be surveyed include school achievement, the number and quality of his relationships with peers, and the extent of friction with siblings. The purpose of this exploration with the parents is to compare the child's present level of functioning with the initial presenting complaints.

The therapist also discusses common responses that children and parents undergo during the ending phase of treatment. The parents should be prepared for the fact that the child may experience brief relapses to the presenting complaints, as if to test the parents' and the therapist's expected responses to the end of treatment. The therapist and the parents should also explore the child's and the parents' mixed feelings of relief, sadness, anxiety, and concern about the loss of the ongoing support offered by the therapist.

> I wouldn't be at all surprised if you have some fear that all the old symptoms and problems will come back and some concern that Johnny's gotten more irritable lately, or that you see great happiness and sense of relief and accomplishment for ending the treatment and having more free time available.

Interpretations illuminating possible motives for the child's reactions as described to the therapist or the parents' reactions might be appropriate.

> I wonder if Joey's temper tantrum today is because he's angry, feeling as if I were leaving him?

> I think you're feeling anxious and in a way that you, yourself, are being deserted by me, whereas I've been a source of support in the past.

It is helpful to suggest that parents discuss their mutual reactions freely with the child.

It is important to communicate the therapist's understanding of, and empathy with, the parents' anxiety and to reassure them that what they feel is common to parents who are about to assume full responsibility for the care of their child. (For another discussion of these feelings, see the section on ending treatment in Part II, Parent Training.) The parents can be reminded of how they have been able to manage many situations effectively and can be reassured that there is no objective reason why they should not continue to do so in the future. Emphasis on their competence and efficacy with their child is crucial in work with the parents at this time.

In reviewing the cause of treatment, the therapist recapitulates the goals that were formulated at the beginning of treatment, how the treatment has proceeded, what has been accomplished, and what the parents have learned. The parents' affective response to this review is an important indicator of their readiness to end treatment. If optimism and confidence are the general tone of their response, then the process is proceeding well. If despair and helplessness dominate, then the collaborative effort with the parents must continue. In some instances, the therapist may choose to continue working with the parents after treatment of the child has ended. It is also appropriate to consider at this juncture whether one or both parents should continue or undertake individual treatment. In other cases, marital treatment may be indicated. All these possibilities should be considered as the review process compares gains accomplished with tasks left undone. The purpose of the review process is to make clear to the parents the work that has been jointly accomplished, to communicate the therapist's appreciation of the parents' achievement, and to provide guidelines for future parenting.

PART II

PARENT TRAINING

SARALEA E. CHAZAN, PH.D.
ROBERT S. KRUGER, PH.D.

5

Overview

PROBLEM behavior is inadvertently developed within the home and sustained by maladaptive parent-child interactions. A common result of these maladaptive patterns of interaction is the development of insecure attachments between parent and child, which can be manifested in a conduct disorder. The goal of the parent-training program is to enhance feelings of mastery for the parents, which will in turn enhance their feelings toward their child. The increased sense of mastery is positively reinforcing for the parents and acts to further the growth of secure attachment between parent and child. In describing parent training, we will be following the formulations of social learning theory, which has demonstrated that parents of children with conduct disorders engage in practices that promote aggressive behavior and suppress prosocial behavior. These practices include directly reinforcing deviant behavior, making frequent and ineffective use of commands and punishment, and failing to attend to appropriate behaviors (Patterson 1982).

In this parent-training program, parents are taught effective ways of interacting with their children. Sessions are conducted in a clinic setting with individual sets of parents, rather than groups of parents. The training includes both a general description of how misbehavior occurs within the family unit and direct training in a number of discrete parenting skills. The therapist serves as teacher and guide, assisting parents through instruction, role-playing, and modeling. The parent practices these skills with the therapist, who provides feedback and clarification. The parents keep a log of the interactions that occur within the home, and together the parents and the therapist conduct a continuous evaluation of the effects of intervention. The extent to which changes within the home are generalized to other settings, such as school and the community, is also monitored, as are the parents' feelings about themselves and their competence as parents.

Parent-Child Interaction

The process of formation of secure relationships between parent and child has been the topic of intense research inquiry. John Bowlby (1958) was the first to observe the importance of parental availability, later referred to by others as maternal referencing (Emde and Sorce 1983), in the development of early relationships between parent and child. Erikson (1950) termed the early epoch of human development the period of formation of *the capacity for trust,* which lays the foundation for the later development of human concern and mutuality. It is not only the availability of the parental figure in a consistent manner that is essential, but also the parent's availability for attunement with and empathy for the emotional states of the child (Stern 1985). In addition, D. W. Winnicott (1965) observed that the parent should be "good enough" and not "perfect," leaving space for the autonomous self of the child to emerge. He described an ongoing duet of harmonious communication in synchrony with the emotional lives of both parent and child. Thus, in the expected course of events, the parent contributes to developing attachment bonds with the child in several ways: (1) emotional availability in a consistent manner; (2) attunement to the child's emotional needs; (3) empathic understanding of the child's needs, which leads to appropriate responses; and (4) a "good-enough" response to the child by the parent, which leaves a margin for lack of attunement and error.

What occurs in the emotional development of a child with behavioral difficulties is an asynchrony in this early duet between parent and child. It is an asynchrony based on feelings of aggression, which result in injurious levels of anxiety, anger, and frustration for both members of the pair. Instead of containing the child's aggressive feelings and frustrations, the parent is brought into the conflict experienced by the child. At those moments of peak intensity, a distortion in perception occurs: the parent ceases to perceive the child objectively. Rather than setting limits firmly and consistently, the parent responds in contagion with the child and returns aggression with aggression. In these families, when a child misbehaves, the parent becomes overidentified with the child's intense anger. The parent may rationalize that this is the way he or she was treated as a child and the way that children have been treated for generations.

In these circumstances, it is understandable that the child experiences difficulty in learning and applying rules, as these children characteristically do not pause and reflect but respond impulsively. Instead of testing the external world, anticipating consequences or considering alternative ways of responding, they immediately respond to their own inner needs, in the immediate way that their parents did. They do not navigate as autonomous persons but rather remain in fused interaction with their parents. This deficit in autonomous functioning is demonstrated in the arena of understanding and responding to rules. It can be seen as the consequence of the failure of "good-enough" parenting and the formation of insecure attachments between parent and child. The core of the problem seems to be the lack of empathy between parent and child and mutual regulation of intense feelings of aggression. In looking for the causes for this failure in autonomous functioning, we believe it is helpful to consider separately the children with conduct disorders and the characteristics of their parents.

The Children

Alexander Thomas, Stella Chess, and Herbert Birch (1968) and others have found temperamental differences (for example, activity level, regularity of sleeping and eating, reaction to new stimuli, intensity of reaction, threshold of responsiveness, quality of mood, and distractibility) among children during the first year of life. Some children display virulent or erratic levels of these characteristics and become difficult to manage. In addition, some parent-child pairs do not work smoothly because differing temperamental characteristics result in problems of "fit." In such instances of mismatched temperaments, the normal ebb and flow of reciprocal interactions is disturbed. In addition, there are developmentally difficult periods for all children, such as the "terrible twos," when even the normal child's behavior becomes increasingly negative and resistant to control. During these ubiquitous periods of expected conflict, there is additional strain on the dyad to adapt to each other.

Many child behaviors, such as whining, yelling, noncompliance, teasing, and hitting may be experienced by the parent as unpleasant. Gerald Patterson (1982) found what characterizes the aggressive child is frequent unpleasant social interaction, which is protracted and explosive. He also found that aggressive behaviors are not random but contingent; that is, they are more likely to occur in the presence of certain family members. Gerald Patterson described a pattern of reciprocal interaction between aggressor and victim: the child's actions are used to produce a reliable impact on the victim, and the victim's reactions prolong the duration of the immediate interaction and produce the long-term effect of increasing the child's tendency to act aggressively. In this process, the reactions of the child's victims contribute substantially to maintaining a negative balance with the aggressive child. Parent and child are in unwitting collusion toward the creation of a status quo that results in aggressive behavior. Gerald Patterson termed these interactions between parent and child *coercive interaction patterns.* The coercion is the deviant behavior on the part of one person (for example, the child) that is rewarded by another person (for example, the parent).

The Parents

Interpersonal processes between parents (for example, marital hostility) and between parents and child appear to be causally related to aggression in children. Karen Wells and Rex Forehand (in press) have identified several characteristics of family life that seem to result in aggression: parent-parent and parent-child relationships characterized by high degrees of hostility or negativism; criticism and indifference among family members; low rates of family cohesiveness and positive attention; and laxity in supervision and effective consequences of negative behavior. There is little evidence of genetic transmission of socialized forms of conduct disorders. Rather, depression and anxiety in parents may result in aggressive behavior in one of several ways (Griest and Wells 1983). First, because of symptoms associated with depression such as agitation, irritability, difficulty in concentrating, and insomnia, parental depression may result in lowered tolerance for normal variations in child behavior, which in turn causes increased hostility, negativism, and use of punishment. On the other hand, parental depression manifesting itself as decreased energy level, hypersomnia, and feelings of despair and hopelessness may result in decreases in parental positive attention and supervision. Finally, parents who view their children's behavior as aversive, uncontrollable, and unmanageable may experience "learned helplessness," which further exacerbates parental depression and withdrawal from the child (Wells and Forehand, in press).

Methods

The main goal of parent training is the alteration of aversive interaction patterns occurring in the home between parent and child. Toward that end, the parents are trained to identify, define, and observe problem behaviors in new ways. They learn specific techniques in management, including the use of positive reinforcement (for example, praise or tokens for prosocial behavior), mild punishment (such as omission of reinforcement or loss of privileges), negotiation, empathic responding, contingency contracting, and other procedures. In addition, the parents acquire a general understanding of the principles that govern the occurrence of problem behaviors.

During the sessions, parents use modeling and role-playing to practice the techniques. As part of their training, parents keep logs of interactions in the home. The training sessions then provide opportunities for the parents to review how the techniques are being implemented and the changes that have occurred. At first parents are taught to use their new skills on relatively simple behaviors that can be observed easily. As they become more proficient, the focus of the program can shift to the more severely problematic behaviors and consider settings outside the home, such as the school.

As a consequence of the increased competence in parenting skills, it is expected that the parents' frustration tolerance will increase along with their enjoyment of their child. The result would be a heightened sense of parental competence and the development of a secure attachment between parent and child.

Phases of Treatment

The treatment program consists of four phases. In the first phase, the parents' use of management techniques is assessed. The therapist and parents reach an understanding of how these techniques need to be improved so that the parents will be better able to help their child. In the second phase, the parents are taught several general principles regarding the development of behavior problems and how they can be changed. In the third phase, the parents learn several specific techniques for managing their child. They are also given instructions in keeping a behavior log, which helps the therapist to assist them in learning to adapt these procedures to their family's needs. In the fourth phase, parents are responsible for providing continuous input to the therapist on behaviors that occur within the home. The therapist charts the gains and recommends ways to maintain them.

In parent training, although the parents are defined as the patients, they are not in the same type of therapeutic relationship as is indicated in individual psychotherapy. The focus is on counseling concerning the management of their children's behavior. Therefore, rigorously applying the hierarchy of verbal interventions would not be productive. However, these categories are at times relevant in a general way and will be cited when appropriate to specific phases of training.

Indications and Contraindications

These training procedures are intended for use in families whose main interest is symptom reduction, which implies reducing the child's aversive behaviors. The major criterion for families included in these procedures is a capacity to comply with instructions. The parents must be capable of understanding the therapist's suggestions and be willing to comply with them. It is not essential for both parents to come to all the training sessions—one parent can share the content of the sessions with the other—but both parents must agree to participate and cooperate.

This mode of treatment is not indicated for children who require intensive intervention directly from the therapist. Although the levels of interaction between the therapist and the parents may vary in intensity, this relationship is not the main focus of treatment. Also, these therapist-parent interactions are available only secondarily to the child through his parents. For these reasons, a child who requires an intensive individual approach because of more internalized problems would not be a candidate for parent-training procedures, although such procedures might be used to augment his individual treatment. Similarly, if the parents are unable to benefit from a direct, didactic approach because of their own difficulties (such as impulsivity, guilt, confusion, or anxiety), parent training is not indicated. Parent training by definition is concerned primarily with symptom amelioration, not with the deeper issues of conflict resolution and unconscious motivation. The major focus is on helping parents to learn new management techniques and to understand why these techniques succeed or fail. The therapist thus assists parents in improving their management of their family situation; he does not intervene directly at the level of personality development.

In training parents, the therapist is sensitive to psychodynamic issues.

Examination of these deeper issues is not pursued, with one exception. When the parents are either overcompliant or noncompliant, the therapist must consider the underlying dynamics. In either instance, however, if the parental reactions do not yield to didactic suggestion, then the family unit is not capable of integration using this approach.

An additional note of caution. Because the techniques being taught involve behavioral control, it is incumbent upon the therapist to monitor the parents to ensure that the techniques are being used humanely. For example, if the parents report having to limit disruptive behavior, the therapist must inquire further to ascertain the specific techniques the parents used, as well as the parents' feelings about the child and the ways they dealt with their emotional reactions. Overly strict parental application of these techniques could harm the child. It is not the goal of these training procedures to develop quiet, docile children but to enhance the pleasure of family interaction (Risley, Clark, and Cataldo 1976).

The Participants

The Patient: The Parents

The patients in this modality are the parents, who seek guidance and instruction in changing the negative interactions within the home that breed the child's disruptive behavior. In this book, references to one parent will often use the female pronoun, for several reasons. In families with conduct disorder children, the insecure attachment is almost always with the mother, if not with both parents. Further, in a high percentage of single-parent families, the single parent is the mother. Finally, even in two-parent households where both parents work outside the home, the mother most often bears the major responsibility for child-rearing. Of course, all references to the parent in this book refer equally to mother and father. It is important to note that although the parents are identified as the patients in parent training, they do not develop the same type of relationship to the therapist that occurs in individual psychotherapy. The focus here is upon counseling the parents in managing positively their child's behavior. The child receives treatment via the parents. He meets the therapist briefly but does not develop a relationship with the therapist or have any ongoing contacts with him. The therapist is engaged by the parent, and the child is the recipient of changed patterns of parental management.

The Therapist

Therapists are clinicians experienced in working with children and their parents and have been specifically trained in parent-training procedures. Their general demeanor is supportive and active; openness and warmth are major characteristics. They must be able to communicate effectively, to establish congenial rapport, and to give corrections in a positive manner. Therapists not only provide information but serve as viable attachment figures for the parents. They are available to the parents and will contact them on their own initiative for feedback. Therapists perform positive parenting functions for the parents and thus serve them as parents. As models of tolerance for delay of gratification, they assist the parents in binding their anxiety and providing appropriate reassurance. Through their empathic understanding and limit setting, the therapists provide immediate models for the parents' referencing of flexibility and patience.

The Supervisor

The supervisor is responsible for monitoring the progress of treatment and of the therapist-patient relationship. Specifically, the supervisor meets with the therapist at the beginning of each new phase of treatment and reviews progress being made by the family, making suggestions for possible improvements in parental techniques. The therapist informs the supervisor of instances of noncompliance by the parent, and together they explore possible reasons for the lack of cooperation. The supervisor also discusses with the therapist issues of motivation that may not be immediately obvious and yet may be indirectly affecting treatment, such as the therapist's discouragement or disapproval. The role of the supervisor in maintaining the parent-therapist relationship is discussed in greater detail in chapter 9.

6

Phase One: Assessing the Parents

THE successful use of parent training as an intervention with conduct disorder children depends largely upon certain parental characteristics. The parents' attachment to the child must be strong enough to provide motivation for healthy individuation; moreover, parents must be able to display warmth and affection appropriately and consistently as a reward for desirable behavior as well as to use negative reinforcement (such as punishment or correction) judiciously and consistently. They must have a genuine desire for direction and instruction and the capacity to form a positive attachment to the therapist sufficient to allow him or her to become a benevolent authority for them.

Of these characteristics, we consider the last to be the most critical. Because of the significance of faulty parent-child attachment in the development of conduct disorders, we believe that it is essential for the therapist to enact selected aspects of the parental role with the child's parents. This enactment involves both modeling appropriate parental behavior—such as limit setting and consistent use of appropriate positive and negative reinforcement—and nurturing the parents in their efforts to care for their child.

Epidemiological studies of delinquency and conduct disorders (see, for example, Rutter and Giller 1983) have found that many parents of children with behavioral problems are psychologically impaired in their parenting abilities because they were not adequately nurtured and parented as children and therefore do not possess the requisite skills or emotional re-

121

sources to foster their child's growth. By acting in a nurturing, empathic manner that does not threaten the parents' self-esteem, the therapist can in certain ways become the "good-enough parent" to the parents. In this role, the therapist guides and supports the parents in allowing the child to separate from them in a noncoercive way. In addition, the therapist simultaneously defines appropriate behavioral limits for both parents and child, as well as defining with them the most effective ways of achieving their goals.

From this perspective on the relationship between therapist and parents, it is clear that the parents must form a benevolent, positive attachment to the therapist and vice versa. The efficacy of training as well as its ultimate impact depends upon the strength and resilience of the therapist-parent bond. When the relationship between therapist and parent is characterized by conflict, the most likely outcome is noncompliance: the parent is inconsistent in carrying out the therapist's directions or dismisses therapist-initiated interventions outright.

The assessment of the parents as candidates for parent training is therefore not primarily concerned with the parents as individuals or with the child's difficulties but rather with the extent to which the parents can form a positive attachment and working relationship with the therapist. It is this firm parent-therapist alliance that will enable the therapist to work with the parents to change their child's behavior. Parent-training paradigms are designed to include a broad range of parental maladaptive behaviors. It is important to note again, however, that these paradigms are not intended for use with more extreme instances of parental psychopathology, such as psychosis or substance abuse. Other factors that might contribute to the failure to form an alliance need to be considered as well—for example, the therapist's gender and personality characteristics and the fit of these aspects of the therapist's personality with the parents' personality characteristics. When a mismatch occurs consideration needs to be given to the selection of a different therapist.

Verbal Interventions

During the assessment phase, therapists intervene verbally primarily to elicit information and provide support, including reassurance, education, and understanding.

Ordinary social behavior occurs, such as responses that welcome the parents to the setting and guide them through the various interactions, up through leave taking. It is important for therapists to use these conventions to defuse anxiety about the treatment setting and indicate their essential humanity.

Statements relating to the therapy provide information about the assessment and treatment procedures and should clarify for the parents the purpose of treatment: what it is about and how it unfolds. Therapists make their roles as guides and positive attachment models clear to the parents, both implicitly through their manner and explicitly through verbal interventions (for example, "I am here to work with you on those situations").

The therapists' requests for factual information provide the adequate data to conduct the assessment procedures. The information gathering clarifies issues and permits contact between parent and therapist that promotes the development of a therapeutic alliance.

Using supportive interventions, the therapists demonstrate encouragement and empathy critical during the assessment phase to convey to the parents their acceptance and recognition of parents' problems. Included as supportive interventions are any suggestions or direct advice offered by the therapists. Although giving directions is inappropriate at this phase, general suggestions can be communicated in a nonthreatening manner, with such phrases as, "You might try . . . ," and ". . . . might be effective." Dispensing advice at this stage is entirely in the service of diagnosing the potential for parental alliance, and though not essential, it should not be avoided if advice is explicitly solicited by the parents. Guidance may have some immediate positive effects in terms of reducing anxiety and forming the parent-therapist bond.

The First Visit

The first visit should last approximately sixty to ninety minutes. The duration should not be indeterminate, but it should be longer than that of an ordinary therapy session (usually forty-five minutes) to permit parents to express their concerns unhurriedly and to facilitate the formation of an adequate working relationship between parents and therapist. In initial sessions, significant topics often do not emerge until what might ordinarily be the end of a standard therapy session.

Assessing the Parent-Child Bond

Collecting information about the strength and nature of the parent-child relationship should initially be done by allowing the parents to talk freely and discursively about their child and his difficulties. Following Stanley

Greenspan (1981), we advocate relatively little structuring by the therapist at the beginning of the first interview to allow parents to express their concerns in their own way. If, however, the parents do not spontaneously volunteer information that the therapist needs in order to understand the nature and intensity of their attachment to the child, the therapist should begin about halfway through the interview to ask specific questions. These queries can be general and should be introduced in the natural flow of conversation. They need not be presented in any particular order, but the therapist should adhere to a mental checklist that covers the following: (1) how each parent and the child spend time together; (2) historically, who has spent the most time with the child and how; (3) how affectionate and loving the child is; (4) how affectionate each parent views himself/herself to be; (5) how easy or difficult each parent has found the child to manage at home; (6) the occasions on which the child's behavior frustrates or angers each parent, and how frequently these occasions occur; (7) how likable the parents feel the child is; (8) how likable the parents feel they are; (9) what kind of relationship the parents feel they have with the child; and (10) how the parents compare their relationships with the child *vis à vis* their relationships with other children in the family. It is important to remember that the child has presumably been extensively evaluated already and that the standard developmental and family historical data have been recorded. Reviewing developmental and family history at this time while being alert to clues to the questions asked above is fundamental to this assessment. If an adequate history has not been recorded, then this is the time to ask additional relevant questions.

Assessing the Parents' Capacity for Warmth

The parents' capacity to display warmth and affection in a consistent manner can be assessed by simply listening for descriptions of parental displays of affection as well as by observing parental nonverbal interactional style in the interview. By *warmth* we mean parental verbal and other behavior that communicates positive affect to the child. Displays of warmth generally involve many nonverbal and vocal actions that can be modulated or expanded in range to convey mild to extreme states of pleasure. These include smiles, laughter, positive speech content, hugs, and affectionate touches. Gerald Patterson and colleagues (1975) have reported that parents of conduct disordered children often have difficulty expressing affection consistently toward their children. Unfortunately, the rule in many families in which children are aggressive is that as long as the child does "nothing" (that is, nothing aversive to others), behavior is ignored.

A Trial Assessment

During the course of the initial interview, the therapist asks the parents to describe two or three recent episodes of noncompliant behavior involving themselves and the child. Most parents seeking professional consultation for behavioral management of their child are extremely cooperative in anecdotally elaborating upon the behavior that disturbs them. The clinician should also attempt to have the parents clarify the types of troubling behaviors and interaction sequences by asking, "Can you tell me about different kinds of actions by your child that bother you?" As the parents begin to categorize behavior (for example, "doesn't listen" or "talks back"), the therapist should note these and, once the list is complete, ask for specific recent instances of each.

In preparation for the second visit, the therapist asks the parents to continue to observe and record interactions within the family. This information will assist the therapist by providing additional information about how they and the child spend their time together and the kinds of difficulties they experience. Specifically the therapist asks the parents to keep a diary, recording how much time each of them spends with the child, how the time is spent, and what types of problems occur. The instructions should be left ambiguous, to permit the parents wide latitude in executing the details of the task. If the initial instructions about keeping the diary are somewhat vague, the task becomes a useful projective test of parental motivation and style with regard to directives from the therapist.

Because parent training requires the parents to follow instructions, the therapist must clearly assess early on how the parents will cope with tasks presented in this way and, correspondingly, how they respond to the therapist as teacher. Parents who do not comply or who are psychologically disorganized in keeping records and reporting their own or their child's extra-therapy behavior are poor candidates for parent training. There are two exceptions to this general exclusion rule, however: parents who are generally diffuse in their thinking but respond well to focused direction and parents in multiple-problem families who are simply overwhelmed by the number and complexity of the difficulties presented by their children. Parents in such families may respond well to parent training; indeed, they may adopt new parenting techniques with alacrity as they discover that these techniques lessen their problems and enable them to cope more effectively. If parents are not comfortable using writing as a tool, they may rely on some other form of record keeping, such as keeping a memorized list or audio taping.

The Second Visit

The second session should take place about two weeks after the first. This time lapse enables the therapist to determine how the parents have followed the limited types of directives given them during the first session and how they are responding to her verbal interventions and efforts to form a relationship with them.

While parent training focuses on altering parental responses to the child, it is valuable for the clinician to meet the child and have the opportunity to observe directly the interactions between the child and the parents. In some instances these observations can be gathered through a home visit, but home visits are usually logistically difficult to arrange. A more convenient technique is to have the parents bring their child to the therapist's office, making the parents' second visit a family play/observation session. Equipment in the therapist's office includes various toys and games, as well as an easel with drawing paper and crayons, to facilitate a range of interactions between parent and child. The parents are instructed that the purposes of this visit are to permit the therapist to observe them with their child in an unstructured setting, to learn more about how the child responds to parental initiatives, and to learn more about how the parents respond to the child's various behaviors.

During this session the therapist should act primarily as an observer, limiting her role to asking whether behaviors observed are typical and how frequently they occur. The therapist should attempt to record as accurately as possible who does what; this record will facilitate subsequent reconstruction of patterns of interaction. Specifically, it will allow the therapist to ascertain under what circumstances the child engages in provocative and undesirable behavior, how the parents respond to it, and the probable effect of parental responses on the child's future behavior. The therapist is particularly interested in whether parental behavior reduces or increases the likelihood of future noncompliant behavior. These observations can then form the basis for valuable feedback to the parents during later visits. This feedback should be used to teach parents, either discursively or through role-playing, about ways of altering their behavior to produce desirable changes in the child's noncompliant behavior and achieve previously agreed-upon goals.

The Third Visit

At the third interview, as in the beginning of the first session, the therapist should allow the parents to raise whatever issues are immediately of concern to them. He should not initially bring up the diary; but if they begin by talking about it, the therapist should follow their lead. If they do not mention the diary and give no indication that they will, then no later than halfway into the session the therapist should explicitly inquire about how they have been using it. Discussion of the diary should focus primarily on how the task was executed (if it was) or why it was not. Ample time should be given for the parents to express their assumptions about what they imagined the therapist wanted or needed to know.

It is anticipated that parents will return to the third session with data that show two patterns: first, relatively little time is spent with the child in positive or affectionate interchanges, and second, problem interactions are frequent and tend to be characterized by aggressive and/or coercive behavior by the child or the parents.

In gauging the extent to which parents are capable of consistently affectionate behavior, the therapist must listen to and, if necessary, request elaboration of the parents' experience with the child. The therapist is particularly interested in finding out how articulate the parents are in describing what the child does that pleases them, how much detail the parents employ in describing circumstances under which the child misbehaves, and how well the parents are able to modulate their responses in relation to the quality of the child's behavior and expressed affect.

Parents vary in their ability to describe in detail their own feelings about, and perceptions of, the child on a given occasion. Moreover, some parents are more able than others to infer the child's motives and to make connections among motives, affects, and actions. Parents who tend to view the child in monolithic terms and are unable to appreciate the complexity of influences on a child's behavior are also unlikely to appreciate their own role in precipitating aggressive or other untoward behavior by the child. In general, the greater the degree of complexity and elaboration in the parents' narratives about the child and their reactions to him, the more probable that they will appreciate and use therapeutic interventions and training.

The therapist should also listen closely to the parents' descriptions of their efforts to exercise self-control and to respond differently to the child's various affect states and actions. In evaluating parents' narratives about their responses to the child, the therapist primarily assesses their flexibility and their capacity to focus on the parent-child interaction. Being flexible

is an effective antidote to coercion by the child. The child will use escalating tactics in an attempt to upset the parents. A flexible parent is attuned
to the child in an adaptive way that does not passively ignore the child's
requests, demands, and provocations. Flexibility implies reasoning and
foresight, offsetting the possibility of impulsive and unplanned responses
that may result in too harsh punishment, violence, or inconsistently en-
forced threats.

Corrective parental action often requires that the parents understand the
meaning of their child's unacceptable behavior. For example, parents may
complain that their three-year-old is a "problem" because he "lies" or
"tells fibs" and, in response to questioning, say that he behaves this way
because "he's difficult." Such parents may be unable to accept the possibility that a child of this age does not consistently distinguish between reality
and fantasy and that fibbing is normal behavior at this age, especially for
a verbal child. In this instance, the therapist should carefully evaluate to
what extent these parents can use information about normative child
development to alter their viewpoint about their child. Thus, having informed them that fibbing is common in three-year-olds and does not
particularly portend a fault in moral character development, the therapist
would note whether the parents persist in their negative views or whether
they stop labeling story-telling as "bad" and perhaps even take delight in
it, finding it humorous, as many parents do.

The Evaluation

For parents to be capable of affectionate response and measured corrective
action, they must comprehend the relationships between situation, motive,
and action in the child's past. That is, parents should display, in response
to questioning, a rudimentary appreciation of the links between the child's
reasons for acting in certain ways and when and how behaviors occur.
Parents who express difficulty in answering "Why?" questions regarding
their child's behavior or who have difficulty perceiving patterns in the
child's disruptive behavior may not be especially good candidates for
parent training.

Parents who do not form an adequate attachment to the therapist as a
teacher and guide or who display an inability to modulate their own
behavior consistently in relation to the child's are also poor candidates for
parent training. There may be many reasons for parents' not forming an
attachment to the therapist. The therapist may not initially have behaved
in a sufficiently warm or supportive manner or been empathic enough with

the parents' plight in coping with a difficult child. The particular therapist and parent might be a mismatch. Alternatively, if the therapist has displayed a sense of omnipotence or grandiosity, he may have antagonized the parents. Therapists who have been trained to reflect upon their own emotions when working with patients, however, are less likely to precipitate these reactions. Some parents simply have difficulty in forming stable relationships with others. Indeed, their relationship with their child is probably just one instance of this difficulty.

What sort of parents experience difficulty in forming attachments to their children or to significant other persons in their lives? It can be safely inferred from research on attachment and separation that adults who manifest these problems have most likely been neglected or abused, physically or emotionally (or both), as children (Robins 1970). Accordingly, in interviewing parents the therapist will want to talk about the parents' parents and, more specifically, the parents' experience of their own childhoods. The therapist's questions should be directed primarily toward finding out how bonded the parents felt themselves to be to their own parents, how physically and emotionally available they perceived their parents to be, and how affectionate and emotionally nurturing they recalled their parents' behavior toward them.

In evaluating the responses to such queries, the therapist should examine not only the content of the parents' replies but also the affect that accompanies them. The therapist should also use his impressions of the parents' affective styles, derived from his own interaction with them. This impression provides a corroborative indicator of the parents' capacity to be warm and responsive as well as to become attached to an authority figure. If it becomes clear by the end of the second assessment interview that one or both parents are not likely either to learn how to behave affectionately toward the child or to form a positive attachment to the therapist, then the therapist should suggest other modalities for treatment.

Parental psychopathology may also rule out parent training as the modality of choice. Parental psychopathology that particularly interferes with the effectiveness of a parent-training regimen includes those clinical conditions and personality disorders that are difficult to treat successfully in individual psychotherapy or for which parents have not sought treatment. Thus, various depressive, phobic, or anxiety disorders, as well as substance abuse, can all be successfully treated if recognized and treatment is sought. If a parent does not identify himself or herself as suffering from a psychological disorder, however, or is unwilling to seek treatment despite his or her recognizing a disorder, that parent would not be a good candidate for parent training. A parent who is actively impaired and not in treatment is likely to undermine the effectiveness of any therapeutic intervention, and especially a treatment utilizing parental action. Psychologically impaired parents are generally preoccupied with their own difficulties and thus unable to implement the therapist's suggestions adequately. For parent training to be beneficial to such parents, they must begin to recognize their own difficulties and, when possible, seek professional assistance to ameliorate them. This qualification does not eliminate some form of concomitant parental counseling as appropriate for parents with identified, untreated psychopathology. Rather, it is an exclusion criterion for the application of the specific parent-training paradigms described in this book.

How does an interviewer, in three sessions, evaluate parental psychopathology and its impact on the child? There are several specific steps that can be taken. Initially, one should ask, in the course of taking a family history, to what extent either parent has suffered from psychological symptoms and/or sought psychological treatment. If the parents answer negatively, one should ask further about specific symptoms such as fears and worries, depression, impulsive behavior, and volatility. One should also ask parents to describe themselves, as well as their child, on each of the nine temperament variables (described in this book in chapter 7, p. 135). Additionally, one should inquire about past and present drug and alcohol use, driving habits, legal difficulties, marital conflict, occupational satisfaction, physical health, and significant life events, such as the death of friends or family members, job changes, and moves. Any of the foregoing can constitute stressors for a given person and render the emergence of parental psychopathology more probable.

While unsophisticated parents may tell a clinician that there is no family or personal history of pathology, they may describe themselves in temperamental terms that suggest a personality disorder or may identify other behaviors (for example, frequent job changes or moves) that suggest psychopathology. We will not review here the components of a competent psychiatric interview and history. What is important for the purpose of conducting successful parent training is the parents' awareness of their own pathology and the therapist's ability to spot such pathology when it is denied.

Formulating a Treatment Plan

During the assessment phase, the clinician is concerned with collecting data that illustrate the nature and degree of parental attachment to the child, the nature and degree of parental psychopathology, and the characteristic patterns of maladaptive family interaction initiated by the child's antisocial behavior. If the parent-training paradigms seem appropriate for the family, at the end of the third visit the therapist should proceed to make another appointment with the parents to discuss specific techniques that could be employed with the child. Many therapists also find it helpful to request parents to read one or two books about parent training. Parents may be given selected sections from chapter 7 to read as suitable educational material.

The therapist should not attempt to begin treatment at this point but should leave ample time to discuss the parents' concerns about initiating treatment, the amount of time involved, the therapist's role, and his or her availability during the training. Above all, based on what the parents have said about their concerns, the therapist should specify some preliminary goals of the treatment and strive for a consensus on the value of achieving these goals and the priority of each one. It is essential that the parents indicate which behaviors are most bothersome to them and why. Without a clear agreement about goals and an understanding of their importance, all further therapeutic work will be compromised.

The therapist should specify insofar as possible, a tentative timetable for achieving these goals. He should also indicate clearly how often, when, and where the sessions will be held, as well as the fees to be paid and a schedule for payment. The remainder of the third evaluation session can be spent on any remaining logistic details. Finally, the therapist should indicate how he can be reached during an emergency, providing brief guidelines about what he considers to be an emergency. Without the latter, many parents leave the session unclear about the circumstances under which it is reasonable to call the therapist outside sessions and when the therapist wants to be called.

Although the sequence of assessment has been outlined to cover three sessions, it can be done in more visits at the therapist's discretion. The assessment procedures, however, should not consist of fewer than three meetings.

7

Phase Two: Beginning Parent Training

MANY researchers have found that both parental satisfaction and generalization of effects are enhanced when parents are taught the principles that underlie behavioral change (Forehand and Atkinson 1977; Patterson et al. 1975; Weathers and Liberman 1977). The purpose of this phase is to give parents a theoretical framework within which to understand their child's behavior and to provide a basis for meaningful dialogue with their therapist. Not all parents benefit from a complete review of the principles; in some cases, a didactic exposition of the rationale underlying the techniques is appropriate. In other cases, the therapist may not feel that elucidating generalities in the abstract is at all helpful and will stick to understandings derived only from specific examples of difficulty.

Verbal and Nonverbal Therapist Interventions

Determining the appropriate manner in which to introduce these more general principles into therapy and to adapt them to the patients' needs in the form of guidelines is one of the therapist's first tasks in establishing the alliance with the parents. It is essential to the continuation of treatment that the alliance be maintained in the spirit of mutual respect and pursuit of a common goal. The therapist must communicate empathy, encouragement, and support both verbally and nonverbally. Supportive statements become crucial during this phase. In addition to providing education, the therapist attempts to allay the parents' anxiety and increase their sense of competency, mastery, and self-esteem through suggestions, encouragement, reassurance, and empathy. The therapist suggests essential attitudes and behaviors that mediate change, as well as indicating those that are counterproductive. He encourages the parents to respond to his comments and communicate their concerns. He resonates with their thoughts and feelings by labeling and echoing their perceived affects. The therapist provides reassurance that change can occur and maintains a positive attitude toward all parental efforts and concerns.

The following two sections, Basic Principles and Building and Maintaining a Secure Parent-Child Relationship, can be used as a separate entity. A little book-within-a-book, these sections organize and enunciate in a step-by-step manner the rationale underlying our approach to parent training. The material may be copied and given to the parents to read and consult with, independent of treatment sessions. Alternatively, the therapist may elect to introduce the material directly as a unit or indirectly to aid in the understanding of specific examples of problem behavior. In either case, it is essential the parents come to understand these concepts and perceive them as relevant to their immediate parenting experience.

Basic Principles: Secure Parent-Child Relationships

Behavioral disturbances in a child reflect inner difficulties that are not an obvious aspect of the problem behavior itself. The behavior is only the tip of the iceberg. In order to gain an understanding of the behavior, we must inquire into the nature of the relationships that have surrounded this child since conception, as well as the family relationships that have had an indirect effect on the child through their impact upon his parents. Although problem behavior affects others negatively and disrupts family organization, it does not originate with these goals consciously in mind. A child's behavior and the parents' reaction to it are not always under their conscious control and occur for reasons they cannot always understand. One of the ways to gain control over the negative cycle of parent-child interactions is to become aware of the specific events that trigger the behavior, the meaning these events have for parents and child, and the effects these parent-child interactions have on subsequent events.

The child's basic relationship with the parents establishes a model for relationships with others—siblings, peers, and teachers, for example. Establishing a secure relationship with his parents is fundamental to a child's maintaining self-esteem and a secure inner feeling of trust in the world. Usually the basis for this sense of trust is begun in the first three years of life, although it continues to develop throughout life.

Secure attachment to the parents results from separation and individuation: the child achieves a sense of independence and competence, separate from his parents. The key to this process of separation, carefully studied by Mahler (Mahler et al. 1975), lies in a parent's attunement to the child's feelings and ability to respond in a manner appropriate to the child's age.

Parents resonate to their children's communications by interpreting the children's signals on the basis of their personal life experiences, including that of having been children themselves. The parents' response is rapid and intuitive. It can be misattuned for various reasons, some based in the child and some in the parents. In general the parents' function is to provide first a warm and nurturing environment within which the child is accepted and can thrive, and second, a sturdy environment, one that will withstand the emotional storms of the needy infant. Limit setting and love are the essential ingredients that lead to a strong inner sense of self. Emotional closeness and distance are the two dimensions that measure the optimal relationship for a given child at a given age.

Several developmental concepts can contribute to an understanding of how an insecure parent-child relationship might develop. In different cases, different components may be relevant. In some instances, all or none of these components may be implied, but in most cases, some combination of the factors outlined in the following section is key to understanding a particular maladaptive parent-child relationship. It is the therapist's role to facilitate discussion of these factors and, together with the parents, to discern their relative impact on the ongoing problem behavior experienced by the family.

The Difficult Child

Alexander Thomas, Stella Chess, and Herbert Birch (1968) of New York University conducted a thirty-year study (the New York Longitudinal Study) in which nine temperamental traits, identifiable at birth and continuing throughout life, were traced in a group of children from birth to early adulthood. The nine temperamental traits are

1. *Activity Level:* How active is the child in general?
2. *Distractibility:* How easily is the child distracted? Can he pay attention?
3. *Persistence:* Does the child stay with something he likes? How persistent or stubborn is he when he wants something?
4. *Adaptability:* How does the child deal with transition and change?
5. *Approach/Withdrawal:* What is the child's initial response to novelty, such as new places, people, foods, and clothes?
6. *Intensity:* How loud is the child generally, whether happy or unhappy?
7. *Regularity:* How predictable is the child in her patterns of sleep, appetite, bowel habits?
8. *Sensory threshold:* How does the child react to sensory stimuli, such as noise, bright lights, colors, smells, pain, warm weather, tastes, and the texture of clothes? Is she easily bothered? Is she easily over-stimulated?
9. *Mood:* What is the child's basic mood? Do positive or negative reactions predominate?

Stanley Turecki and Leslie Tonner (1985) described a general system for assessing a child in eight of the areas. Their descriptions are as follows:

Temperamental trait	Easy	Difficult
Activity Level	Low	High
Distractibility	Low	High
Adaptability	Good	Poor
Approach/Withdrawal	Approach	Withdrawal
Intensity	Low	High
Regularity	Regular	Irregular
Sensory threshold	High	Low
Mood	Positive	Negative

Depending on how many areas of temperament fall on the difficult end of the spectrum, and to what extent the resulting behavior poses a problem for the parents, any given family may be dealing with a child who generally fits into one of the following categories:

• Basically easy but with some difficult features: The parents are coping but may need to learn some management techniques and principles of discipline.

• Difficult: The child is hard to raise and there is strain on the mother and usually on the family.

• Very difficult: Both the child and the family are in trouble.

- Impossible: The child is a "mother-killer." (Turecki and Tonner 1985, p. 15)

The children we deal with in this book can all be placed somewhere on this continuum of difficult children.

Difficult Phases in Child Development

At certain ages, most children experience some marked difficulty in adapting to their surroundings. These ubiquitous difficult developmental periods usually occur at times of transition between one period of development and another. Most parents are acquainted with the notion of "the terrible twos," but they may be unaware that the span of this period may begin earlier—in some instances as early as fourteen months—and continue until later—as late as three years—than is usually anticipated. It is helpful for parents to be aware of these normal developmental stresses. Another critical juncture occurs when the preschooler enters grade school. Problems in adaptation may be evidenced as early as five years or as late as seven years. Following a relatively stable period of school-age adaptation, the child again manifests normal upheavals and tensions during preadolescence. In our culture, preadolescent stress for some children begins as early as ten years of age, while for others it may be delayed until fourteen years of age. At these transitional periods, children share a propensity for oppositional, angry, persistent, and uneven responses to their environment. The usual, predictable pattern of response is broken, and the intensity of responses may run the full gamut from unbearable to barely noticeable. At these times children universally present with perplexing and provocative patterns of behavior. The therapist must help the parents to discern how these predictable periods of turmoil have affected their child and the parent-child relationship.

Difficulty in Parent-Child Interaction

The occurrence of a temperamental mismatch between parent and child has been termed the *problem of fit*. For example, a slow-to-warm-up child may be paired with an active, intense parent, who initiates approaches to her child and expects an immediate response. The number of incompatible patterns is considerable, and the consequences of mismatching are harmful to both parent and child. Frustration, anger, anxiety, and disappointment interfere with the synchronous functioning of the parent-child pair, and disharmony develops.

Two common difficulties that impair parental functioning are lack of specificity and a lack of individuation. A parent who lacks specificity is unable to attune to and focus on the messages communicated by the child. She is distracted or for some other reason blocked from receiving the signals given by the child and either does not respond or is misattuned, responding inappropriately. On the other hand, a parent who lacks individuation fails to perceive the child as an independent being, separate from her own needs or desires. There are two major sources of this lack of individuation. First, patterns of response deriving from the parent's past may distort her understanding of the child's needs. The child is perceived as repeating some prior experience of the parent, and the result is misattunement and an inappropriate response. Second, there may be reversal of roles. Because of feelings of parental anxiety and inadequacy, the child is given too much power. The child, rather than the parents, is in control of the situation, determining how limits will be set and how his or her needs will be met. Whenever the child is not individuated from the parent in an age-appropriate manner, the parent is prone to distorted perceptions that affect parent-child interactions adversely.

The Good-Enough Parent

Donald Winnicott (1965) was the first to describe the good-enough parent. The good-enough parent is far from ideal: adequate to the task, but not perfect. She provides the child with sufficient opportunity to experience his angry, aggressive, hurting feelings within the confines of a relationship that assures safety, both from physical assaults and from emotional injury. Injuries and mishaps do occur, but they occur within the spectrum of manageability. The spectrum itself is flexible and adapted to the child's needs and strengths. Through his experience with the less-than-perfect parent, the child learns to endure a world that is not perfect and not under his omnipotent control. The end result of the pairing of a good-enough parent and her child are the child's feelings of self-esteem, which parallel the parent's feelings of competence.

It is the object of this book to deal with good-enough parent-child relationships, in the recognition that the pursuit of perfection is folly. In fact, the pursuit of perfection itself undermines the goal of parenting, which is the gradual relinquishment of the child to a less-than-perfect world.

Building and Maintaining a Secure Parent-Child Relationship

A secure relationship between parent and child is the framework that provides both parent and child with a sense of organization of boundaries between self and other, as well as the regulation of separate and mutual roles. *Organization* refers to the limits and structure that determine how a relationship will be constructed. *Roles* involve those behaviors that are performed as part of this organizational structure, translating the relationship into everyday activities. Maintaining control within the relationship requires that these rules and roles be explicitly defined, understood, and practiced as part of daily routine.

A secure relationship combines three basic ingredients: warmth, firmness, and consistency. We will explore how each of these components contributes to the formation and maintenance of a parent-child relationship. We will also describe specific ways to communicate a sense of warmth, firmness, and consistency to the child.

Providing Warmth, Acceptance, Reassurance, and Support

Positive feelings act to strengthen and enhance a relationship. If desirable behaviors occur, the probability that they will recur is enhanced by positive consequences. These positive effects will be referred to as rewards, or reinforcement. To be strengthened, a behavior must be rewarded; if it is no longer rewarded, it can be weakened. Positive feelings allay the universal experience of anxiety and insecurity that one is unwanted and unloved. If the only way to acquire a response from parents is through negative behaviors, then these behaviors will be strengthened. We call such behaviors *negative attention-getting behaviors.* They achieve the reward of being attended to and therefore are repeated. In the extreme case, a child comes to understand that only by being difficult, mean, or bad can he receive the love he desires.

A new adage, "Catch your child being good," (Becker 1971) implies that if you do not reward, or reinforce, your child when he is being good, you will get less good behavior. The child looks to the parent for messages of approval or disapproval, love or rejection. Perceiving the child for who he is and rewarding any approximate efforts at positive behaviors will enhence the parent's relationship to him. These positive behaviors may be minimal at first, but the impact of the positive response from the parent will enable these fledgling behaviors to become full participant behaviors in the secure relationship.

Establishing Firmness, Strength, and Objectivity

Firmness implies parental strength and lack of ambiguity. The clear message of acceptance of some behaviors and nonacceptance of others helps to structure behaviors in a positive manner. It is important for the parents to convey the message that they accept the whole child, including both his or her good feelings *and* bad feelings, without qualification. This acceptance is conveyed through emotional availability for attunement, empathy, and reflection. At the same time, parents must firmly and clearly enunciate the limits. While the child's full array of emotions is open to scrutiny and mutual understanding, negative actions cannot be permitted. Often these limits must be communicated in the heat of confrontation, but it is crucial that the parent not be enticed into a battle situation with the child.

Whenever possible, limits—and the consequences of exceeding them— should be explicit in advance. In the heat of confrontation, no extensive conversations should be attempted. The parent should apply the limits to the child clearly, nonthreateningly, but firmly ("You are shouting, therefore you must go to your room"; "If you do not follow the rules, there will be no TV"). Maintaining stable affect and firmness permits the boundaries between parent and child to remain in place. The parent remains apart from the heat of the battle and firm in his or her position as adult. Discussion may be delayed for several days or may not occur at all. In either case, the child comes to anticipate a firm, unwavering, unambivalent parental response to his or her behavior that is as important as anticipating the consequences of actions. Being firm reinforces the parent's position as adult and communicates to the child feelings of competence and self-assurance in his or her parental role.

Maintaining Consistency, Regulation, and Organization

The parent's consistency acts as a secure base for the child's behavior. His or her regular, dependable response is a reference point to which the child returns again and again. At first this reference point is external to the child and depends upon the parental presence. Gradually the child comes to accept the warm, firm, consistent parental response as his own, internalizing it as part of his personal repertoire. The toddler who looks at a sharp object and says, "No, no," is talking to himself, having internalized the voice of the parent.

Although it is important that the parent be consistent and at first relatively rigid and inflexible, some variability within limits is possible with time and growth. The child can begin to anticipate a variety of parental responses, depending upon the circumstance. For example, when a positive response is required, the parent needs to decide if the appropriate expression of approval would be material (involving money, tokens, privileges, candy, and the like) or social (a verbal expression, a hug, or pat on the back, for example). Social responses are more variable and more readily available than material rewards; indeed, they are endless in supply and more useful for both establishing and maintaining a behavior. Material rewards are effective initially but less effective in maintaining behavior. The parent must decide what reward would be appropriate for his or her child. If the reward is too large, the child will become tired of it quickly; if the reward is too small, it will not motivate the child to change his behavior. Selection of the appropriate reward requires foresight and planning. It cannot be made on the spur of the moment or at the impulsive whim of the parent.

The parent must also be consistent in her attitude of availability, both for self-referencing and for self-regulation. Exactly how this attitude is expressed will vary with different parent-child pairs and with each pair over time, but the consistency of parental response should be reliable and dependable.

To summarize, an efficient strategy for providing a reward for the child includes the following factors:

1. The reward is meaningful and relevant to the specific child. Selecting the appropriate reward requires a knowledge and careful consideration of what matters positively and negatively to the child.
2. The child must know about the selection of the reward and the contingencies for receiving it well in advance of its utilization. The reward strategy needs to be made public, so that everyone acting on the child's behalf behaves consistently.
3. Deprivation of the reward should not be something the parents deem their child would experience as exceedingly cruel. Some degree of protest, which may be extremely intense initially, is to be expected as the child's wishes are thwarted and gratification denied.
4. The reward strategy should be possible to administer in a foolproof way for as long as necessary.

The Damaging Effect of Negative, Rejecting, and Punishing Responses

Extensive punishment sets up escape and avoidant behaviors that may be more harmful to the relationship between parent and child than is the behavior being punished (Wittes and Radin 1968). The consequences of punishment that originate in anger or frustration are anxiety for the child, and guilt for the parent. Punishment that is the outcome of punitive parental impulses will probably reduce noncompliance for a while, but it does not eliminate the child's motivation for engaging in negative behavior. The behavior is likely to reappear shortly. To be effective, punishment must be administered every time the negative behavior occurs, but because the parents are not with their child every second, this standard is impossible to achieve. The behavior therefore actually gets stronger.

Moreover, since punishment loses its effectiveness with frequent and continued use, more and more severe punishments are required. If physical punishment is used, the parent provides a model of aggression for her child. The punishing parent loses effectiveness with her child in several ways: first, the child will avoid her; second, because she is continuously associated with punishment, her value as a positive influence on her child decreases; and finally, she becomes a target for the aggression that she is modeling. This position within the family further increases the child's negative behavior toward the parent (Forehand and McMahon 1981).

Many people find it difficult to accept this view of punishment, for they were punished as children as the sole means of discipline. If we want to succeed as parents, we must have a strong desire to offer our children something we did not receive, thereby strengthening relationships within the family for future generations. Reciprocity implies that among family members, "You get what you give" (Patterson 1975, p. 20). To receive positive behavior from another family member, you have to give it first. If you give negative behavior to another family member, you should expect it in return. Positive parenting leads to positive responses from children, which further enhance the relationship between them. Reciprocal negative responses, on the other hand, lay the groundwork for fear, anxiety, and insecurity, even though the short-term effects may be gratifying. The disciplining parent, like the misbehaving child, must learn to delay gratification. The security of long-term ties between parent and child is endangered by misusing power and resorting to punishment. Secure bonds are built on the basis of reliable and firm parental expectations, accompanied by warm feelings and acceptance of the child along with all his diverse feelings.

8

Phase Three: Practicing New Understandings

W E have discussed the importance of the three essential components—warmth, firmness, and consistency—in structuring a secure parent-child relationship. How can these qualities be instilled as part of parent-child interaction?

During the third phase of parent training, the therapist continues her supportive role, describing new techniques of management, teaching new skills, and encouraging parental participation, exploration, and experimentation. In the context of trial and error, the parents come to depend upon the therapist for her understanding and guidance. The therapist can often help them to view behaviors from a different perspective, enabling change to occur.

Verbal Interventions by the Therapist

In addition to her supportive, empathic stance, the therapist now expands her repertoire of verbal interventions to include facilitative statements that focus upon what the parents are doing and experiencing. The therapist initiates, enhances, or maintains communication with the parents through invitations to continue, review statements, and directing the parents' attention to specific events and the connections between them. The therapist conveys ongoing attention to, interest in, and comprehension of what the parents have said. She may initiate conversation about a topic, or she may request expansion or additional information after a topic has been introduced by the parents. The therapist also paraphrases, summarizes, or integrates what the parents have said or done up to that point or in the past. Role-playing may be used to dramatize the actions described.

Finally, the therapist confronts the parents to make them begin to examine and direct their attention to the patterns that link thought and feelings with action. As the parents grow in their capacity for frustration, tolerance, and self-reflection, the therapist can encourage them to look at increasingly broader spans of their patterns of interaction. It is important that the therapist pace her confrontations well, avoiding the negative effects of overload or overwhelming experience. The purpose of the therapist's confrontational statements is to point out the conditions and their consequences that form the familial patterns of interaction within which the problematic behaviors arise thus enabling the parents to observe the consequences of their actions within the family. At times these statements by the therapist link behaviors to thoughts and feelings that were not available previously to the parents' conscious awareness. Interpretations of parental behavior might refer to defenses, wishes, or motives of underlying current or past parental behavior.

Setting up the Behavior Log

The behavior log was first introduced as part of the assessment procedure. In that phase, parents are introduced to the notion of the usefulness of recording their children's behavior. The instructions given are minimal, and parents are free to record whatever seems relevant to them. Their selection of events as well as their understanding of them is useful to the therapist in beginning to identify types of parental response.

In phase three, the behavior log is reintroduced, but this time explicit instructions are given for the format. Parents are asked to acquire a separate notebook for this purpose, to be kept handy at all times. They are asked to record the following information: (1) the date and time of day the behavioral event occurs; (2) a description of the event; (3) their response to the event; and (4) the consequences—for example, what happens following their intervention. Parents are instructed to record their actions, thoughts, and feelings—as well as their child's behavior—that are associated with the specific parent-child interaction. The log is brought in weekly to be discussed and provides a major focus for the training sessions.

In some instances, several sessions may be required to motivate the parents sufficiently to keep the log. In such cases, the therapist begins with whatever information is reported by the parents, even if it has not been recorded, and demonstrates how the event could have been written in the log. If after several sessions the parents still are not keeping the log, the therapist must inquire further to ascertain the factors underlying this resistance. Among these factors may be parental lack of confidence, laziness, or an unwillingness to devote time and effort to the problem outside of regular sessions. Although these reasons need to be explored and worked on, it is also important to demonstrate the importance of a behavior record (kept either in writing or in memory) to the progress of training. In fact, if the parents do not report in a consistent way, the process cannot proceed.

Improving the Physical Environment and Parental Administrative Skills

The therapist needs to understand the physical layout of the home—its various rooms and the different functions they serve. Particular attention is given to sharing of rooms, possible crowding or isolation, noise factors, and the situation of the home in the larger environment (for example, is it a private home, an apartment, in the country or city?). The therapist must be aware of the stability of the physical home environment— whether there are plans to move or change it, who has ownership, and so on—and must consider how these factors impinge on family interaction and what changes are feasible and which are not possible. In the case of the latter, the therapist assists the parents in coming to terms with, and making the best of, a difficult situation.

The other aspect of family living fundamental to the therapist's inquiries is the family's routine. Daily time schedules often reflect hidden facets of family relationships that need further exploration. Chaotic schedules, overly rigid scheduling, or the lack of a time schedule for a particular family member can contribute to a child's difficulties. The therapist may have to help the parents set up an age-appropriate schedule for the child, including time allotted to homework, TV, and after-school activities, as well as set hours for going to bed and getting up. The therapist can be useful in pointing out how activities might be rearranged to facilitate progress.

Other aspects that can be explored include family responsibilities and decision making, the advisability of an allowance, self-help skills at mealtimes and dressing, and the use of leisure time. Although each of these areas may be addressed specifically when relevant to a particular problem, the therapist also evaluates the overall administrative aspects of family functioning in order to suggest age-appropriate means of organization.

Improving Parental Interpersonal Skills

Focusing and Attunement

Focusing means directing the parents' attention to their child in ways that will help them understand the child. The therapist directs the parent to focus on relevant behaviors, verbalizations, and feelings. The therapist is like a parent, who points a finger to guide the child's attention to the relevant stimulus event. The therapist thus becomes a participant in the event, although she often receives information secondhand and relies upon parental report and her own internalized vicarious response. At first the parents may be heavily dependent upon the therapist for direction and clarity of vision, but gradually they will come to maintain a consistent focus of their own. The parents come to learn their child to the point of imitation and are able to evoke the specific repertoire of responses they have observed in memory. This capacity for evocative memory of their child's responses acts to enhance the development of affective attunement.

Affective attunement (Stern 1985) refers to the sharing of a feeling state, which is responsive but not necessarily directly imitative. By focusing on their child's behavior, parents can eventually progress to attuning to the feelings that underlie the behaviors. Indeed, as their attunement grows, they may discover that a relatively small number of feeling states can account for a wide variety of disruptive behaviors. These core feeling states are often intense (for example, terror, not just mild anxiety) and therefore indicate the extent of disorganization and the resistance of the behavior to change. It is experiencing these feelings with the therapist that enables the parent to endure them with relative equanimity in the presence of their child. By attuning to their child's feelings in this manner, the parent is reaching behind the external behaviors and is concentrating upon the quality of feeling being shared. Before this attunement can be attained, however, it is necessary to begin by focusing upon external behaviors. Often something that occurred in early infancy has resulted in misattunement between parent and child. These disparate strands of feelings and behaviors must be retrieved to reweave a new quality of textured interaction between parent and child.

Empathy and Facilitating Communication

Empathy (Demos 1984; Stern 1985; Hoffman 1978) involves not only resonating with a feeling state but also abstracting knowledge from the emotional experience and integrating this understanding into a response. At these moments the parent is truly identifying with her child. Not all parents are able to reach a level of empathic understanding, but for those who are capable of self-reflection and impulse control and who have access to memories of their own childhood, these understandings follow attunement. Empathy involves distance and self-observation, not only an ability to focus on and attune to present events but also the capacity to reflect upon one's life and feelings. It is a creative recall based upon immersing oneself in the present and integrating relevant components from one's personal past.

The empathic moment shares many of the attributes of an "a-ha!" experience, eliciting a profound sense of sharing and deep understanding. The therapist may exercise her empathic response to demonstrate its essence to the parents. In fact, what she brings to bear when the parents describe their own trials and tribulations is often a new experience for parents who have never known the feeling of being understood in a nonjudgmental, nonthreatening relationship. This is the kind of understanding that, it is hoped, they will learn to provide for their own child.

THERAPIST: Tell me more about John's difficulty with his brother.

MOTHER: It's not only his brother. It also goes on at school. He's always hitting the other children and hurting them.

FATHER: He seems to have no understanding of other people's feelings and just wants to hurt others.

THERAPIST: He seems to want to hit and hurt others. Can you tell me more specifically how this happens?

MOTHER: John, who's ten, and his brother Tom, who's two years younger than he—although they're almost equal in size—are always arguing. It seems that they argue over anything and everything: who sits where at the table; who gets to the bathroom first; what TV program we will watch.

THERAPIST: Any decision or choice seems to be an argument.

FATHER: Tom will just argue, but John, he will fight, hit, and do whatever he has to do to get his way.

THERAPIST: Tell me more about one incident.

MOTHER: Well, the other evening we were just ready for dinner, and I heard a lot of noise coming from the living room. I rushed in, and there were the two boys fighting over a baseball card. Each one insisted it was his. Tom was ready to give in, it seemed, and John just raised his hand and hit him on the shoulder. At first he seemed to only want to frighten him, but then he just let him have it. It really makes me angry to see him get physical that way.

THERAPIST: Does anyone else get physical in the family?

FATHER: Well, Mother never does. But, on the other hand, I do. She and I are very different. That's how I was raised when I was a kid, and it worked. So, if he gets physical, I just get physical back with him.

THERAPIST: How did it feel when your father hit you?

FATHER: It would make me angry. I would get so angry I would want to hit him back. But—well, we knew we kids couldn't get away with that, and besides, he was bigger. But . . . I sure would get mad, really mad.

MOTHER: I get mad too when John hits out. I walk away. It's not that I'm not angry, but I find walking away is the only way I can keep my temper under control. I used to yell a lot, but nothing seemed to matter.

THERAPIST: How do you feel when you walk away?

MOTHER: I still feel angry, and I guess John does too. Maybe he feels I don't love him then, because I walk away. And I don't love him—at those moments it's hard to love him when he's hurting someone else. My mother and father would never allow hitting in our home. I just can't understand how John dares to hit out that way.

FATHER: Yeah—he was born that way, a tough kid. Nothing seems to bother him, and he assumes nothing bothers anyone else—even getting hurt. I've seen him come home with a black eye. I ask him, "What happened, John?" He says, "Nothing." Nothing will change that kid, nothing.

THERAPIST: It sounds like you are both pretty discouraged. It seems like nothing can help John. How do you think John feels about his hitting and hurting others?

FATHER: I don't think he has feelings. He just hits out.

THERAPIST: It sounds as if he and you both use hitting as a way of expressing your feelings.

FATHER: I only hit when it's the last resort—there's no other answer. I just feel one good swipe and it'll all be over. It just can't go on this way. Something has to stop this behavior.

THERAPIST: So you hit in order to stop—to put an end to something—bad behavior, which is unacceptable. Does it work?

FATHER: Well—it sure gets out my feelings. Once they're out, I feel relieved and for the moment all is quiet.

MOTHER: When Phil's not home—when it's just me and the kids—I'm beside myself. When Tommy gets hit, I yell and yell. I say things I'm sorry for later, like "Get out of here, you rotten kid. You can't be a member of this family. Go away and don't come back."

THERAPIST: These are very strong and painful feelings.

FATHER: Well, you should be in our house when this fighting goes on—and it's always John's fault. It just has to be stopped.

THERAPIST: It just has to be stopped. I wonder if John doesn't feel the same way. Something terrible happens—a baby is born and seems to take his place; nothing is his any longer—his toys, his books, even his parents are not just his any longer—and he feels it needs to be stopped.

MOTHER: Do you think John has any feelings when he's hurting someone else? It seems as if he has no feelings at all. He sometimes frightens me.

FATHER: Well, maybe we all share the same feeling—that things are impossible and need to be stopped.

THERAPIST: John certainly has feelings, although he doesn't talk about them. Instead, he acts them out. He is using actions to express some very strong feelings—that life with Tom is impossible and something needs to be done to stop him. John also can't stand the feelings of anger he has inside of him because of Tom's presence and what he does. So he shows you through his actions how badly he wants this impossible situation to stop.

MOTHER: He resented Tom's arrival so much. It seemed he was so happy until then. It's even hard to remember how sweet he could be before Tom came on the scene. I think he never forgave us for having a baby— especially me, the mother. How angry he was when I had to give my attention to the baby. I remember feeling that way, too, when my baby brother was born. I never forgave my parents.

FATHER: What can we do to reach John? My hitting doesn't seem to be the answer.

THERAPIST: Hitting does give some immediate relief, but over the long haul, it just leads to more anger and more hitting. John sees you hit and learns from you that that is the way to solve problems.

FATHER: I never thought of it that way. But, of course, over the long haul, it simply doesn't work.

THERAPIST: Let me suggest that after the time-out procedure we discussed earlier, when John is calm, you might talk with him about what happened. You might give him words that would help him express his anger.

FATHER: But he will only get angry again—about the baseball cards, or whatever, and insist that his way of seeing things is the right way.

THERAPIST: When we are intensely upset, it's often difficult to see another point of view. What would help John is if you would join him, join him in experiencing what he is feeling and give words to it.

MOTHER: You mean—just say, "You're angry now, son, very angry."

THERAPIST: That's right. Now let's try and role-play it together. This time, you be John and I'll be the mother.

MOTHER: Let's see—he'd say, "You just don't understand. You never do understand. Tom took all of my cards—all of my cards."

THERAPIST: You are very, very angry with me. You feel I do not understand. It's so impossible when I don't understand. It feels so lonely to feel no one ever understands. You are angry, and you feel it is all Tom's fault.

FATHER: That's all? Just say back to him what you think he is feeling?

THERAPIST: That's it. Share with him. Let him know that you can feel what he feels—the pain, the hurt, the humiliation.

FATHER: But what if he gets overheated and angry again?

THERAPIST: Then send him back for another time-out and try to reopen the dialogue when feelings are cooler and the atmosphere is less tense. Often, just letting John know you can share his feelings will lighten the atmosphere enough to allow tensions to dissipate and new, more constructive behaviors to occur.

This first exercise in attunement and empathic understanding needs to be worked through in many different versions, in many sessions, until it becomes an acquired skill. In this family, the perpetuation of old family patterns of acting out, aggression, repeated loss of control, and the split in roles between husband and wife—all reflect typical constellations of punitive familial behavior. The parents will need considerable support and rehearsal in putting their new understanding into practice.

Relating their own life experience to the experience of their child is important to the parents' understanding of their child and his feelings. Telling the child of their own similar experiences is not helpful, however; it imposes another block to communication. This is a way in which parents with all of the best intentions often err in communicating with their children. To enhance a child's experience of being understood, the parents must attune to him, joining him and reflecting his feelings and experience. It is this mirroring of feeling in a caring manner that helps their child feel they have been able to join him in his distress and to alleviate his pain and aloneness. Role-play is an important facilitator in this parental learning. The use of time-out procedures and other limit-setting measures, to be discussed later in this chapter, are important adjunct skills that also must be discussed and rehearsed.

Self-Reflection and Problem Solving

As the parents become more focused and attuned to their child's feelings, they come to understand the connection between feelings and behavior. Specifically, negative behaviors can often be understood as the child's attempt to gain warmth and approval from his parents. When he has been unable to receive it in a positive manner, he then pursues a more negative means to achieve his goal of recognition.

A parent must learn to reflect upon her own response to her child's need for interaction. Self-reflection may lead her to delay an immediate response and initiate a process of problem solving. The first question to be asked is "What is going on here?" followed by a further query, "What am I feeling?" then, "Why do I feel this way?" and finally, "What can I do about it?" Parents need to be supported in delaying their response, pursuing an understanding of what is happening, and exploring various alternative modes of responding.

From the behavior log, the therapist and the parents may select examples and enact them, exploring various possible ways of responding. Parents must be brought to the understanding that a single event may be the outcome of various different causal inputs and that the appropriate response might vary, depending on what aspect of the event the parent chooses to focus upon. Rather than responding immediately, deferring a response and taking the time to explore several alternative solutions might give the parent the chance to choose the best possible response.

Delaying a response also allows the parent to modulate it, and thus the intensity of the negative behavior is not matched by the intensity of the response. In fact, different skills are suitable for different phases of intervention. During the heat of the conflict, firmness and containment are needed. When the conflict and emotional intensity have diminished, verbal explanations and reasoning can be introduced.

Parents need to rehearse and experience the various levels of emotional intensity in order to be able to focus on what is going on and to respond appropriately: It is difficult for them to fathom that a response does not have to be returned in kind; rather, it can be given with understanding. If parents are able to grasp this principle of problem solving and delay, they will have taken a major step in breaking a sense of coercion in the parent-child interaction.

THERAPIST: I notice from reviewing your behavior log that you're particularly bothered by Sean's interrupting while you are talking together, or when one of you is talking to someone else or is on the telephone.

MOTHER: Yes! He constantly interrupts and doesn't seem to be able to wait until I'm done to ask his question or say what he wants.

FATHER: I notice the same kind of thing, only with me, it's when I'm on the phone. If Sean's around, whenever I pick up the receiver it's his signal to start talking to me or doing something I'm sure to notice and not like, like teasing the dog.

THERAPIST: Do either of you have any idea why he behaves like this?

MOTHER: It seems as though he wants our individual attention—as though he can't stand it when we're talking with each other or someone else.

THERAPIST: How do each of you usually feel when Sean behaves this way?

MOTHER: I usually feel extremely angry—very irritated, to say the very least. At times I get so angry that I break off my conversation with whoever I'm talking to and yell at him.

THERAPIST: Does this help?

MOTHER: No, unfortunately not. Sean just usually cries or has a temper tantrum, which completely disrupts my conversation, because then I have to deal with his behavior.

THERAPIST: [to Father] What about your reaction?

FATHER: Well, I usually get angry and tell him very firmly to stop what he's doing.

THERAPIST: Does this work?

FATHER: Not usually. He generally whines or says, "No!" and then I have to deal with that.

THERAPIST: So both of you end up discontinuing your conversation to respond to Sean?

FATHER AND MOTHER: Yes.

THERAPIST: Well, it certainly seems as though Sean has learned how to divert your attention and keep it. Why do you think each of you becomes so angry when he interrupts?

FATHER: Well, I guess I feel that I've done enough with him for that day and that I'm entitled to some time to myself to do my thing.

MOTHER: In addition, it's not as though we don't pay attention to him. When he's not in school, I spend almost all my time with him in one way or another—he goes everyplace with me.

THERAPIST: How do you mean?

MOTHER: Well, instead of leaving him at a friend's or with a babysitter, I'll take him with me if I have an errand to do, or something.

THERAPIST: Why do that?

MOTHER: Well, frankly, it's often easier.

THERAPIST: What sort of message do you think the behavior of always taking him with you might be giving an eight-year-old boy?

MOTHER: Well, I'm not sure . . . maybe, that I want him with me?

THERAPIST: Or, perhaps, that he should be with you, or that it may not be safe not to be with you. When you talk to someone else or make a telephone call, do you tell Sean you're about to do this, how long you'll be, and ask not to be interrupted?

MOTHER: No—not that I recall. Why? Should I?

THERAPIST: What do you think about that?

MOTHER: Well, what would be the point?

THERAPIST: Let's try and imagine why Sean is acting this way. One theory might be that he is a spoiled brat. Do either of you think that?

FATHER: No, I don't think so because he's not very demanding in any other circumstances. He doesn't expect a lot of toys, or want what other kids want. He just seems to demand a lot of our time and attention.

MOTHER: I'd agree with that.

THERAPIST: Well, let's think of another alternative explanation. What about the possibility that he is so attached to you that he becomes anxious when you divert your attention away from him to someone else?

MOTHER: You mean talking to me is a way of being with me?

THERAPIST: In a way.

MOTHER: And when I talk to someone else, I'm leaving Sean alone?

THERAPIST: That's the idea.

MOTHER: Well, then, I guess I get so angry because he never seems to be able to be left alone.

FATHER: Yeah, he always seems to want something, more attention.

THERAPIST: Sometimes, when children are frightened of being alone, they may use any opportunity or tactic not to permit themselves to be left— including being obnoxious.

MOTHER: If that's true, what do we do about it?

THERAPIST: The first step is to recognize anxiety as the cause of Sean's behavior. The second is to find some ways of enabling him to feel secure while being left alone—in little ways at first and then in bigger ways.

MOTHER: How do we do that?

THERAPIST: One possible way is to introduce the experience of being on his own gradually. That's why I asked if you ever warned Sean ahead of time when you were about to make a phone call. For example, you might say to Sean, "I'm going to make a quick call—two minutes—and then I'll be off. If you can leave me alone for that time, I'll be very pleased and you can have a cookie." Then you try and make your call and keep it to two minutes or less. If Sean is successful in not disturbing you, praise him lavishly and give him a cookie. If he's unsuccessful, then you know two minutes was too long for him to wait.

MOTHER: Should I punish him if he doesn't wait?

THERAPIST: How do you feel about that?

MOTHER: Well, I guess I'd be angry, but since punishing doesn't work, probably not. But then what should I do?

THERAPIST: What about simply sharing with Sean what you've learned? Namely, that two minutes by himself is too long for him to tolerate without seeking out contact from you. You might add that next time he might be able to wait a minute and a half.

FATHER: You mean we might need to break him of this behavior gradually?

THERAPIST: Well, I wouldn't call this procedure "breaking him"; rather, it's more helpful to think of increasing Sean's independence. Once we think of the problem this way, we can also think of the corresponding problem of reducing his anxiety. This way of thinking, then, allows us to think about what kind of solutions would be most effective.

In this example, parental lack of awareness of the probable origin of the child's behavior has resulted in a negative cycle of interaction between parent and child. While the mother has some inkling of the child's intense desire for attachment, she does not appreciate the extent to which she reinforces his attachment-seeking behavior and his corresponding difficulty with separation. Both parents are aware that uninhibited expression of anger on their part is not effective in limiting the child's undesirable behavior. The therapist utilizes this awareness, as well as the insight that attention seeking may be due to separation anxiety, to assist the parents in devising alternative strategies for responding more effectively to the child. A fundamental feature of this approach is that parents are asked to evaluate different explanations and identify possible causal connections between a specific hypothesis and the behavior they observe. Here, both parents are able to reject the commonplace hypothesis that the child is demanding because they do not frequently set appropriate limits (for example, he's "spoiled"). They know from their experience with the child that since his demanding behavior is exhibited selectively, another hypothesis is required. Separation anxiety seems likely, because both parents report the experience that the child seems to want primarily "time and attention." Whether this working hypothesis is correct can be determined only when the parents attempt to implement the therapist's desensitization procedure and report on its progress.

Effective Limit Setting

Gerald Patterson (1982) presents the following essential criteria for successful parent training. The parents must learn to stay out of coercive interchanges. When they do get involved, they must use the kind of responses that are effective. They must win every time they engage the child in this manner.

To help parents improve their limit-setting skills, the therapist trains them to use several techniques: rewarding and ignoring, giving commands, the time-out procedure, the quiet-time procedure, and the playtime procedure. We will examine each of these techniques in turn.

Gerald Patterson (1982) notes one invariable characteristic of parents of aggressive children: they cannot, or do not, punish well. Instead of applying effective consequences to aggressive behavior, they engage in other behaviors, such as scolding and threatening, that do not productively confront the behavior. Gerald Patterson refers to this parent behavior as *nattering,* or *irritable aggression.* This is a negative verbal response that is not backed up by constructive punishment.

Although we generally agree with Patterson, we do not find punishment per se a constructive behavior modification technique. Rather, we have found that parental disapproval, time-out, ignoring of behavior (when indicated), and, of course, physical restraint of aggressive behavior, when necessary, are far more viable than aversive stimulation. Moreover, consistency and promptness in applying these techniques, as well as rewarding desirable behavior, are generally sufficient to limit a child's noncompliance. It is important to stress that all behavioral management strategies are most effective when parents have acquired skills in attuning, empathizing, and rewarding. The persistent use of aversive techniques tends to undermine the quality of the child's attachment to the parent while not necessarily deterring the child from acting negatively in the future.

Rewarding and ignoring

Rewards occur following a specific behavior and specifically evaluate that behavior as positive. Rex Forehand and Robert McMahon (1981) teach parents three kinds of rewards: (1) physical rewards, various kinds of physical affection, such as hugs, kisses, and pats on the back; (2) unlabeled verbal rewards—praise statements, such as "Terrific," "That's great"— although positive in evaluation do not tell the child exactly what is being reinforced; and (3) labeled verbal rewards, statements that specify the behavior the parent is reinforcing—"Thank you for cleaning up the table"; "You really helped Johnny a lot"—not only praise the child but also attend specifically to the ongoing activity.

Rex Forehand and Robert McMahon also emphasize four general guidelines: "(1) Rewards should immediately follow desirable behavior; (2) rewards should be specific; (3) rewards should be used consistently; (4) once the behavior is well established, the rewards should be reduced in frequency to a more intermittent frequency" (1981, p. 67). The parents need to rehearse giving rewards with the therapist, using role-playing. As the parents become skilled in the techniques, the therapist rewards them appropriately.

Counterbalancing the use of positive attention by the parents is the use of withdrawal of attention, or ignoring minor annoying behavior. To withdraw attention means to disengage, to turn away from the child physically and give no verbal, eye, or body contact to the child. The parent should explain to the child the purpose and intention of her actions before she actually begins to employ this technique; any explanation while using it would destroy its effectiveness. The child senses that the parent has lost interest, has withdrawn contact, and is not available for communication. When the negative behavior is discontinued, contact with the child is resumed.

This is a technique the parent can employ when she herself is losing control. Rather than confront the child with the intensity of her own rage, she can withdraw to an adjacent room until she is under better control. The disadvantage of this approach is that the parent loses touch with what is happening with the child; it can therefore be used only under circumscribed conditions, in which the behavior can be easily contained without leading to a spiral of further aggressive behavior.

Giving commands

Several researchers (Peed et al. 1977; Roberts et al. 1978) have demonstrated the importance of parental command behavior in influencing the child's compliance. The command-training segment of our treatment program corresponds to that described by Rex Forehand and Robert McMahon (1981). Parents are taught to give commands to their child in the following manner:

1. Be specific and direct. First get the child's attention. Call the child by name, and pause until eye contact is established. The voice should be firm and slightly louder than usual. Phrase the command as a "do" command, rather than as a "stop" command, in order to tell the child what behavior is expected of him or her. Say exactly what you expect and phrase the command in words the child understands. Use gestures to illustrate the meaning of the command whenever possible.

2. Give commands one at a time. If there are several tasks to be completed, a separate command should be given for each one.
3. Pause and wait for the child to comply. No further commands should be issued until the child initiates compliance.

If the child does not comply with the order within a short time, the parent should apply the consequences established for noncompliance. On the other hand, if the child initiates compliance within a short time, the parent should reward him or her as described in the previous section. Compliance should be rewarded promptly and frequently. Giving the child attention is particularly useful in maintaining compliance to a task that takes some time to complete. Labeled verbal rewards are most appropriate for the initiation and completion of compliance.

The time-out procedure

Time-out is an interruption of the focus of an interaction. It is a logical extension of ignoring, but in this case the child is sent out of visual contact with the parent, preferably to his own room, as a holding action. Just as the young child is physically restrained and contained by the parent's physical body, the older child is contained by the confines of his room. With younger children it may be preferable to use the stairs or a time-out chair as the specified location. Time-out periods vary from five to twenty minutes, depending upon the age of the child. The amount of time used is always consistent and is decided upon in conjunction with the therapist.

The purpose of the time-out procedure is not necessarily punitive in the painful sense. Although the child's activity is interrupted, he is allowed to pursue activities of his choice within his room. Thus, he may choose to read, rest, play, or engage in a quiet project. He may not come out of his room, however, until the parent indicates that the allotted time is up. If at the end of the time the child is still in a tantrum, another time-out segment is assigned. These time-out periods are strung together until control is reinstated. This use of time-out precludes the necessity for physical punishment. Although some parents may feel that only physical punishment can be effective, that approach should be strongly discouraged.

If the disruptive behavior occurs outside the home, the child is given time-out segments that are put into effect when he gets home. The child may accumulate as many time-out segments as the parent deems necessary. Any verbal exchange regarding the choice of action, the reason underlying the decision, or the connection between aggressive behavior and its consequences must follow the time-out procedure. Verbal discussion need not follow immediately; it may be delayed from the event by days or a week. The time-out procedure itself, however, must follow as immediately upon the initiation of noncompliance as possible.

Time-out is initiated by parental command, and there is no further contact until the time-out period has been completed. In the case of a child who will not remain in his room or time-out chair, it may be necessary to hold him for a time. In doing so, the parent uses her own body as a physical restraint. She talks to the child, saying, "I do not like to hold you this way. I will not let you hurt me. I will not let you hurt yourself. I am holding you until you are calm and able to be quiet on your own." The parent's voice must remain calm, and her grasp on the child must be firm and comforting. She may not let the child out of her grasp until the child is ready to follow the command for a time-out. (In the case of a fearful child, the parent may need to remain within view of the child while he is in his room.) If the child does not comply with the parental command for a time-out period, then additional time-out periods are given. The child is given a warning that additional time-out periods will be the consequence for noncompliance. The time-out procedure begins once the child is sufficiently quieted to comply on his own. In the case of a large child, it may be necessary for two adults to restrain the child. In this case, it is very important that the parents' voices remain calm and that verbal communication be maintained with the child during the holding procedure.

It is most unusual for this holding procedure to require more than a few applications. If it is done thoroughly, the child experiences an understanding of his parents' firmness and intentions. This is an image of the parent that the child can recall—one that will then facilitate future compliance. In asserting her authority, the parent must not lose her sense of self-control. If she feels this is about to happen, she must withdraw from the child until she is able to maintain firm and strong composure. Once the child has become accustomed to time-out procedures, he may initiate them on his own. This capacity to calm oneself is essential to self-regulation and attests to the achievement of a capacity to be alone.

The quiet-time procedure

In addition to time-out procedures, the parents can include as part of their repertoire a quiet-time procedure. Quiet time is also time spent by the child alone in his or her room, but it is not a consequence of disruptive behavior. Rather, it is regularly planned time that allows the child to settle down and achieve a degree of comfort in being alone with his or her thoughts and activities. It is designed to help instill within the child the capacity to be alone, referred to by D. W. Winnicott (1965); unless time is set aside for such solitary activities, the child may not develop this capacity. Parents can use regular allotments of quiet time to anticipate disruptive periods during the day and thereby avoid them. The quiet-time notion can also be helpful in communicating to the child that the parent also requires time alone for repose and refueling. Thus, the separation that occurs in the normal course of events can contribute to the strengthening of boundaries.

The playtime procedure

Regularly scheduled and anticipated quality time shared between parent and child is an important antidote to negative interactions. Playtime between parent and child assures the development of new relating skills. Cooperation, sharing, reciprocity, taking turns, following directions, sensitivity to another's feelings, and tolerance for frustration and delay are all skills that can be acquired during playtime.

Playtime between parent and child can range anywhere from passive observation by the parent of the child's activities to the active pursuit of some joint venture. It can range from playing a game with rules, to preparing a meal, to taking a spontaneous walk outdoors. The possibilities for play are infinite, and the therapist should explore them with each parent. Whatever the playtime is used for, the important thing is that it be regularly scheduled and that intrusions not be allowed. Optimally, playtime would be one on one, with a ratio of one parent to one child, but this pattern can be varied based on the needs of parent and child. Allocating this time is not contingent upon good or bad behavior. The interval between scheduled playtimes, as well as the length of the playtime, is dependent upon the individual needs of parent and child.

It may be necessary for the therapist to model playfulness to the parents and help them to explore various alternatives. It is important that the affect shared be pleasurable. If it is not possible for a parent to engage her child playfully, this fact must be explored at greater length. In such a situation, the parent might begin with a more passive observer role, maintained for a short duration. Again, it is within the context of the therapist-parent relationship that parents may first feel at ease to explore playfulness, a discovery that enriches the entire family.

FATHER: Sam just seems to have a lot of trouble getting along with other kids.

THERAPIST: Can you give an example of that?

FATHER: Well, last week I was at a soccer match—I'm the coach of his team—and I heard him calling one of the other kids names. A scuffle broke out and Sam got a bloody nose. I had to take him out of the game. But this goes on all the time.

THERAPIST: What did Sam have to say about it?

FATHER: He said, of course, the other kid started it.

THERAPIST: How do you usually handle these problems?

FATHER: Well, I'm afraid I tend to yell at him. I tell him that people won't like him if he keeps it up, that he'll be a social reject.

THERAPIST: Does Sam seem to understand that?

MOTHER: No, I wouldn't say so. At least it doesn't keep him from doing the same thing again.

FATHER: He also says that he doesn't care what the other kids think, that he doesn't want them as friends anyway.

THERAPIST: It sounds as though he has a hard time admitting he's doing anything that bothers other people.

MOTHER: I think that's true. I think he knows it bothers others, but it's so difficult for him to accept that. In fact, I wonder if he doesn't want to be liked so much that when he doesn't get the response he wants he gets mad.

THERAPIST: What makes you think that?

MOTHER: Well, at home he often asks for reassurance, asks how well he's doing in school, seems to want to show off when he's achieved something.

FATHER: Yeah, I notice that on the soccer field. He seems very proud when he scores and really basks in the praise the other boys give him. But when he makes a mistake—look out!

THERAPIST: What happens then?

FATHER: He gets very irritable and cranky. Can't take criticism at all, even if it's constructive. Even if another boy says something positive like "Nice try!" he gets upset and often says something nasty like, "How would you know?" Obviously this kind of answer doesn't do much to win friends.

THERAPIST: It sounds as if Sam is very hard on himself, as though he finds it hard to accept his own mistakes and constantly worries about his performance.

FATHER: I'd say that was true. He's probably fairly insecure from what you're saying, and he's only happy when he's doing well.

THERAPIST: Or being told he's doing well.

MOTHER: Yes, that's a good point. I guess because he's so insecure, he doesn't judge well how he's doing, and so he needs to be told that he's doing okay.

THERAPIST: Conversely, he doesn't seem able to judge when he's doing poorly with others.

FATHER: Except by their reactions.

THERAPIST: Well, even there he often seems to deny the effect of what he does or distorts the nature of his action when he talks about it.

FATHER: Yes, that's true.

MOTHER: Well, what can we do about it?

FATHER: And about his aggression?

THERAPIST: I think the first thing is to communicate to Sam that you understand that he wants to be liked very much, and that he worries about this. Further, I'd tell him that you know that sometimes he's cranky when he feels others don't think he's doing well or when he feels he's not doing okay. I'd point out to him that when he's cranky, he might say or do things he doesn't mean but which bother other people anyway.

FATHER: You mean help him accept the results of his behavior without blaming him?

THERAPIST: Exactly! I'd also tell him that, whether he means it or not, his crankiness gets him into trouble and that that's something which makes him more unhappy—and makes you unhappy when you see it occurring.

FATHER: Okay, suppose we do this and nothing changes?

THERAPIST: That's just the first step. Sam has to agree to some extent before you go any further. It's not essential that he buy this whole scenario, but it's important that he not completely reject the idea. So you should spend some time encouraging him by telling him that it's normal to want to be liked, that no one likes making mistakes, but that it's harder for him than for most people to accept mistakes and that this sometimes gets him into trouble.

MOTHER: I think he'd be relieved to hear that. I think he'd feel that, at last, someone understands him and is trying to help.

THERAPIST: I would guess you're probably right. He might feel less blamed and more understood.

FATHER: Well, what next?

THERAPIST: The next step is to tell Sam that, even though you understand why he sometimes antagonizes others, you know he may have a hard time stopping himself. Therefore, you'll try to help him with this.

FATHER: How?

THERAPIST: By teaching Sam how to use the time-out procedure, which we've already discussed, when he's not at home. When, for example, you and he are on the soccer field, I'd tell Sam that when you notice that he's beginning to look annoyed or sound argumentative, you'll gently remind him to take some time out. From what you've said before, you often seem to know when trouble is brewing.

FATHER: Yes. He gets a distinct frown and his voice sounds irritable.

THERAPIST: Well, if you can head him off, that would help. But it's not enough to tell him to take time out. I'd explain that the time-out is mental. You might teach him some of the breathing or relaxation exercises we've talked about and encourage Sam to "take a breather" by moving away from the person to whom he's talking and be by himself for a bit.

FATHER: What if he refuses?

THERAPIST: Then you should resort to voice control and give a command, trying to sound firm, yet intense. If he doesn't react to that, you might put your hand gently on his arm and guide him away from the scene of the action. Before you resort to this tactic, however, I would talk to Sam ahead of time and explain to him that you're going to touch his arm lightly when you think he's out of control, and that's his cue to move to the side or away from the scene. In fact, I'd practice doing this with him several times at home, with you, Mom, perhaps role-playing the other child.

MOTHER: That sounds like a good idea.

THERAPIST: However, the time-out alone won't reduce the frequency of negative behavior unless Sam feels more self-assured.

MOTHER: How do we achieve that?

THERAPIST: Well, you've said he seems to enjoy praise, especially when told he's done a good job.

FATHER: Yes, that's true.

THERAPIST: Then it's important to respond positively to Sam as much as possible. In practice, this means trying to notice whenever he does anything that pleases you, even mildly. I would try to say something positive to him at least five or six times a day. These comments don't have to be about anything major, but they should let Sam know you don't just talk to him when he's in trouble. Moreover, they should be frequent enough that he feels that it wasn't so long ago that one of you said something positive about him.

FATHER: Okay, we'll try that. But what are some of the positive things we could say?

THERAPIST: To increase Sam's self-esteem, I would start out by praising him for some actions he's likely to do under any circumstances. For example, if he comes down in the morning and gets himself breakfast, I'd tell him you appreciate his taking care of himself in the morning, that it saves you time, what a help it is, and so on. If he performs routine chores, like setting the table, I'd praise him for that. But you should also praise him for other types of behavior. If he behaves kindly toward his younger sister, or even just says a kind word to her, I'd let him know. I'd also especially praise him every day he is able to go without an argument or a fight with a peer. In that instance, I'd let him know that you view such restraint as a sign of maturity. If he does slip and have a fight with a peer, I wouldn't criticize him but, instead, I'd encourage him to approach the other child and attempt to apologize. You might want to model how to do this through role-playing, with one of you taking the role of the other child and the other playing Sam. This might help Sam gain some distance through observing the two of you enacting an apology without either becoming too distraught or upset. If you would prefer, we can practice this type of role-play here before you introduce it to Sam.

MOTHER: Yes, I think I would like to try that. Are there any other things we can do at home?

THERAPIST: Yes. One technique, which is often helpful in improving rapport and strengthening a child's bond with the parent, is spending a limited but specific amount of time playing with Sam each day.

FATHER: Playing?

THERAPIST: Yes. Play is a central vehicle for children to express and learn about feelings as well as to learn interpersonal problem-solving techniques. By sharing your child's play, you are communicating an interest in what he feels, and you are participating with him in a highly pleasurable activity. This gives both of you an opportunity to interact in an unpressured, enjoyable way. You can also learn a good deal about what typically frustrates Sam, how and why he gets so angry, and how he can be helped to be more flexible with others and tolerant of his own mistakes. I would suggest playing with Sam for a half-hour each day. But it's very important that you let him set the agenda. You are to be simply a participant trying to observe Sam's behavior. We can talk further about the significance of his play in subsequent visits.

FATHER: That sounds interesting. I wish there were some way to help Sam avoid trouble with other kids before it starts. If I'm not around, how will he learn to stop himself?

THERAPIST: One further suggestion you might try is to encourage Sam to identify the feelings of frustration and anger that lead up to his exploding. If he can begin to do that, then you might suggest that he seek out an adult at those times and ask for help.

MOTHER: What should he say to an adult?

THERAPIST: He should say he's feeling angry or upset and is afraid he might say or do something that might hurt someone. If either of you are available, it would, of course, be best if he came to you. But if he's not near you, then a teacher or other adult in authority would probably be able to help. The very act of going to an adult and labeling what he's feeling will probably help defuse the situation. The most difficult part in using this technique is helping Sam know what he's feeling at the time he feels it.

MOTHER: I agree.

THERAPIST: I've given you a number of suggestions and ideas to think over. Why don't we meet in a few weeks and see how these strategies are working?

9

When Parents Do Not Comply

D ESPITE the fact that they have come to a therapist for assistance some parents consistently fail to follow the therapist's instructions. We view such failures as noncompliance. Parents, like children, have many reasons for opposing efforts to change their behavior, even when those efforts are self-initiated.

In recent years, social learning approaches (Barkley 1981; Forehand and McMahon 1981) have introduced the use of trained parents as adjunct therapists in the treatment of conduct disorder children. Social learning theorists, however, have invariably neglected to address a fundamental obstacle to the implementation of their programs: patient (or in this case parental) noncompliance. Most behavioral theorists seem to adopt the *rational actor* perspective so prevalent in economics—that is, people behave rationally to maximize goals that are clearly in their self-interest and avoid choices that produce undesirable outcomes or perpetuate problems. Clinicians have known since Freud that the "rational actor" hypothesis is a myth.

Noncompliance in the Initial Phase: A Failure of Attachment

In a parent-training model, the therapist acts as a consultant whose role is to teach parents more effective management skills with respect to the child and to enable parents to use these skills consistently in order to change conduct disorder behavior. As we have noted earlier, to be an effective teacher and enabler, the therapist must form a trusting relationship with the parents, becoming a secure attachment figure for them. The therapist's failure to become a secure attachment figure constitutes the primary reason for parental noncompliance.

There are several reasons why a secure therapist-parent relationship sometimes fails to form. The most common reasons include parental psychopathology; the therapist's lack of warmth; the therapist's lack of empathy with the parents' plight; the therapist's failure to be clear and explicit about the nature of expected tasks; and the therapist's failure to provide consistent, positive reinforcement for parental efforts. While the last two reasons have been commented on in earlier chapters of this book, the first three reasons will be described here in greater detail.

Effects of Parental Psychopathology

Parental psychopathology of certain kinds has been noted as a contraindication for undertaking parent training. It should be added that, in addition to Axis I disorders (DSM-III-R 1987), Axis II psychopathology (personality disorders) constitutes a major obstruction to successful parent training. In particular, borderline, narcissistic, passive-aggressive, and antisocial personality disorders are especially problematic in parent training, owing to the difficulty in treating them psychotherapeutically. Although every effort is made to eliminate these parents in the assessment phase, nonetheless, their pathology may not be detected early on. Among other factors, a pseudocompliant attitude or the forcefulness of the parents' plea for help may have obscured their underlying pathology.

Parents displaying significant psychopathology of Axis I or II types often experience considerable difficulty in effectively modulating their own behavior in relation to that of their child and thus often do not implement the therapist's directives or provide productive reinforcement. Moreover, owing to the difficulties in personal relationships created by people with personality disorders, such parents do not relate in a positive, unambivalent way with the therapist. They may, therefore, deliberately or unconsciously undermine the therapist's efforts and may in turn elicit negative behavior from the therapist, thereby establishing a conflictual, as opposed to a cooperative, relationship between parents and therapist. Obviously, such relationships are counterproductive in reducing conduct disorder behavior.

The Effect of a Therapist's Lack of Warmth

The therapist's indifference, or coldness, is an obvious factor interfering with therapist-parent bonding. Just as lack of parental warmth and affection contributes to the child's conduct disordered behavior, similar behavior by the therapist can contribute to parental noncompliance. Parents who do not form attachments with their difficult children may be quite anxious about attachment and separation in general and may require displays of encouragement by the therapist to feel comfortable with him. Without such overtly warm behavior, parents may not trust the therapist's judgment about what to do with their child.

The Effect of a Therapist's Lack of Empathy

Similarly, a therapist's lack of empathy with a parent's distress over coping with a difficult child may interfere with the parent's relating to the therapist. A clinician need not be cold or insensitive to be perceived as unempathic. It is sufficient that the therapist fail to acknowledge, verbally or nonverbally, how troublesome the child can be and how disturbing the parent finds this. A depressed parent may be particularly sensitive to the therapist's failure to empathize enough and may perceive even a warm therapist as judgmental or rejecting if he pays insufficient attention to how the parent feels about the child's misbehavior.

Perceiving the therapist as supportive is important to psychologically healthy parents as well, however, because they may feel guilty and inadequate when they experience rage and frustration toward their child. Many parents labor under the misconception that one should experience positive, loving feelings for one's child at all times. Feeling angry or hateful toward a child is often viewed by parents as a weakness or, worse, a sign of psychopathology. Moreover, many parents are frightened by the intensity of their aggressive feelings toward their child, and they may worry about their ability to contain their aggression.

Exploring how parents feel when their child misbehaves is always helpful. Parental attachment is often strengthened by comments upon how difficult coping with such a child can be, how frustrating for a parent it is, and how such anger and frustration can lead parents to feel inadequate. Moreover, the therapist may wish to comment that many parents become so angry with their children that they feel as though they might hurt the child if pushed much further. These remarks can be made within the context of describing normative parental reactions to a conduct disordered child. Parents are then reassured and can feel the therapist truly understands their plight. Supportive comments should be made at the beginning of the initial phase to communicate, first, that the therapist views the parents' anger with the child as expectable, given the child's behavior; and second, that the therapist does not blame the parents for feeling angry, irrespective of how the parents may judge their anger.

Noncompliance in the Middle Phase: Failure to Sustain Attachment

While the preceding reasons may be the source of parental noncompliance at any time in therapy, they are particularly characteristic of the initial phase and typify the origins of early failures in therapist-parent attachment. It is frequently the case, however, that parents successfully relate to the therapist in the initial phase only to become noncompliant during later phases. This emergent noncompliance in parent training clearly has an analogue in patterns observed in individual psychotherapy.

During the middle phase of parent training, two reasons for parental noncompliance are common. Both are concerned with issues of individual control, autonomy, and parental perceptions of their competence. Parents for whom issues regarding independence, control, and authority are still unresolved cannot sustain a secure relationship with the therapist. These are the parents most likely to display noncompliant behavior during the middle phase of parent training.

Parental Envy of the Therapist's Mastery

One reason for parental noncompliance in the middle and late phases of parent training is the parents' envy of the therapist's mastery of skills in managing children. Parents initially consult the therapist because they recognize that they are experiencing considerable difficulty in limiting or eliminating their child's aversive behavior. Many parents who are selected for parent training make successful use of the therapist's instructions and support, and their child's behavior improves. Some of these parents, however, retain persistent doubts about their competence, despite the obvious behavioral evidence of it. They may resent what they view as the therapist's skill and feel more inadequate than they did on entering training.

Accordingly, they may begin to behave less cooperatively than heretofore and may actively undermine the behavioral foundation carefully laid by the therapist and themselves for a healthier relationship with their child.

In responding to this noncompliance, the therapist should constantly focus upon the parents' feelings of inadequacy, envy, insecurity, and antagonism toward what they perceive as an overwhelmingly competent authority. The therapist should usually attempt to enable the parents to articulate such feelings and to resolve them. In some cases, however, explicating the parents' conscious or unconscious reasons for not complying is inadvisable. Some parents, for example, are inarticulate and may have difficulty elaborating what they feel. Other parents for various psychological reasons feel vulnerable to what they imagine would be the therapist's punitive, harshly judgmental response to the open expression of such feelings. For still others, acknowledgment of these emotions directly contradicts their consciously avowed concepts of themselves as parents (as "helpful," "effective," and so on). Recognizing emotions and attitudes at variance with these parental self-concepts would require radical revisions of the way these parents perceive themselves, and the parent may be unprepared or unwilling to undertake such a revision.

If the therapist decides that clarification of the foregoing reasons for noncompliance should not be attempted, he may choose to counteract noncompliance in other ways. For example, he may consistently emphasize that successful outcomes result primarily from the parents' efforts. Moreover, the therapist should note, whenever possible, how the parents' mastery of skills is developing and how much more competent they have become than they were at the start of training. The therapist should also emphasize that his contribution to successful outcomes is largely that of consultant when snags arise and not that of a therapist treating their child, reminding the parents frequently that they are the primary therapists.

Similarly, just as he gives the credit for successful results largely to the parents, the therapist should make the parents understand that the responsibility for any other outcome is also theirs. When parents are able to accept such responsibility, they are less likely to blame the therapist for adverse outcomes. Blaming the therapist is another major reason for noncompliance. Along with enabling parents to accept their role in creating desirable and undesirable results, the therapist should attempt to convey acceptance of the parents' behavior and feelings while observing the consequences. Throughout, he should emphasize that change is always possible, provided parents are willing to attempt it. This idea serves as an important counterbalance to the despair and hopelessness that can easily arise when parents feel they have exhausted all their psychological resources and alternatives.

Parents' Overidentification with Their Child

Another reason for noncompliance with the therapist's directives is that a parent may overidentify with the child and take vicarious pleasure in the child's behavior. Such parents also have difficulty separating from their children and tend to attribute their feelings to their children. They may minimize the severity of the child's behavior, rationalize its origins, or both. Typically, such parents are inhibited in the normal expression of aggressive affect or have been so in the past, and they may experience the child's aggression as fulfilling a conscious or unconscious wish. The parents may be reluctant to work with the therapist to help the child inhibit the aggressive behavior, even though they may pay lip-service to the desirability of doing so. As a result, they may sabotage the implementation of the therapist's directives.

Similar overidentification with the child may occur if parents are aggressive or were so as children. Often such parents will tell the therapist that they were aggressive as children ("and didn't turn out badly") and that their child is exceptionally bright and is merely "bored" or "not challenged" sufficiently in school (or wherever the behavior occurs). In such cases the failure to separate psychologically from the child makes it more likely that the parents will view the therapist as directing his efforts at them, rather than at the child and the parent-child relationship. Since these parents are probably deeply enmeshed in their relationship with their child, they will most likely view any attempt to enable the child to separate and become psychologically distinct as quite threatening. Although the parents have voluntarily sought assistance (usually because they have been required to do so by the school or some other agency), they actually do not want to change.

The key to changing the noncompliant behavior of parents who identify with their children is initially the therapist's observation and communication that they are failing to comply. It may take some time before the therapist recognizes that the parents are consistently failing to implement directives upon which the therapist and parents have agreed. As in individual treatment, the parents may produce numerous excuses and rationalizations, each of which seems quite plausible in its own right. Effectively managing parental noncompliance, however, requires the therapist to point out to them that agreed-upon plans are not being implemented and objectives are not being achieved. At this juncture, the therapist may choose to review the original goals agreed upon and the priorities assigned for their achievement. Beyond these observations, the therapist may decide to explore some of the reasons for their noncompliance. The focus then would be upon the parent-child relationship, its intensity, and the apparent difficulty the parents are experiencing in separating from their child. As a result of this further exploration, a referral for individual treatment may occur. Sometimes, however, support and empathy are enough to help the parents through a period of frustration and noncompliance with the therapist's directives.

THERAPIST: Let's review together Tommy's progress. How has he been doing at home?

MOTHER: Just terrible. I can't seem to get him to listen. I tell him not to bother his baby sister, and ten minutes later he's back bothering her again. I just can't get him to mind.

THERAPIST: Tell me more about what happens.

MOTHER: Well, you know we've told you about how Tommy is stubborn. He just has his own way of doing things and won't hear of anything else. Sometimes his ideas are okay, but other times I just don't have the patience to keep explaining to him why what he's doing isn't right.

THERAPIST: So it can be very frustrating trying to set limits. He simply won't listen.

MOTHER: And then I get upset, and the next thing you know I am yelling again. I hate it when I yell—it just makes things worse. I tried those time-outs you talked about, but they simply don't work.

FATHER: It doesn't seem to faze him. Send him to his room, and he plays with his toys or reads a book. What does he care? No—I'm sorry, they simply don't work!

MOTHER: I did just what you suggested—sent him right to his room. The next thing I knew, I heard him singing. Now, you know that doesn't help! He doesn't even realize he's been bad!

THERAPIST: Tommy is really a handful. Yelling seems to be the only way he will listen.

MOTHER: Yes. He does listen. But, then, the next time I have to yell louder! That makes me feel awful.

FATHER: Sometimes it sounds like the house is falling down. Those times, if I am home, I just settle it quick with a hard slap on the rear end, like I got when I was a kid.

THERAPIST: We always tend to repeat what was done to us. Does it work?

FATHER: Well, it sure does! Right away he listens! He feels hurt, of course, and runs away. Last week he was caught beating up a kid in the playground. He explained to me he was showing the other kid he was wrong. I didn't know what to say. After all, that's how I had treated him!

THERAPIST: That is a dilemma. Almost sounds like no way out. You hit him, and then he hits others!

FATHER: But just sending him to his room—how would that help?

THERAPIST: The idea is not to hurt him, although sometimes he may feel time-out hurts. The idea is to interfere—to disrupt any behavior that is unacceptable to you. Then Tommy learns to control himself as you controlled him. The time-out in his room gives him a chance to repair and feel better again.

MOTHER: I can't believe it will work. I just imagine him in there enjoying himself—playing! When I was little, my parents were strict. We never dared be sassy or talk back.

THERAPIST: It must be very upsetting when Tommy chooses to do things you would never have done with your parents.

MOTHER: Well, [smiles] sometimes I chuckle a little, thinking what it would feel like to do what he's doing.

THERAPIST: Sounds like part of you might even enjoy misbehaving!

MOTHER: Oh—I guess so. It was so long ago. But we were never allowed to misbehave, and I just think about how it would feel.

FATHER: That's when she gets soft on him, and I have to step in. Being so fresh to his mother! I can't tolerate that nonsense. But the hitting doesn't help. Sometimes, I just walk away to keep from hitting him.

THERAPIST: Sounds like he gets you so angry, you give yourself a time-out!

FATHER: Well, it does help. If I walk away, I'm not around him anymore and gradually I find myself getting calmer. I need to get away from my wife too!

THERAPIST: Time-out gives time for repair, and then the issues can be dealt with more calmly.

MOTHER: Maybe we should try again with time-outs.

FATHER: I'm willing. But let's understand again exactly how to do it. I want to write it all down so I get it straight this time. It's hard to keep records, you know. I tried it, but just let it go after a while.

MOTHER: Seems like we just lost hope that anything could change.

THERAPIST: When things just go on and on, it seems impossible to hope they could change. Let's review the specifics of consequences of different kinds, and be sure to bring up all your questions and comments.

The therapist has navigated a difficult impasse and apparently has gotten the training alliance back on course. He did not confront the parents in their frustration and despair, but rather offered support in the form of attunement and empathy. As the parents felt less threatened by the possibility of being judged, they were able to be more open and to share their feelings of overidentification with their child and their ineptness as parents. After experiencing the warmth of the therapist's acceptance and understanding, they were able to request further input from him about parenting techniques. Only after their initiative did he offer didactic suggestions and corrections. The parents' renewed motivation is expressed in their willingness to invest additional effort and to revive their hope of reaching their parenting goals.

The Role of Supervision in Maintaining the Parent-Therapist Relationship

The supervisor stands midpoint between parents and therapist: that is to say, in this capacity she monitors the degree of tension and noncompliance versus the progress and growth of the therapeutic process. This equilibrium of progress versus resistance is always a dynamic variable. If the balance in the therapeutic process is sustaining to both parents and therapist, this stability can be attributed in part to the participation of the supervisor. The supervisor's role is that of participant observer, who steadfastly surveys the drama that ensues. Specifically, the supervisor must be assured that the therapist has a thorough understanding of the parent-training paradigms. She provides ample opportunities for the therapist to rehearse his understandings of these principles and their application. On a more abstract level, the supervisor is allied with the therapist in much the same way the therapist is allied with his patients. She provides a nonjudgmental, supportive model of an experienced person available for consultation. If the therapist is afraid of being judged negatively, then the process will go awry. The entire system depends upon a collaborative effort, in which observations are made in a constructive, tactful manner. The supervisor attempts at all times to allay the therapist's anxiety, which might stand in the way of progress.

Each phase of treatment is considered separately in terms of its challenges for supervision. In the initial phase, the therapist can share with his supervisor his initial impressions of the patients and the feelings they evoke in him. These first impressions are crucial. They will form the background for the work to be done and thus carry a weight far greater than might be estimated by calculating simply the contact time spent with the parents. The supervisor must probe these feelings and help the therapist become aware of his reactions, which might impede the development of the secure therapist-patient relationship critical to therapeutic outcome. It goes without saying that the parallel process of initial feelings between supervisor and therapist must also be considered. Usually, the parents' and therapist's initial desire is to accomplish the treatment goals, and this desire serves as an impetus to establish both a positive supervisory and therapeutic relationship.

The way to present the didactic material, which we have labeled Phase Two, is dependent upon the parents' characteristics and the therapeutic style of the therapist. The supervisor not only ascertains that the therapist has a grasp of the didactic principles but also assists him in presenting these principles in a manner most comfortable for himself and the parents. The supervisor also helps the therapist to attune to the parents' overidealization of his wisdom and knowledge, which must be diffused with care if progress is to continue.

The supervisor monitors the relationships between the parents and the therapist and gives special care to issues of noncompliance. It is her task to point out negative reactions and their potential before they develop into problems. This delicate balance between friend and guide must be maintained to assure the safe journey of all through the potentially hazardous course of treatment.

10

Phase Four: Ending Parent Training

I DEALLY, terminating treatment is a joint decision between parents and therapist. It should evolve from a consensually shared judgment that significant amelioration of symptoms has taken place and that additional training sessions are unlikely to produce further gains. At this point in parent training, it is appropriate to plan for a gradual tapering off of training sessions.

Problems

The prospect of ending training sessions creates its own set of problems. The parents may regress to earlier behaviors not in evidence since the start of training and may begin to demonstrate noncompliance with treatment goals. The source of noncompliance in the ending phase of treatment depends on the specific case. Some typical reasons for noncompliance within this phase are easily identifiable and, indeed, can be anticipated. Some parents return to earlier behaviors because of their fear of separating from the therapist. Parents commonly experience anxiety about their ability to sustain competent parental behavior without the therapist's guidance. Furthermore, despite their motivation to end training, some parents may experience anger, which undermines their previous efforts and achievement.

If we are correct in postulating that parents of conduct disordered children have difficulty in forming secure attachments, it is not surprising that they find separations more troublesome than most people. As the end of training approaches, the parents may become anxious, irritable, and less willing to continue implementing previously successful behavior management strategies. They also may be angry with the therapist for lapses in the child's behavior.

Alternatively, the parents may become overcompliant, presenting themselves as inept and unable to act without the most explicit directions from the therapist. This type of parental behavior clearly communicates a wish to continue to be advised by the therapist. By allowing the child to become symptomatic again, the parents express a demand that the therapist delay ending.

In some cases, parents may openly express their fears of being unable to act effectively after ending. Occasionally they may display flagrantly inconsistent and arbitrary behavior at this time, as if to emphasize the reasonableness of their fears. Again, the therapist should be alert to such behavior when it constitutes a clear change in heretofore capable adults. If the therapist is aware of the origin of this noncompliance, articulating it and exploring its causes, along with reassurance, are usually quite helpful.

During the treatment, the therapist has fostered the formation of a positive bond between himself and the parents. If this effort has been successful, it can be expected that the parents will experience the ending of training as a loss of the therapist and that some parents will resent the clinician for inflicting this loss upon them. Exploring the reasons for this anger will further the parents' understanding of the conflicts they experience in forming secure relationships. This understanding will help them realize that they can sustain therapeutic gains without the therapist's constant input and support.

Some parents may not be overtly hostile but may report a resurgence of aggressive and/or other distressing behavior by the child. Examining the circumstances surrounding this behavior usually reveals a lack of parental consistency and a failure to utilize previously successful interventions. When parents are requested to explain these lapses, they may be at a loss. Further questioning may indicate that the parents feel that ending means the therapist is "giving up" on them. They, in turn, are "giving up" on the child. Moreover, the parents may believe that the child's redevelopment of symptoms demonstrates to the therapist that he didn't do such a good job after all and that he cannot now end training, because the child isn't "cured" and the therapist therefore cannot "abandon" them.

Because parents may view the therapist's terminating their training as rejection or abandonment, cautiously discussing their emotions, wishes, fears, and expectations regarding its ending and its aftermath should be integral to parent training. The therapist should allow ample time for this discussion and should not be surprised at the intense emotions, especially anxiety and anger, that ending training precipitates in the parents.

Therapist's Verbal and Nonverbal Interventions

We suggest that the therapist gradually reduce her activity and the scope of her interventions as the ending of training approaches. During the final phase of training, the therapist should focus increasingly upon the parents' actions and their consequences for the child, articulating how the parents' choices have brought about certain desirable and undesirable results. Emphasis should be given to why and how certain parental interventions work and others do not.

As the therapist reviews training procedures with the parents, she uses various techniques, including (1) attending to parental feelings and behaviors as they rehearse the skills and reenact sequences experienced at home; (2) modeling and role-playing to facilitate an understanding of how to use these new skills; (3) confronting the parents with the cause-effect relationships in the interactions they are reporting and suggesting ways to change dysfunctional behaviors; and (4) problem solving, trying to fit the most appropriate technique to a specific situation or to anticipate future outcomes of given parental techniques and strategies.

As suggested in earlier phases of treatment, if the therapist has any doubt about what happened during an event reported by the parents, the therapist should ask them to role-play the interaction. In this fashion, the therapist thoroughly reviews, and directs the parents' attention to, causal sequences involving the child's provocations, the parents' emotional responses, the parents' interventions, and the child's behavioral responses. In the final phase of parent training, the therapist becomes more passive about giving directions, structuring parental activity, and initiating interventions. Rather, she primarily encourages the parents to verbalize their emotional responses to their child's behavior and their notions of managing troublesome situations effectively.

The purpose of this shift from a more directive approach to a relatively reflective one is to demonstrate to the parents what they have learned in training and to support their independent choice of effective strategies. As the parents notice that their thoughts about their child's behavior and their decisions regarding responses to it approximate the therapist's, they should begin to appreciate their newly acquired skills and thus to feel more competent and confident in their parental roles.

The Process

At the beginning of parent training, the parents reported what types of child behavior they wanted to change and the therapist assisted them in identifying the behaviors that were reasonable targets for change. In addition, the therapist assessed the child's temperament and ascertained which management strategies would be most effective for their child. Finally, the therapist assessed the nature and degree of the parents' attachment to their child and the extent to which this bond required alteration. Accordingly, ending training can be proposed when the therapist observes consistent evidence over an extended interval (two to three months) that (1) target behaviors have improved and the changes have been maintained; (2) the use of agreed-upon strategies seems to account for the behavioral changes in the child; and (3) there has been a strengthening of the parents' positive attachment to their child, accompanied by adequate support for the child's developmentally appropriate efforts to separate psychologically from the parents and move toward individuation.

The termination phase of parent training should be conducted in accordance with a clearly defined timetable, which specifies increasing time between sessions and a definite stopping point. Sessions should be decreased gradually, first from weekly to biweekly, then to monthly, then to trimonthly, and finally to biannually. The therapist should be flexible, however, and be prepared to resume training on a limited basis at any stage if new problems emerge that warrant additional consultation. Each therapist must determine for himself the criteria for additional sessions. Unless the child's behavior has significantly worsened, however, and/or other changes in the parents and their life circumstances have occurred, the therapist should encourage parents to attempt to cope with difficulties as they have in the past, only calling upon the therapist as a consultant. Thus, in the final phase of training, the therapist maintains a passive-reflective stance and only after due deliberation alters his approach. Whenever a new problem emerges, the parents are given sufficient time to utilize previously acquired skills and are encouraged as much as possible to manage their situation independently.

Timetables should be tailored to meet the requirements of individual parents and therapists. One possible plan is for sessions to be held every other week for three months, then monthly for three months, and then after two three-month intervals, and two six-month intervals. This model allows 24 months for termination. Given the usual extremity of conduct disordered behavior and the intensity of parental attachment difficulties, we view this timetable as appropriate. Parents may decide that three-month visits or six-month visits are unnecessary. If the therapist is concerned about the relative staying power of the gains made, he should voice his doubts openly and encourage parents to return after an extended time, even if they do not appreciate the value of these later visits. If the parents persist in their refusal to return, then the therapist should propose a follow-up in the form of a brief telephone call at stipulated intervals.

A Final Note

It is important to keep in mind how to measure whether our efforts at changing parents' behavior have been successful. Parental satisfaction takes many different forms of expression. As clinicians, we recognize that an increase in perceived parental confidence—expressed as either increased self-confidence or enhanced self-esteem and pleasure in interactions with the child—are the ultimate indications that parents believe their training was effective. Lasting change of benefit to both parents and child takes place through fostering the parents' autonomy, their capacity to reflect about their emotional responses to their child, and their ability to act judiciously but with affection.

PART III

PLAY GROUP PSYCHOTHERAPY

JO ROSENBERG HARITON, A.C.S.W.
PAULINA F. KERNBERG, M.D.
SARALEA E. CHAZAN, PH.D.

11

Overview

FOR all children, the peer group takes on new importance when they reach school age. At this age, children have a developmental need to gain mastery of newly acquired skills and to become more independent of their adult caregivers. Learning the values and norms of behavior of their age group through interaction with peers helps them to become more autonomous and to proceed with their development.

Many children with conduct disorders are unable to use the peer group to fullest advantage, because they have great difficulties interacting with others in an adaptive manner. They tend to lack self-awareness and to misjudge the social cues of others. Consequently, they do not achieve sufficient social skills to develop friendships. Their deviant behaviors, which may include lying, cheating, stealing, fighting, running away, and blaming others for their own acts, tend to make other children avoid them. Conduct disordered children are prone to intense affective reactions and to cognitive deficits in which memory becomes blurred, and thus they lose awareness of their part in creating difficulties. They tend to associate with peers who, like themselves, are active and aggressive. Their problems are therefore compounded by the fact that their friends cannot be counted upon to provide them with useful feedback.

Within the school system, these children are the troublemakers. Their "bad-child" images have led to low self-esteem, which has become entrenched over time and is difficult to change. Frequently they have received inconsistent parenting and are distrustful of adults. Teachers are authority figures whom they perceive negatively. Adults feel frustrated with these children and often give up on them. As a result, the children are less likely to receive appropriate feedback, and a vicious cycle ensues.

We use the term *play group psychotherapy* (PGP) to refer to the methodology and approach to group treatment described in this book. Group psychotherapy refers to the use of a small, carefully planned group of children specifically chosen for treatment because of their behavior problems. The group participants are aware of the purpose of the group and accept it as a means of obtaining relief from distress and modifying their disruptive behavior. Our model of play group psychotherapy is influenced by Saul Scheidlinger's (1982) conceptualization of group therapy, as well as by Samuel Slavson and Mortimer Schiffer's (1975) description of play group therapy. Whereas Slavson and Schiffer originally conceived of play group therapy for young children with neurotic conflicts, we utilized interpretation of play and other nonverbal and verbal behavior for the school age, conduct disordered child. Interpretation of the children's play is an essential curative factor of the treatment. Because conduct disordered children are frequently active and many lack a facility with language, play is a way to express feelings nonverbally. In PGP, children are considered as individuals, as members of dyads and other group constellations, and as members of the group as a whole. Thus, the PGP model encourages the scrutiny of group members within a variety of relationships.

Who Can Be Helped?

Play group psychotherapy is intended for a particular subgroup of the children who meet the criteria for selecting therapeutic candidates described in Part I, Supportive-Expressive Play Psychotherapy (SEPP, see chapter 1). PGP should be considered as the primary treatment modality for any of the following children:

1. Children whose maladaptive behavior in school or elsewhere tends to focus primarily around peer relationship problems. This group includes children who are bullies, who are severely scapegoated, or who tend to be excluded by others of their same age.
2. Children whose individual psychotherapy is at an impasse, whose target symptoms, such as poor impulse control, are not being resolved. These children tend to be concrete and unable to talk about what is occurring in their lives. They need the opportunity to experi-

ence the difficulties that they are encountering with others, beyond the one-to-one relationship of individual treatment.

3. Children who react to adult authority figures so negatively that the individual treatment alliance cannot get started. For these children the peer group format provides an alternative to the negatively tinged one-to-one relationship.

4. Children who seem so impervious to social interaction that a group is needed to offer a more forceful and intense opportunity for feedback from multiple sources.

5. Children who show focused conduct disordered behavior when they emerge from other, more severe psychiatric disorders, such as bipolar depression or schizophrenia.

6. Children who lack social skills and have not learned to participate in games or play with peers.

From a pragmatic perspective, group treatment is also indicated when there are not enough therapists available to work individually with the children in need of treatment in a clinic setting. Obviously, the group modality allows more children to be treated.

There are some specific kinds of children for whom PGP is not the recommended modality of treatment. In addition to the exclusion criteria cited in chapter 1 for SEPP, PGP would not be recommended for the following children:

1. Children with Attention Deficit Disorder as the primary diagnosis. The amount of stimulation in the group would tend to be confusing and overwhelming for such children, who do better in individual treatment.

2. Children who are too deviant from the other children in any particular group. Groups are organized by sex, age, and level of ego functioning, as well as by a balance of mild, moderate, and severe cases within a diagnostic entity. Whenever possible, we do not place a child in a group in which he will be the only one of his age or his race or the only one with a physical handicap, although these are relative counterindications.

3. Children who are so depressed that acute suicidal ideation or gestures are presented, which require individualized and prompt management.

The Participants

The Children's Group and Its Therapists

In keeping with the common preference for same-sex peer groups during latency, group membership in PGP is made up of children of the same sex. Children are assigned to groups that generally have no more than a three-year developmental span based upon chronological age and/or maturity. Groups have no fewer than three children and, given the volatile tendencies of these children, are generally limited to six. The group meets once a week for an hour.

In our model, each group has two co-therapists. The presence of two therapists is particularly important with this population to ensure that the group remains a safe place for all members. Moreover, we believe that co-therapy provides a model of appropriate interactions for the group, as the therapists help each other maintain the boundaries of the group. A co-therapy model also allows one therapist to work with an individual in need of one-to-one attention while the other focuses on the rest of the group.

The role of the therapists in PGP is to create a facilitating environment in which the group members can begin to feel safe and in which interpersonal behaviors can become the therapeutic focus. To these ends, the therapists must convey their authority to set limits and establish group norms, and yet remain flexible enough to adapt these norms to the specific group with which they are working.

In addition to the qualities discussed in chapter 1 that a therapist must have in order to work with children in individual treatment, we have identified qualities necessary for working with children in group treatment. PGP therapists require a capacity to set limits and provide structure, to offset the chaos that emerges in these children's groups. They must be able to collaborate with another therapist and to deal with uncertainty. Therapists in PGP must also have the capacities to contain regressive behavior and channel it constructively, to absorb aggression, and to remain calm under group stress. It is important that they not have a great need for gratification from the group; as the children project their low self-esteem onto the therapist, and the group transference can make an insecure therapist feel inadequate and incompetent. The ability to withstand rapid fluctuation in affect states is essential, for children may hug them one moment and reject them the next. They must be able to maintain an even, hovering attention in order to identify group themes and at the same time keep every group member in mind. They must be ready to support the most vulnerable group member when that support is needed. Finally, the therapists in PGP must have the capacity to use humor to prevent demoralization and to bring in another perspective to deal with despair.

The Parents' Group and Its Therapist

PGP works more smoothly when a parents' group is held at the same time as the children's group. A therapist meets weekly or every other week with the parents, and all the parents must know how to reach their parents' group therapist should emergencies arise.

It is the parents' responsibility to attend the parents' group regularly and to understand the structure and the purpose of the children's group. The parents need to inform the parents' group therapist of new events that might be affecting their child's behavior and to bring up issues of concern to them in raising their child. In addition to understanding more about their child, the parents learn to relate with other parents around the similar difficulties their children are experiencing. Tensions arise in the parents' group, which parallel tensions in the children's group. The opportunity to discuss these issues with the support of other parents in the group helps the parents to relate to their children, as the children seek a resolution with their peers. Personal growth as well as increased competence as a parent is the result of participation in the parents' group.

By being supportive, the parents' group therapist is able to develop an alliance with the parents. He should be knowledgeable enough about group dynamics to allow the parents' group to address its salient issues. He should help the parents maintain appropriate boundaries between the parents' group and the children's group, serving, when necessary, as advocate for the parents with the children's therapists. A thorough understanding of the therapeutic group process being used with the children will enable him to answer the parents' general questions about it. Directive and able to focus the group members on child management issues, he should also remain flexible when the parents want to use the group to meet their needs as parents or as individuals. The therapist must balance the parents' personal issues with the group's need to address child management issues.

The Supervisor

In PGP the supervisor plays a complex and diversified role. She supports and facilitates the therapists' understanding of what to expect of the children and their parents so that the therapists can anticipate and react appropriately to the processes of the group treatment. She should make the children's group therapists aware of their authority with the children and the importance of structure. The supervisor also teaches group dynamics as they apply to the phases of the group and the specifics of peer interaction.

The supervisor helps the children's group therapists to integrate the material shared from the parents' group therapist* to prevent the children's being treated without important input from the parents. One person may serve as supervisor to both the children's group therapists and the parents' group therapist, meeting with all three together, or the supervision for the parents' group may be performed separately by another supervisor. It is important, however, that all supervisors realize the necessity for integrating process material from the two groups for the therapists' being supervised.

For both parents' group therapist and children's group therapists, the most important function of the supervisor is to provide support, clarifying painful learning experiences about being therapists of a group and allaying the self-criticism of their evaluation as part of the children's projections or the parents' projections upon the therapist.

The supervisor facilitates the observational skills of the children's group therapists, which tend to be impaired by the impact of the group. With the supervisor's assistance, the therapists come to see they can be reliable participant observers. They learn to prioritize levels of interventions according to the stages of the group as outlined in this book. They scrutinize the content of interventions to promote the development of improved social skills, increased self-esteem, and impulse control. Examining the impact of the children's group on the co-therapy couple is a consistent focus of supervision. Attempts of the children to ignore one member of the co-therapy team or to play off one therapist against the other by exacerbating differences in style or approaches are to be expected. Other roles, which members of both groups often enact in relationship with the therapists, include father-mother, boyfriend-girlfriend, adult-child, two buddies against the rest of the group members. The ongoing observation by the supervisor can help the therapists be attuned to these dynamics occurring within the transference. In the children's therapy group, if the personality or training of the co-therapy team is mismatched, the supervisor must be alert to the possible necessity for reassignment.

The supervisor also plays a crucial role in clarifying the emotional impact the children have upon the children's group therapists and the ensuing countertransference. The countertransference reactions include emotional withdrawal, masochistic submission to the group, feelings of

---

*In Part III, we will, for the sake of convenience, adopt masculine pronouns for the parents' group therapist and feminine pronouns for the supervisor. We imply neither a preponderance of one gender over the other in these roles nor a suitability for these roles.

helplessness, overbearing anger, rescue fantasies, and perceptions of the parents as critics of the group.

Countertransference problems that need to be examined by the supervisor vary from one phase of the group to another. The beginning phases frequently induce in the therapists intense reactions of fear, loss of control, hopelessness, and despondency. The therapists in turn portray these same feelings in each group member. These feelings might lead the therapists to become paralyzed and unable to deal with the ongoing interactions within the group and with the misbehavior of individual children. The therapists then experience the feeling that they are not in control of the group. In the middle phase of treatment, the therapists may overestimate the children's capacity for elementary social behaviors, out of a disbelief that these youngsters could be so greatly impaired. A therapist may also evidence fear of parental criticism, which leads to the therapist's becoming impatient, avoiding parental contacts, and blaming the parents. In the ending phase, the therapists may step out of role and reveal more of themselves than is appropriate as a means of compensating the children for leaving them. This inconsistency is problematic, because children may interpret this behavior as a deprivation in that the therapists were not behaving in this manner all along. It also interferes with the children's right to go through a mourning process by working through anger about the therapist's leaving. Similarly, countertransference issues arise for the therapist of the parents' group and need to be viewed along with ongoing group dynamics in the children's group. Given the various countertransferences that can occur in PGP, it is vital that they be integrated into the supervisory process to enable the therapists to analyze their own feelings and to understand better the group process and their role as therapists in working with the children and their parents.

How Does PGP Work?

PGP affords children with disruptive behavior an opportunity to benefit from a peer group under the watchful eyes of adult therapists who set the framework for interpersonal learning. As the children display their maladaptive social behavior in the group, immediate feedback from their peers and the therapists helps them to work through the problem behavior in a benign, supportive environment. Working on troublesome behaviors as they occur decreases the children's tendency to deny their problems and the difficulties their behavior is causing. Since membership in the therapeutic group remains constant, the children are able to practice new behavior with the same children with whom they previously experienced trouble. They are offered a chance to achieve validation, to develop self-observation skills, and to rehearse ways of relating that can carry over to life outside the therapeutic group.

PGP works in several ways to help children work through their problem behavior. They include providing structure, fostering group cohesiveness, and encouraging socialization.

Providing Structure

Structure provides the predictable framework in which the children's interactions and activities can unfold as freely as possible. The purpose of the group structure is to create a consistent environment in which the children can feel safe and secure, knowing that they will be taken care of by the group therapists. We define structure as *containment*, the experience of being firmly and securely held within the group framework. The supportive atmosphere created within the framework of treatment depends upon several elements of the therapeutic group situation, including the setting, the materials used for play, the limits set on behaviors, and the authority of the group leaders. Considerable structure is needed not only at the beginning but throughout the entire process. Adequate structure is not used to keep the children under control but to help reduce their anxiety to a tolerable level so that the children's chaotic, intense feelings and impulses can be expressed and shared in ways that are not overwhelming for the individual child and other group members.

Structure also helps children internalize the rules established independently prior to the group session. Moreover, it serves to protect the therapists from their countertransferences, which might otherwise be acted out through arbitrary measures at moments of intense turmoil during the session. With basic rules and limits known in advance, group members and therapists are able to proceed in a calmer, more predictable fashion. Limit setting can also give these children an opportunity to experience mastery and competence in acquiring a skill they had not previously developed. Thus their low self-esteem and sense of inadequacy can be countered in a constructive way.

Fostering Group Cohesiveness

The group therapy experience can create a new beginning out of which the participants can regain a feeling of belonging and become optimistic about changing their own behavior. Because all the children know that they are working on similar kinds of behavior problems, they can be more accepting of group goals. Children need to belong to a peer group. It can be helpful for them to see that others in the group have problems similar to their own. The children can teach each other, and the therapists can also demonstrate ways of behaving that can be more appropriately gratifying than what they have known previously.

The opportunities for mutual giving and receiving that occur within the group help the group's members to feel that they have something to offer each other. This sense of reciprocity can lead to an increased sense of competence, both on an individual level and within the group as a unit. Scheidlinger's (1982) concept of the group as "benevolent mother" is relevant to this growth of identifications within the group that leads to the resolution of ambivalent and hostile attitudes and the emergence of supportive relationships. The experience of group cohesiveness that withstands the stress of threatening intragroup conflict results in strengthened ego functions for its members. For the child with a history of disruptive behavior, these impaired ego functions have resulted in disobedience, impulsivity, temper tantrums, fighting, and low self-esteem. As a result of the experience of belonging to a therapeutic group, these children demonstrate an increased capacity to delay gratification and to attend to the task at hand. Group membership enhances both a sense of belonging and a feeling of individual identity and effectiveness.

Encouraging Socialization

Complementing these gains in ego functioning are the child's gains in interpersonal skills and relationships with others. The children learn to put their feelings into words, to share, to take turns, and to form and maintain a friendship. Through the interactions within the group, the children improve their skills in observing the feelings and behaviors of others, which in turn help enhance their self-understanding and relationships to other children.

Irvin D. Yalom (1970) conceptualizes the major curative aspects of group psychotherapy as including interpersonal learning, catharsis, cohesiveness, commonality of problems, altruism, and recapitulation of the family experience. All the components relevant to the interpersonal processes are involved in PGP. In PGP, catharsis occurs as the children are permitted to discharge affect, but within limits that help them channel their aggressive behavior into more socially acceptable ways of behaving. Therapists facilitate the channeling of affective expression by providing activities that help broaden sublimatory experiences (such as building projects, basketball games, and bringing snacks) and by encouraging verbalization to replace action. The learning of social skills, which include how to begin, maintain, and end interactions with peers, is fostered through activities, games, and role-playing as well as through the interchanges that occur within the group. The group experience helps its members come to see that they must take responsibility for their own actions and that passing blame onto others does not free them of accountability for their behavior. In sum, within the group the children begin to learn what real friendships entail.

The Process of Group Development

As the group develops in PGP it undergoes a process of differentiation. One focus of the therapy group is organized around specific tasks. This orientation would include games, activities, and discussions. Another focus of relationships that emerges is organized around unconscious, irrational forces within the group. Bion (1959) identified these two separate systems and termed them the *work group* and the *basic assumption group*. The "basic assumption group" assumes dependency, fight-flight, or pairing formations that can become shared fantasies and perceptions among group members. These formations are then acted out within the group, serving either as adaptation or resistance, depending upon the context of the group process in which they occur.

Although Bion's theory was not designed for a children's therapeutic group, his formulations about group processes are included in the theoretical rationale of our therapy model because they account for the children's unconscious perceptions of the group as a whole, including the regressive forces within the group. Using Bion's formulations we can understand the choreography of the transferences that emerge in the group.

When dependency is the primary formation, the therapists are seen as omnipotent, idealized figures who are there to take care of all the group members. Fight-flight formations represent an unconscious wish of the members to become leaders in their own right by aggressively attacking each other, with flight as a defense against this fighting. In children's groups, rebellion against the therapist is a common initial form of fight-flight group formation. The formation of pairing is the shared group fantasy of members coming together to produce a new member, or solution, or Messiah, to save the group. Pairing also gives rise to a sense of belonging and being cared for by the partner to the exclusion of the group. Sometimes shared secrets in the group may be an example of pairing that promotes commonality in the group. In the children's group, pairing of a child with the group therapist is especially significant. In pairing with the therapist the child is expressing a wish for an exclusive relationship with the therapist. The wish attests to insecurity and compromises the child's autonomous position with his peers. Tension inevitably arises when the basic assumption does not lead to a resolution. The three basic assumptions are not sequential, but one or another does assume dominance at a given point in time.

In addition to separate themes, in PGP groups a common theme or "common group tension" (Ezriel 1950) emerges as a result of the combination of individual fantasies within the group. The therapist provides both group-as-a-whole interpretations of the common underlying tension and individualized comments to each child as they relate to the group theme. Thus the therapist in PGP focuses upon overall themes and how individual members contribute to them. We believe that group themes should be identified in our children's groups to help decrease the sense of isolation that conduct disordered children feel as they come to see how their behavior contributes to an overall group process.

In our experience with PGP, we have found that an integration of individual and group-as-a-whole approaches works very well. We believe that flexibility in the choice of approach to the group is especially important. Conduct disordered children are prone to projections that are readily acted out in the group. Group themes inevitably emerge, and sometimes these children are better able to hear an intervention if they see that others are also told similar things. On the other hand, individualized interventions provide each member with the recognition that they are unique and worthy of attention. This individualized focus bolsters mastery, self-esteem, and identity formation. We do not always link individual interpretations to group themes. The type of intervention to be used depends upon the therapist's clinical judgment and the readiness of individuals and/or the entire group membership to process what is being said.

The Goals

The goals of PGP include those of SEPP and additional aims specific to the group modality of treatment. The following goals may be shared with the children in treatment. Based on a list prepared by Barbara B. Siepker and Christine S. Kandaras (1985), they have been adapted by us to fit the needs of conduct disordered children. Each child in the group selects with the therapist the goals that would be appropriate for his or her treatment. The list is by no means exhaustive and is stated in simple, concrete terms that children can readily understand. The children may want to write additional goals of their own to individualize the program to meet their needs.

1. To diminish conduct disordered behavior:

   a. To stay in the room for increasingly longer periods of time

   b. To refrain from physically hurting anyone

   c. To refrain from whining or hitting

   d. To talk instead of hitting

   e. To increase participation in discussion time

   f. To refrain from destroying property

   g. To refrain from throwing supplies

   h. To keep the supplies in the group room

   i. To behave appropriately in the waiting room and corridors of the clinic

2. To improve social adaptation:

   a. To learn to trust and be open

   b. To learn to make friends and become a friend

   c. To learn to understand feelings of peers and siblings

   d. To learn to share

   e. To learn to observe how others handle conflicts

   f. To learn alternative modes of looking at and responding to situations

   g. To learn to understand the feelings of adults

   h. To learn to get along with adults

   i. To learn to play games by the rules without cheating

   j. To learn to lose without blaming others or denying responsibility

   k. To learn not to break up a game when losing

   l. To learn how to be a leader and a follower

3. To increase self-esteem:

   a. To learn to recognize, label, and talk about feelings

   b. To learn to talk about oneself (what one wants from oneself and others)

   c. To learn to get feedback about one's behavior and personality

d. To learn what impact one is having upon others

e. To learn to cope and handle stress

f. To learn new ways to soothe and comfort oneself

g. To develop a positive social self-concept

The Phases of Group Development

Within each group meeting, both regressed and advanced behaviors occur. Each meeting may therefore be conceptualized to varying degrees as both a repetition of the past and a forecast of the future (Bennis and Shepard 1956). It is crucial for therapists to bear this concept in mind so that they neither overestimate a group when it is functioning at a higher level nor underestimate the group's potential when it is in a regressive phase. Recognizing the swings in group development helps to protect the therapist from disappointment and disillusionment about the members when the group is in a regressive trend.

Warren G. Bennis and Herbert A. Shepard (1956) cited two major areas of uncertainty that are central to group development: the group members' orientations toward authority (dependence) and their orientation toward one another (interdependence). Authority conflicts appear first, and only if these are fully resolved by the members do issues of interdependency and intimacy come into play.

They characterized each member as joining the group with his or her own typical responses to authority figures, such as submitting, rebelling, or withdrawing. Within the initial authority phase, the group moves from one of these preoccupations to the other toward a resolution of the dependency problems. Following this phase the group can focus more on problems of intimacy (interdependence). Individual responses to interdependence conflicts are characterized by destructive competitiveness, emotional exploitativeness, or withdrawal. In the intimacy phase the group also moves through various subphases until intimacy conflicts are resolved. The orientation in both phases is directed toward "enslavement of the other in the service of the self, enslavement of the self in the service of the other, or disintegration of the situation. Hence, they prevent the setting, clarification of, and movement toward group shared goals" (Bennis and Shepard 1956, p. 417).

In order for a group to reach maturity it must pass through all the subphases. Regression frequently occurs, as do lower levels of development coexisting with more advanced levels. Some groups may become stuck at a certain level of development and never resolve the crucial issues around authority and intimacy. The skill of the leader as well as the personality of the members can facilitate the progress of the group process. These two polarities in group development will be useful to us as we trace the development of children's groups in PGP.

Group Beginnings: The Preaffiliative Phase

After the preparatory period, when the group has been selected and each set of parents and child has met at least once with one of the therapists, the children begin the group process. This is a time of heightened anxiety in which children are tenuously related. We therefore call it the preaffiliative phase. The sessions are chaotic and full of turmoil. Although relationships with peers and therapists exist, the children's disorganized functioning makes it appear that the children do not relate to each other or to the therapists. Instead they destroy toys and run in and out of the room, and the scene comes close to pandemonium. This onset to the group process has been called the *fragmented stage* (Bracklemanns and Berkovitz 1972). Bion (1959) characterized it as psychotic, with paranoid behavior predominating. Saul Scheidlinger (1982) points to the group as a benevolent maternal matrix with negative transferences split off and directed onto the leaders.

For conduct disordered children, joining and forming a group is so sabotaged by anxiety that the group appears as a chaotic, fragmented cluster of individuals. These early sessions appear devoid of structure, despite efforts by the group therapists to impose it. The regression inherent in the group process and the social failures of these children combine like a centrifugal force that pushes away structure and creates fragmentation. There is little or no acknowledgment of the leader by the children. This behavior can last from weeks to a few months. Frequently therapists feel bewildered, defeated, and angry as they try to counteract this dispersal of the structure they are trying to impose.

The *preaffiliative phase* is determined by the dynamic tasks that the group members are trying to resolve, the tasks involved in joining and forming a group. Each member must confront questions such as "Who am I within this group?"; "Will I be recognized and heard?" The children feel alone and trust no one. Hypervigilance is common as the members scan the environment for ways to feel safe and protected. A pecking order among the children develops: who is the strongest and most to be feared and who is the most fragile and easiest to scapegoat?

The therapists' task is to help the children understand that it is the newness and strangeness of the experience that create anxiety. What may appear as the escalation of out-of-control behavior may actually be a reflection of intense anxiety in the children, who are worried that no one will protect them in the group. Some of them initially fear they will be destroyed. A passive stance by the therapists at this point may serve only to heighten the anxiety and should be avoided.

The Middle Phase: Issues of Membership in the Group

For conduct disordered children, the middle phase of PGP may be the time in which most of the productive work is accomplished during the academic year. This phase is reached when the dynamic tasks of forming the group have been resolved. The children can now acknowledge the authority of the therapists, and the dominant submission-rebellion issues can be worked through.

In the preaffiliative phase, no such relation to the therapists is acknowledged in group sessions, although individually the children may behave quite differently. Now the therapists are more openly acknowledged, and authority-dependency issues are more in the open. With conduct disorder children, however, we have seen that conflicts about authority and dependence are so severe that they are never fully resolved and occur throughout the group process.

The child's status within the group, including issues of inclusion, acceptance, and rivalry, are of central concern. Subgroups form, and play scenarios occur involving "good" and "bad" group members and acceptance or rejection of the therapists. Auxiliary therapist roles may be formed among the children as they vie for a place in the pecking order of the group.

The earlier part of this phase is a reactive period, during which the individuality of the members is evident as the children compete with one another to have their needs met. During periods of optimal functioning, children can begin to "hear" one another as they have verbal exchanges and share activities in an effort to gain acceptance from other children and the therapists. Children may rally together to challenge the therapists through play scenarios, which are now more organized through negative comments. The rebellion that is characteristic of this phase is a sign of early group cohesion. It also sets the stage for working through the magical expectations that children tend to have about adults and allows a more realistic appraisal of the therapists and the group to emerge.

As the group members learn that the therapists are there not only for themselves but for the entire group, members begin to turn to each other for support. They are also more ready to deal with the inevitable frustrations of group life. They experience the group as more benevolent than they did at first, and a sense of "we-ness" develops as the sessions become valued events. Attendance improves during this phase; sometimes members want to give the group a special name, and a clublike feeling among members emerges. Snacks are more readily shared at this time.

Fantasies about being special to the therapist can begin to be worked on at this point, and sibling rivalry is addressed. To further the development of cohesion, the therapists can help the children choose a name for the group, acknowledge group history, establish commonalities among the members, and provide group and individual confrontations and interpretations. One can expect to find metaphors in the play that can be identified and worked with, and in some sessions of optimal functioning, verbal interventions about the children's interactions can be taken in by the group and the individual members.

The Ending Phase: Issues of Separation and Competence

PGP groups are correlated with the academic school calendar, and the ending point falls naturally in June. Terminating the group is in some ways an artificial construct; it does not automatically imply that the group and all its individual members have achieved their goals, and some children will continue in group treatment for a second year. Nonetheless, it is important for all members to acknowledge the end of this group and bring their experiences during the year to some closure. A time-limited group promotes a progression through all phases that gives the children at least an experience of an entire group process, which can be growth inducing.

An ending process gives the children the opportunity to address the real separation and feelings of abandonment that a summer break will entail. Those children who have sufficiently improved will finish their group treatment at this time. Some children may require other modalities of treatment; others may no longer need any treatment. Children who still require group treatment will be referred to a group that will start in the fall. Since at least one of the therapists will frequently not be conducting a group the following year, a process of saying good-bye to that person is provided for in this ending phase. Moreover, some children for whom a second year of group treatment is recommended do not return to the group in the fall because of family relocation, transfer to another modality of treatment, or family problems. A good-bye to everyone helps take into account these factors and lends completion to the group experience.

In the ending phase of PGP, the therapists should try to recapitulate the history of the group and of the progress that the various members have made. Individual children may briefly regress to original symptoms. They may deny the importance of the group. Alternatively, they may wish the group could go on forever. The therapists convey to the children a sense of optimism about their gains, as well as the reality of the finality of the group. The members, then, begin to accept that the group will come to an end. Anxiety about separation should be addressed, as well as the specific way each child reacts to the ending of this group.

Parents will also have feelings of loss, relief, and disappointment that need to be explored in a private session and the parents' group.

Modes of Interaction

Play

An important aspect of PGP, play fulfills children's developmental need to belong to a group and to interact with peers. It facilitates communication between the children and the therapists and helps the children master new behaviors. When children develop the capacity for symbolic play, they can adapt more readily to reality and can assimilate reality, especially traumatic experiences. Mastery and security evolve as children incorporate aspects of the external world through play. They develop tolerance to frustration through representational and fantasy play as they learn that turning passive into active helps to reconcile them to being denied gratification (Slavson and Schiffer 1975). Play in groups allows for the release of anxieties and fears through abreaction and re-enactment. Play has a cathartic effect, which also helps by serving as a channel for expressing primitive impulses. PGP provides opportunities for role-playing, which allow children to develop identification and mastery as they portray the roles of persons in their immediate families and practice behavior that can be put to future use. Role-playing helps children create new solutions for old problems and develop empathy for other points of view. The children's participation in these portrayals facilitates feedback about dilemmas presented during group discussion time.

Play within the group also helps the development of skills. Playing games requires following rules, conforming to the norms of social behavior, and controlling aggression. Many conduct disordered children do not know how to play cooperatively, and learning how to play games should therefore be viewed as a therapeutic experience for social adjustment. The child's perception of peers and awareness of his or her interaction with peers receive immediate feedback from other members of the group, either validation or lack of support. To be reconfirmed by a peer has an important impact on self-esteem and underscores the significance of play as a way to help children learn to value peers and to take an interest in being understood. Through cooperative play, the latency-aged children learn to consider other points of view and to care about how others view them. They learn to read cues from, and to take into account the motivation of, other group members. Play within the group setting thus enhances the children's empathy one for another. The group therapy setting can also enable the child to begin to deal with peer group pressures and to protect his or her individuality in the light of group demands (Grunebaum and Solomon 1982).

Each PGP session should be held in a specially designated room, large enough to allow for motoric activities of the group as well as for individual play. A one-way observation mirror and microphones, videocamera, work table, chairs, and toy cabinet are necessary equipment. The group session should be a minimum of one hour. The time may have to be used as a limit-setting device, curtailed early on if the group becomes chaotic. Clinic personnel should be instructed not to interrupt the session once it has begun to permit group boundaries and confidentiality to be maintained.

Play materials should be chosen by the group therapists to facilitate socialization and communication experiences. The materials offered throughout the various phases of the group will vary from simple games and structured activities, to activities allowing more free play and cooperative interaction in the later phases. Materials should be chosen carefully to meet the group's tolerance for emotional expression, consistent with its level of anxiety. Early in the development of the group, it is better to have the room sparsely furnished with objects than to have too many choices available. One activity per session may be all the children can handle initially. Supplies are added at later points as the group shows an increased tolerance for them. Further discussion on providing structure within sessions will be provided in chapters 12 to 14 on the individual phases of PGP.

Verbal Interventions

In PGP the therapists' verbal interventions reflect the group process as it unfolds, targeting interactions within the session and not focusing on the historic development of these behaviors from the child's earlier development and family dynamics. The verbal interventions are categorized using the same schema outlined for SEPP, including the four specified modalities of communication. (See the Introduction, pp. 12–17.)

Ordinary social behavior

The therapist uses appropriate conventional expressions of greeting, leave-taking, and politeness, addressed to individuals or the group as a whole.

→ Billy couldn't attend today. He called the group to say that he had a bad sore throat.

← Thanks for asking whether my cold is better.

Statements relating to the treatment

The therapist specifies the procedures, boundaries, and rules of PGP in terms of the structure of group sessions, the children's behavioral limits within the sessions, the group process, and the therapist's role.

→ The group needs to be a safe place for all children and the therapists, and therefore we can't allow physical fighting or dangerous behavior toward any member here.

← Our roles as doctors will be to help you to get along with each other, and to be better able to put your feelings into words.

Requests for factual information

The therapist asks a child or addresses the entire group for objective information to fill informational gaps.

→ When we plan snacks in here, we need to know if there are special foods anyone is allergic to or can't eat for some reason. This way when we take turns bringing in the snacks, we'll all know in advance what is acceptable.

Supportive interventions

The group therapists utilize support to teach the children new ways of coping and to broaden their range of functioning.

Educational statements supply factual information or correct misinformation on matters other than therapy or teaching new skills.

→ Tony, I'll teach you how to build the airplane so it won't fall apart.

← You kids look surprised at my appearance. I have a new haircut; I am still the same person.

(→) It isn't safe for the "robber" to lean out the open window in our group room. He could break a leg if he fell off a window ledge this far up.

The therapist's suggestions introduce ideas or alternative courses of action for the children. These suggestions may become more emphatic in PGP due to group pressure on the therapist.

→ You boys all want to play knock hockey now. Yet by grabbing for the hockey sticks at the same time, you get into a fight and then no one has a chance to play. Usually, when kids take turns, no one gets left out. Let's decide upon a time limit so that everyone who wants to play can have a turn. How long a time shall we allow each person?

← When I feel people have been unfair with me, I tell them so they can hear my side. After that, I listen to their side. Then I decide whether or not to continue playing. I don't quit the game until I hear what they have to say.

(→) The boxers can say "stop the action" if they feel the play is getting too rough.*

Encouragement, reassurance, and empathy involve approving actions or resonating with the thoughts or feelings of the child, by labeling or echoing his affect.

→ You didn't want our group to have to end early today and so you refused to fight, even though Mark kept provoking you to do so. Look how well it worked out, even though you thought you wouldn't be able to stop yourself from fighting.

← I feel sad, just like both of you, to learn that Monica's parents are getting a divorce.

(→) It's all right for the pitcher to have quiet time by himself in a corner of our group room if he feels disappointed about losing the game.

Facilitative interventions

The group therapists' role is to help the play activity unfold and when appropriate to comment on the emerging themes of the play, as they relate to the group. The therapists help individual members see the impact of

*The "stop-and-go" rule is explained in chapter 12, pp. 208, 212, 221.

their behavior upon others, as well as the influence the group has on individual members.

Invitations to continue are responses that convey ongoing attention, interest, and understanding to a child or children.

→   Did everyone hear what James said about fighting—that one of the reasons he strikes out is that he feels small and stupid when he doesn't get his first choice of things to play with? James, can you tell us more about that feeling?

←   Richard says he feels like killing me sometimes. Who else has felt like that? . . . What more can you say about that, Richard?

(→)   Is Batman angry in this play?

Review statements involve paraphrasing, summarizing, or integrating what the child or children have said or done up to that point in the session or in past sessions.

→   You came eagerly to the group room today, but as soon as you entered you started to destroy the new models. Since everyone knows we have to have members leave the session if they break things, you must not be wanting to be here today as much as you seemed.

←   You've all been showing me ways I haven't protected you enough.

(→)   The robber has now shown us from his play the reasons why he needed to steal.

Directing attention

The group therapist alerts the child or the group to specific aspects of ongoing play, expression of feelings, or significant behavior. It is the therapists' role to highlight clearly and distinctly the impact of group members.

Preparatory statements alert the children to the possibility of new meanings in their affects, behavior, play, or ideas.

→   Danielle, whenever we start making the model of the airplane, you start teasing others and make it hard for the rest of the group to work. It happened also when we were planning our afternoon schedule. What do you make of that? Can anyone else in the group help Danielle to understand this?

←   I think that you have ideas about Dr. Brown and myself.

(→)   We need to figure out why the policeman is so harsh with the
       convict.

"Look-at" statements about the present identify and direct the child's
or the group's attention to affects, behavior, play, or ideas that may occur
entirely within the present session.

→   You all look like you want to run out of the room now, when I
       mention that soda was spilled on the rug in the waiting room after
       last session.

←   You avoided looking me straight in the eye when I asked whether
       you meant to knock down Eric's blocks.

(→)   Did the group notice how none of the cowboys could choose an
       activity today?

"Look-at" statements about the past serve to integrate different behaviors over time and to promote continuity by identifying and directing the
child's or the group's attention to affects, behavior, or ideas that occurred
earlier in the group's history.

→   You and Ed were angry last week.

←   Remember when you used to think that I thought it was funny when
       you couldn't complete a project and needed my help?

(→)   The red team always used to fight each other if they didn't win the
       game.

"Look-at" statements about the future identify and direct the child's or
the group's attention to affects, behavior, play, or ideas that may determine
future consequences. These statements make explicit a specific outcome or
contingency of events.

→   If you run out of the room, you will not be permitted to return.

←   If you hit me, it will automatically result in our stopping the game.

(→)   The red team will lose points if the players do not follow the rules.

"See-the-pattern" statements enable the therapists to point out to the
group a problem with a particular child, and the contexts in which it exists;

the observation can then be validated by the other members. In an enabling atmosphere, such observations can be an extremely useful way for members to give and receive important information about themselves. The therapists' sense of timing, empathy, and working alliance with the child and the group help to make confrontations more effective.

→   Every time anyone wants to show us what he has made, Billy acts to distract us by speaking loudly to Andy or one of the other boys. Have you noticed that, Billy? Has anyone else noticed it?

←   You are all speaking at the same time, want to play with the same toy, and want to sit next to me. Have you noticed that?

(→)   The Barbie doll always wants more attention from the mother doll just when it's time for mother to feed the baby.

Interpretations

Interpretation is used in PGP mainly in the middle phase and toward the end of treatment to help the children develop an understanding of the hidden motivations and conflicts behind their behavior. Group norms considered antitherapeutic should be interpreted, as well as anxiety-laden issues that are threatening group cohesion. An issue critical to the existence or functioning of the entire group always takes precedence over a narrower interpersonal issue. Historical material from a child's background is rarely utilized as a reference point for interpretation unless the child has shared information with the group that can be linked to his current behavior. Generally the group sessions (past and present) provide the material from which interpretive comments are made. This is common ground for all the children and thus of value to all of them.

Interpretations about defenses:

→   Alice feels unsure the group will invite her to join in, and she resents that everybody except her is paired together for a game. She tries to split up the group so she won't be the only one alone.

←   You are all angry at me for having stopped the game. Rather than telling me about how you feel, Sam and Bob are fighting with each other, Dick is pretending I don't exist by turning his back to me, and Ronald is throwing chalk all over the place.

(→)   All the good guys behind the fortress try to get rid of the bad guys
        before the bad guys hurt them.

Interpretations about motives:

→   When Andrea feels she can't give clever answers to some questions
        like Nancy, she feels dumb and covers it up by being bossy instead.

←   You wish that Dr. Brown would be absent today so that you could
        have me to yourselves.

(→)   Somehow the robbers get out of control just when it's time to stop
        for today. I think they wish they could have more time with the
        policemen (therapists), and they think fighting would be the way to
        do it.

Chapters 12 through 14 provide a detailed description of early, middle,
and ending phases in PGP. Because the group process and the changes in
it from one phase to another cannot be fully captured in brief extracts, we
will present one complete session from each phase of treatment of one
ongoing PGP group.

12

The Initial Phase of Treatment

Introducing the Child to PGP

P RIOR to the first group meeting, each child should meet individually with at least one of the children's group therapists. Sometimes
the children tell the therapist that their parents have not told them
anything about the purpose of the interview or that they will be
in the group. In some cases this is true; in other cases the children have
failed to register the information or want to have it repeated. It is important
for the therapist to clarify the child's understanding of the purpose of the
meeting and to correct distortions as they emerge. The therapist then
explains the plans for the group.

General Orientation

The therapist first gives a general orientation or description of the session.

→   It's a place for kids. In the first meeting we will go around the room
    so that all the kids can tell their names and the kinds of things they
    like to do.

The orientation with each child should include the number of children
in the group, a brief description of the activities, and the means of commu-

nication between the therapists and parents. The child should be told that the parents are invited to attend a special parents' group to learn more about parenting. During this orientation meeting the child is also told that everyone will take turns bringing snacks to the group.

Explaining the Purpose of the Group

The child is told that a general goal for all the children will be to learn to play and make friends with other children. In addition to the common goal of learning to make friends, the therapist and child should jointly work on a list of specific target areas for the child to work on in the group. The list can be given to the child at the end of the session and shared with the parents, ensuring that all participants agree on therapeutic goals. The therapist also gives the child a telephone number where he can be reached if the child needs him.

The child is informed that the group will meet once a week for an hour for the duration of the school year and that his parents will inform the therapists in advance, if possible, of any absences. He should be told who will bring him and informed about the arrangements to meet in the waiting room after the group session ends. He should understand that whoever brings him will be called out of the parents' group session to help him if he needs quiet time outside of the group or if for some reason he must leave early.

Explaining How the Group Functions

The child should be told that what is learned in group cannot readily be taught in a classroom. To learn best how to relate to other children, they need the experience of "moment-to-moment" interaction with other children in a safe environment to practice what they are learning. Adults alone cannot teach them how to make friends; what helps most is the experience of being with other kids their age. The child needs to understand that children can help each other in the group and that the adult therapists will step in when they are needed. The therapists will function like umpires in a baseball game, helping to run the group and give support and direction to the kids. At this time the child is shown the group room, and any further questions are elicited. The parents and child are given the specific starting date and time for the initial group meeting.

Working with the Children's Group

In the initial phase of PGP, the therapists facilitate constructive play and pave the way for later interactions by nonverbally conveying attention and interest in the children. They establish a predictable sequence by meeting the children in the waiting room, walking them to the group room, having supplies available, structuring the time available for play, discussion, and snack, and preparing for leaving by helping to put away supplies at the end of the session. The therapists try to make sure that each child feels their presence by maintaining eye contact and personal availability when a child seems vulnerable, by providing supportive gestures to encourage what is being expressed, and by setting limits when necessary. The therapists can indicate that expectations for controlling impulsive behavior are to be met by closing the door to prevent a child from running out, holding a child back to prevent fighting, or restricting the use of materials.

Providing Structure in PGP

As we saw in the last chapter, the therapists must convey their authority to set limits and establish the norms of the group and yet remain flexible enough to adapt the norms for the specific group of children with whom they are working. The children will test and retest the limits throughout the formative stages of the group. Contrary to the experience of many therapists who have not worked in groups with conduct disordered children, the group therapists must, from the beginning through the middle phases, remain active to structure the sessions. It is necessary to assist the children by augmenting the controls they have not yet sufficiently internalized. The use of play materials and choice of games should reflect this highly structured approach. For instance, suggestion of an activity such as construction sets or building models serves to pull the group together. The group room should have as little extraneous material as possible to avoid overstimulating the children. These children have difficulty modulating aggression and need activities that will help them contain their impulses, which are so frequently destructive.

The therapists may require practice in working together in the initial phase and may differ as to when to step in and call for limit setting. Sometimes co-therapists find it useful to agree to back the one who feels least comfortable with the aggression presented at a specific point in the session. In this way they work as a team, making it more difficult for the children to split them to add to the chaos. The children need to feel that the adults are in charge at all times and experience this control as reassuring and supportive.

In the beginning sessions, we have found it useful to assign seats to the children for the discussion periods to make them aware that some structure is expected. The co-therapists spell out several rules in the initial sessions and in the preparatory meeting.

1. The group needs to be safe for all the children and the therapists, and therefore no physical assaults or dangerous behavior toward any member is allowed. (This statement will help counteract the initial anxiety common to many children that the group will attack them and that they will be destroyed.)
2. The group room and its contents must be preserved.
3. The children should try to remain within the group room during the entire session, if possible.

The techniques for instituting control should begin with verbal requests to stop the behavior that violates the rules established for the group. Mild, supportive restraints can be added as needed to encourage a child to stop, or to break up a pair of children whose behavior is escalating to dangerous levels. If further steps are needed, these should include separating a child from the others by having a time-out period within the room to help him regain control. One therapist can separate a child from the others when necessary and talk with the child in one-to-one interaction in a quiet corner of the room. We try to have a preselected space in the room designated for this purpose. This procedure helps to allay the child's anxiety and to improve his capacity for control. Alternatively, a child may be excluded from the group for the remainder of the session, but removing the child from the room is done only as a last resort. Shortening the length of the session may be needed if a contagion effect has led the whole group to escalate aggression.

The "stop-and-go" rule (Clifford and Cross 1980) should be made available for the children's use as well as the therapists': a child or a therapist can stop the action at any time by calling "stop" if a child is breaking a rule or behaving inappropriately, such as fighting or taking a toy away from another child, and later indicating "go" when both agree that the incident is over and the play can be resumed. This rule helps give both children and therapists some control of the action to curtail feelings of being overwhelmed in an out-of-control period in the group. It is a rule that is fun, like a game, and that helps to develop mastery.

We have made it a policy that any child who needs to be excluded for the remainder of the session must be supervised by the person who brought him, and that this person must thus leave the parents' group to accompany the child. If we learn that splitting has occurred, so that children behave well in the session but act out in the waiting room after the session, we work on the issue in the group session and inform the parents of the need to supervise their child prior to and after the session. At times it has been necessary to have the children exit from the group one at a time, accompanied by the parents who meet them at the group room door to escort them off the grounds.

A structuring technique especially useful early in treatment is to divide the session into a discussion time followed by a playtime and finally by a snack time in which discussion occurs. In the beginning phase, discussion time should be brief, perhaps five to ten minutes. In later phases of treatment, the discussion period can be increased. The discussion informs group members of important events such as planned absences or the addition of new members and gives members a forum to attend to tasks the group should address, such as how "time-outs" should be called for and how games should be decided upon.

The playtime should follow, as group members will not be able to engage in a discussion for long initially and need to work on their social and problem-solving skills in a free-play period. The duration of playtime should vary, depending upon the group members' tolerance for play following the rules. Generally a half-hour playtime is suitable. Verbal interventions occur in the play period to facilitate the interactions and to help the children follow group norms.

The snack time at the end of the session should be approximately fifteen minutes. This calming-down time serves several purposes: It gives those children who have trouble with transitions time to settle down before leaving. It also allows the children to distance themselves from the play period and gives them a less affectively charged time in which to comment upon their own actions and those of others. The discussion should include some consideration of what occurred in the play period to enable members to focus upon improving their problem-solving and social skills. The comments of the therapists and children can frequently be more readily absorbed by all present in this quieter time.

Play

Initially, therapists make available individual projects for each child, if he or she wants them, to allow for parallel play. Activities and games that can be shared with other children are also provided, but therapists should not push for interaction at this point; the experience of being able to be in the room with other children is enough. A task orientation is needed at first to help curtail the regression that could otherwise become overwhelming for the members. A period of individual productivity is beneficial, because many of the children have lacked such developmental accomplishments. Appropriate initial materials are puzzles, Lego blocks, crafts projects or models, construction sets, bean bag games, dime-store balsa wood airplanes, paper (oversize sketching pads or paper rolls suitable for murals), markers, individual computer games, and cardboard blocks.

Gradually, the therapists introduce materials that encourage cooperative play for pairs or groups of children, and later, activities that include the entire group. In the middle and the final phases of the group, the members can select their own activities. Appropriate materials for cooperative play include knock-hockey, nerf balls and nerf basketball hoop, cards, board games, and pinball machines. Games that elicit feelings and improve communication skills and problem-solving abilities are useful and can be played in teams. Puppets, role-playing, charades, and the use of the video camera for filming and viewing are also appropriate. If the room is large enough, sports such as relay races, freeze tag, and touch football can be introduced. The therapists can modify the rules to increase the structure or decrease competition, as needed. We feel that the selection of materials should also reflect the tastes and enjoyment of the therapists.

Verbal Interventions

In the preaffiliative phase, verbal interventions are directed primarily at the children's anxiety about being members of a group. Ordinary social comments, supportive and educational comments, and facilitative comments help to allay the children's anxiety and fears while increasing their effectiveness in social interaction.

During the first session, the therapists reintroduce themselves and have every child introduce himself or herself. It is important to give all the children the sense that what they say will be taken seriously and with regard for their individual needs. Because some children have short-term memory deficits, limited attention spans, and a tendency to become overwhelmed or disorganized if they are overstimulated, it is sometimes necessary to practice learning names and review the same information in subsequent sessions.

→   I am Dr. Brown and this is Dr. Black, and now we would like each of you to take a turn to say something about yourself, such as your name, the kinds of things you like to do, and what you are like, so we can really get to know you in the group. Johnny, let's begin with you.

If the group is restless and all the children do not get a chance to introduce themselves, the therapists should suggest they continue at the next meeting.

→   So now we know about John, next time we'll listen to David. And then after David, Andrew can introduce himself.

The therapists clarify that this is the room where the children will meet and specify that there are things they are allowed to do and things they are not to do in the group room. They suggest that the children go to the bathroom before group session begins, but the children also are shown where the bathroom is in the event they need to use it during the session.

During the snack period, the therapists review the structure of the session and discuss plans for future sessions.

→   Each time we will be meeting with you as today. We will pick you up in the waiting room and have a playtime, followed by a snack time and a discussion time in the group room. We will prepare to stop the session with everyone helping to return the toys in the room to the order that it was when we started. We'll take turns bringing in snacks. Who would like to bring snacks for our next session? It is also important we know ahead of time if you can't come to the next session.

Confidentiality should also be discussed. The therapists must convey that what goes on in the group is private. Parents can call the therapists to give information, but the specifics of what happened in any session will not be discussed with the parents. If the children want to share information about the group with their parents, they may do so.

During the initial phase, supportive statements are limited to direct communications and statements about the relationship to peers and the therapists. Because children with conduct disorders have not learned how to play with one another, we do not yet expect to see a capacity to use symbolic communication.

→   I'll teach you how to play the game by reading and explaining the rules out loud.

→   Sometimes when you meet new kids, it feels like they are more enemies than friends. It takes several times to get to know them better and to find out whether that is true.

(→)   You can say "stop" to each other when you feel the need for time out or want to stop the action of one of the other kids in here, such as if the King-of-the-Mountain game gets too rough.

←   Tell us whenever you need our help, if you can't decide on the rules of a game. We'd be happy to referee, rather than have you give up on the game.

Encouragement, reassurance, and empathy are used frequently in the preaffiliative phase. They lend support and facilitate the group process.

←*   We know that you don't know each other very well as yet, but see how you manage to play together very nicely.

←   Although you've been busy getting used to each other, you still remember our names.

Invitations to continue and review statements serve to facilitate the unfolding of group process.

→   Uh huh, oh, I see, yes. (These words of encouragement can be addressed to individuals, subgroups, or the whole group.)

←   So, you have been telling us, by jumping all over the room, going from toy to toy, and wanting to leave early that you don't think that we can take care of all of you in this group.

---

*In the following pages, asterisks indicate the therapist's verbal interventions that express his or her feelings, thoughts, and patterns of behavior to the child or group. These statements introduce the child to another person's perspective (for full discussion, see p. 12).

Working with the Parents

Prior to the beginning of treatment, the parents meet individually with the children's group therapists. This initial meeting not only introduces the parents to the therapists who will directly be treating their child but gives them an opportunity to learn more about the child's diagnosis and about PGP as the appropriate means of intervention. It is essential that the parents as well as the child understand the necessity for regular attendance at the sessions. The importance of confidentiality of group members is also discussed. The parents are encouraged to suggest to their child that he bring up with the group incidents that occur at home. They are told that it is important to obtain from the school specific information about the child's difficulties with peers and are asked to sign the appropriate release. Fee schedules, medication issues, and future meetings—one midway in the group process and one at the end—are planned. How to reach the therapists by telephone, if necessary, is also explained. The purpose of the parents' group and the arrangements for it are described fully, and the parents are strongly urged to participate.

The parents' participation in the parents' group serves to promote the treatment alliance and to help the parents feel involved. It is also a way to maximize communication with the home and demystify the treatment process. In addition to offering each other mutual support, the group members provide an ongoing source of information about their children's functioning outside the group. Group meetings afford an educational opportunity for the parents to learn effective behavior management techniques from their group therapist. In addition, the therapist provides an available parental model to the parents and facilitates their sharing of information with one another.

The parents frequently experience the parents' group as a club, as it gives them a firsthand experience of affiliation with a group.

Parents are not considered the patients, and the parents' group therapist must make this clear. The parents' group is designed for mutual support and parental guidance; it is not group therapy intended to resolve personal issues. It is based on the belief that the parents can become better parents if they exchange ideas with one another and experience "being parented" by way of modeling from the group therapist, as well as from the other members.

The parents' group requires a meeting room of its own, scheduled for the same time as the children's group. The parents' group session should end five minutes before the children's group ends to allow the parents time to meet the children in the waiting room when the children are ready to leave.

This arrangement helps to contain the children and to further the therapeutic process. All parents must understand that if a child is asked to leave a group session, it is the responsibility of the parent to leave the parents' group to attend to the child, either remaining with him for a quiet period outside the group or taking him home if that is indicated. If the entire children's group ends early, the parents' session must also stop early so that the parents may accompany their children. No child should remain in the out-patient area unattended.

At the initial meeting, the parents' group therapist greets the parents in the waiting room and takes them to their group room after the children have been taken to their group. The chairs should be arranged in a circle. The therapist briefly introduces himself and suggests that the parents do likewise. The parents are encouraged to share information about their child and why PGP was chosen. We have found that parents have frequently felt left out of prior treatment experiences for their children. They often share these feelings with the group during these beginning meetings and wonder whether this group experience will be any different and of any help to them.

The parents' group therapist discusses the plans for the sessions and the overall duration of the group. He also lets the parents know how to reach him in case of necessary absences or emergency consultations. He explains that most information about the children should be shared in the group, if possible, and that he will pass along to the children's group therapists the information they need. The contacts planned with the children's group therapists in the middle and end phases of treatment should also be specified. The parents' group may also choose to meet with the children's group, together with their therapists, midway in the school year. This joint meeting would further enhance their feeling of participation and involvement.

The therapist highlights specifically the types of information that are helpful for the parents to share about their children. He stresses that major events in the child's life between sessions should be reported, such as running away, assaultive behavior, school truancies or suspensions, or fights with the parents. Stressors at home that may affect the child, such as parental separations, illnesses, moves to a new address, and losses, should also be shared, if possible. Parents are encouraged to discuss disciplinary measures about which they have questions and to use the group to help them develop new strategies to modify their child's behavior. To allow the entire group to support individual progress, parents should also share gains and positive experiences as they occur.

The parents are told that the group is a forum for them as well—one in which they can air the enormous stresses they face as parents of a conduct disordered child. The therapist conveys an interest in them as individuals and invites them to share their feelings as parents. Parents are told they are free to bring up concerns about which they would like help from the group and to let the therapist know if they feel they are not getting the help they need. The therapist informs the parents that they are responsible for setting the agenda for each session.

The parents' group therapist works to facilitate the group process by encouraging all members to have their share of time in the group. He must limit members who monopolize the session, encourage reticent parents to speak out, and identify group themes. "Tell us more about it" or "That seems important to you; perhaps others can learn from your experience if you share it with us" are examples of the therapist's invitations to continue, which assist the group in focusing on its goals.

Prior to the close of each parents' group session, the therapist should integrate what has occurred in the session and relate it to larger overall themes the group is working on. This synthesis helps the members to review what has occurred and keeps them focused on their overall tasks. If the group tends to digress too much, the therapist suggests what the group should discuss in the next session.

An Early Session

Dr. Jones, a male therapist, and Dr. Edwards, a female therapist, have run this boys' group in an out-patient setting. The children in the group are David, Bob, John, Ronald, Adam, and Matthew, who enters at a later time.

David, age 12, the oldest boy in the group, was referred to this particular group despite his age because he is socially immature and isolated. He comes from an intact home, where he has been oppositional and rebellious. In school his social awkwardness has been especially apparent, and his peers have ostracized him.

Bob, age 10, has a history of speech and language problems, and under-achievement in school. He has had periodic aggressive outbursts and difficulty tolerating frustration. Negativistic behavior with peers has frequently led to his being scapegoated. Bob's parents divorced when he was an infant. His mother has been known to physically abuse her son when he becomes defiant.

John, 11 years old, has a history of impulsive, intrusive, and aggressive behavior at home and school. He has low self-esteem and appears anxious. His teachers have felt him to be unmanageable and unmotivated in groups and have recommended a special education setting for him. He is a bedwetter and has previously taken a psychostimulant for hyperactivity. His parents are divorced. He lives with his mother and younger sister.

Ronald is 9 and wears thick glasses for his severe myopia. His symptoms include fighting, exposing himself, lying, stealing, cheating, and oppositional defiant behavior at home and school. His low-average IQ is considered to be below his full intellectual ability. He has been in a special education setting for learning disabilities. Both of his parents have been treated for substance abuse, and his father also has a criminal record for assault. Ronald now lives with his grandmother.

Adam, age 9, has a history of depression, behavior problems, and poor school performance. His peer interactions have been problematic, since he has difficulty allowing others to join him in his play and tends to bully children of his own age. He is particularly demanding of adults, and this has been a problem for his grandmother, with whom he lives. Two years ago his mother, who has a history of substance abuse, moved south to live with her new boyfriend. His father has remained uninvolved with him.

Matthew, age 8, was referred for a trial period in the group. His history includes unruly behavior in the classroom, biting other children, stealing, lying, and distractibility. He does not follow directions and requires a small, highly structured, class. He has a developmental expressive and receptive language disorder. His mother is a single parent who is depressed and unable to set appropriate limits with him.

In this session from the beginning phase of PGP, the therapists set the stage for the emergence of a coherent group structure by clarifying rules and limits as well as by acknowledging the children's concerns for territory and possession. For example, in the circle discussion time the therapists designate a chair as left empty to represent a place in the group held for an absent member. In this way, each of the children feels a sense of belonging to the group and of being valued by the therapists even in their absence. The therapists act as active facilitators of peer interaction and model social skills in a manner that is both supportive and educational. Both therapists introduce the use of words instead of actions through clarifications and review statements. Around the issue of snacks the question arises as to whether each child will get his fair share. This concern for individual needs is contained by adequate provisions made by the therapists. The group unit is not yet independently capable of acting dependably as a "benevolent mother." The therapists in their role as gatekeepers, timekeepers, and culture bearers impart a sense of rules and consistent expectations. The underlying tensions within the group lead to a reliance upon the therapists to assure individual existence. The children's dependence upon the therapists is poignantly revealed in the threat experienced to the group's integrity by the prospective absence of one of the therapists.

Present at this session are Dr. Edwards and Dr. Jones, David, Bob, John, Ronald, and Adam, who comes late.

John enters with David and calls out that Mr. Potato Head is his. Dr. Jones indicates that he is going out to check the video machine to see that it is playing. John twists the head of the baby doll and kicks it like a football, and Bob leans against the one-way mirror, peering through it. David hits the baby doll as John did, but he is even more aggressive with it. Dr. Jones returns and asks John to put something away and then intercepts David with the doll.

DR. JONES: What are you doing, David?	→ Directing attention: "Look-at" statement (in the present)
DAVID: Trying to break the doll.	
DR. JONES: [moves to prevent the doll from being broken] Well, you can't do that.	→ Statement relating to the treatment

Dr. Edwards enters. David and John play a duel with each other. David knocks John with a toy and John hits David.

DR. JONES: [to John] There's no hitting each other, okay? If you start hitting people, then you get time out. Did you hear what I said, John?	→ Statement relating to the treatment ⇄ Directing attention: "Look-at" statement (in the present)
JOHN: Yeah.	
DR. EDWARDS: We start the session by sitting in a circle. [David is sitting next to her.] So you come sit here, John, and sit for a few minutes. [John gets chair.]	→ Statements relating to the treatment

The opening of the session illustrates the need for structure, which helps to control the reckless behavior of trying to break the doll and fighting with each other. The chaos of the preaffiliative phase must be addressed promptly by the therapists. The therapy room is not overstimulating. The therapists have a firm attitude, which conveys to the children that the therapists are in charge. Suggesting that the children sit in a circle at the beginning of the sessions provides structure through limit setting. It gives the group a concrete center in space and time that helps convey predictability and order.

DR. JONES: First thing I want to bring up this week is where were you last week, David? We missed you.	→ Directing attention: "Look-at" statement (in the past)
DAVID: Nowhere. My mom wasn't there.	
DR. JONES: Oh, you weren't able to come to group last week because your mom wasn't there?	→ Directing attention: "Look-at" statement (in the past)
DAVID: Yeah.	
DR. JONES: Well, we missed you. You didn't come? How did you feel about not coming?	→ Ordinary social behavior Directing attention: "Look-at" statement (in the past)
DAVID: Yeah.	
DR. JONES: I don't know what "Yeah" means. Yeah, you didn't come? Or, Yeah, you cared?	→ Facilitative intervention: Invitation to continue
DAVID: Both.	

Dr. Jones requests factual information to determine the reasons for David's absence in the previous week. Indicating that David was missed helps to bolster the boy's self-esteem. "Look-at" questions focus David's attention upon his own feelings so that he can acknowledge having missed the group.

David gets out of the chair with the Mr. Potato Head toy. John knocks it. Bob climbs on top of the stack of chairs and calls out that he's bigger than the others.

Ronald knocks on door and is invited in by Dr. Jones. The kids say "Hi," and Dr. Jones tells him to pull up a chair to join the circle.

DR. JONES: You weren't here last week, Ronald.	→ Directing attention: "Look-at" statement (in the past)
RONALD: Yeah, I was.	
DR. JONES: Oh, it was the week before that you weren't here.	→ Directing attention: "Look-at" statement (in the past)
DR. EDWARDS: We're still missing Adam.	

Each child is individualized by the therapists. Both Ronald and Adam are noticed for being absent.

DR. JONES: Oh, yeah, Adam still isn't here. The other thing I want to mention, I told you guys last group but you may have forgotten. I want to tell you guys I won't be here next Wednesday or the Wednesday after that, so I won't see you for two sessions. [The boys make noise, and Bob sits on top of the stack of chairs.]	→ Directing attention: "Look-at" statement (in the present) ←* Statements relating to the treatment
BOB: We're ashamed of you. You're fired.	
DR. JONES: I'm fired, huh?	← Facilitative intervention: Invitation to continue
DR. EDWARDS: Oh, wow.	→ Supportive intervention: Empathy
JOHN: We'll be here for all of the time.	
DR. EDWARDS: Does anyone have anything else to say about Dr. Jones not being here for two weeks?	→ Facilitative intervention: Invitation to continue
BOB: You do.	
DR. EDWARDS: I do. You're right. Absolutely. I will miss Dr. Jones.	→ Supportive intervention: Reassurance and Empathy ←* Supportive intervention: Suggestion

Dr. Edwards tries to facilitate feelings about Dr. Jones's absence and models for the group that she will miss him.

DR. JONES: Dr. Edwards will be running the group alone.	→ Statement relating to the treatment
BOB: That's not fair. It'll be boring.	
DR. JONES: Do people have more to say before we start playing?	→ Facilitative intervention: Invitation to continue

DR. EDWARDS: I do. I have something to say. A real surprise.	←* Directing attention: Preparatory statement
DR. JONES: [to David] Sit down. More of that, we'll give you a time-out.	→ Supportive intervention: Suggestion
DR. EDWARDS: I thought we would watch the video we made last time.	←* Statements relating to the treatment
BOB: Another time.	
DR. EDWARDS: You don't want to? [Bob shakes his head no.]	→ Directing attention: "Look-at" statement (in the present)
JOHN: Not a good time.	
RONALD: No, he wasn't on video because he was crying.	
DR. EDWARDS: You don't want to see yourself?	→ Directing attention: "Look-at" statement (in the present)
DR. JONES: Bob doesn't like being on video. He's said that a lot of times.	→ Supportive intervention: Empathy

David moves to one-way mirror and partially blocks it with a toy TV/ puppet screen. John does the same to block the mirror.

DR. JONES: Both David and John, by blocking the mirror with the toy TV, are showing by action what the rest of the group is saying, that they don't want to be seen on video.	→ Interpretation: Defense Motive

Videos can be used, but when the children feel insecure they may reject it and feel self-conscious. Dr. Edwards points this out to them with her "look-at" statement. When Dr. Jones notes that Bob doesn't like being on video, he is providing support and showing respect for the patient's wishes.

John stands on chairs and threatens to throw a heavy punching bag at Ronald. Ronald dares him to throw it and John does so. Ronald tussles with him on the floor.

RONALD: I'll kill you! I'll break your face!	
BOB: That almost hit Dr. Edwards.	
DR. EDWARDS: Boys, stop the action. You boys may need time-out now.	→ Supportive intervention: Suggestion

The "stop-and-go" rule can be used by anyone in the group, including the therapists.

DR. JONES: What you're reminding me of, Ronald, is the way we ended last week. You've reminded me of how angry you were last week at John, when John was tripping people.	→ Directing attention: "Look-at" statement (in the past) → Directing attention: "See-the-pattern" statement
RONALD: And he never even said he was sorry. What kind of kid was that?	
DR. JONES: John, I'd like you to talk to Bob about that.	→ Supportive intervention: Suggestion
RONALD: He's a dwork. He's not nice. He beat up my friend Bob and now he's going to be dead.	
DR. JONES: [puts arm around John] John, sit down. I want you and Bob to talk about that.	→ Supportive intervention: Suggestion

Dr. Jones is using a "see-the-pattern" statement to bring up the angry and hurt feelings among the group members. The therapist suggests they talk about the incident and provides encouragement by putting his arm around John.

BOB: I don't want to talk.

In the initial phase of PGP, the children are more prone to action than talk.

DR. JONES: John, look at Bob over there and ask Bob why he was mad at you. Talk to Bob about that. [Bob and John argue about a punching bag. Dr. Edwards puts an arm around Bob.]	→ Supportive intervention: Suggestion

DR. EDWARDS: Sit here, Bob. [One of the boys yells "Fight! Fight!"]

→ Supportive Interpretation: Suggestion

DR. JONES: You guys are all heading for a time-out, cause you are just throwing things.

→ Directing attention: "Look-at" statement (in the future)

RONALD: Well, he's a dwork.

BOB: We know that.

JOHN: You're a retard.

RONALD: He beat up people. That's what happens when you do that. You get revenge. [Ronald takes a pretend swipe at John. John stands on a stack of chairs and picks up a chair as if to throw it.] I dare you to throw it.

DR. JONES: You guys are heading for a time-out cause you're throwing things.

→ Directing attention: "Look-at" statement (in the future)

DR. EDWARDS: I think everyone has a hard time in here.

←* Directing attention: "Look-at" statement (in the present)

DR. JONES: I can't tell if you guys are playing or whether you're serious.

←* Directing attention: "Look-at" statement (in the present)

RONALD: I'm serious.

BOB: I don't know about that.

DR. JONES: [to John] Are you playing or serious, John?

→ Directing attention: "Look-at" statement (in the present)

JOHN: I'm serious.

DR. JONES: [to Ronald] Don't you want to work it out? Or do you want to stay mad at each other? Ronald, you want to stay mad?

→ Directing attention: "Look-at" statement (in the present)

Both Dr. Edwards and Dr. Jones are providing encouragement for the children to look at their own feelings and attitudes. This leads to acknowledgment by the children of their feelings as they work out their dispute between each other.

RONALD: No.

DR. JONES: You want to work it out? → Directing attention: "Look-at" statement (in the present)

RONALD: But he needs to apologize first.

JOHN: I'm sorry.

DR. EDWARDS: Ronald, he just said he's sorry. → Directing attention: "Look-at" statement (in the present)

RONALD: I didn't hear him.

DR. EDWARDS: He just said it. John, come here. John, say it again. → Directing attention: "Look-at" statement (in the present)

JOHN: I'm sorry.

DR. EDWARDS: [to John] You want to come here and look at Ronald when you say it. → Supportive intervention: Suggestion

DR. JONES: It doesn't sound as if John is trying very hard to convince anyone he's sorry. → Directing attention: "Look-at" statement (in the present)

BOB: You should both say it at the same time, really.

JOHN: I'm sorry, if you're sorry.

RONALD: You're not sorry, and I'm not sorry.

BOB: John, listen.

JOHN: I know, he's over there playing while I'm trying to say it.

RONALD: [playing a noisy game] I'm listening.

DR. JONES: But you're also playing a game. I don't think it's entirely up to John. I think you should have to help him. → Directing attention: "Look-at" statement (in the present)
← * Supportive intervention: Suggestion

RONALD: What do you mean? He has to say it first, because he did most of the throwing.

DAVID: I want to fight.

DR. JONES: You want to fight?   → Directing attention:
                                       "Look-at" statement (in the
                                       present)

DAVID: It's boring.
DR. JONES: Maybe if you tried to   → Supportive intervention:
get involved in the discussion,   Suggestion
David, it wouldn't be so boring.

The therapists make various suggestions to facilitate peer interaction. They are taking primarily an educative stance, offering suggestions on how to solve the problem between Ronald and John. Their role as facilitators is primary and includes their work with David, who tries to divert the interaction by saying it is boring.

DR. JONES: [to Ronald and John]   → Supportive intervention:
You and Ronald were going to   Suggestion
make up to each other.
RONALD: I'm sorry.
DR. JONES: What are you going to   → Facilitative intervention:
say, John?   Invitation to continue
JOHN: I'm sorry. [John throws a
ball cooperatively to Ronald,
who catches it.]
DR. JONES: Do you guys know   → Directing attention:
why you are apologizing to each   "Look-at" statement (in the
other?   present)
RONALD: He beat up my friend.
DR. EDWARDS: And what did you   → Facilitative intervention:
do?   Invitation to continue
RONALD: I beat him up, after he
tripped me.
DR. JONES: So you're sorry for   → Directing attention:
reacting that way.   "Look-at" statement (in the
                                      present)

DR. EDWARDS: John, do you want   → Supportive intervention:
to say to Ronald why you're   Suggestion
sorry?
JOHN: I'm sorry I beat up the
other kid.
RONALD: And for tripping me,
and beating up Bob. Well, you
should apologize to me and Bob.
JOHN: I just did.

At this point, Adam comes in. The boys play Monkey in the Middle, and Adam is in the middle, then John, and they continue to play the game. David and Bob are not taking a very active part.

DR. EDWARDS: I think David wants to play.	⇄ * Supportive intervention: Suggestion, Empathy
DAVID: Yes, I do!	
DR. EDWARDS: But no one gives him the ball. [Then David does join.]	→ Directing attention: "Look-at" statement (in the present)
BOB: [on the side, to Dr. Jones] Can we play running bases?	
DR. JONES: We're playing this right now. Why don't you get involved?	→ Directing attention: "Look-at" statement (in the present) → Supportive intervention: Suggestion

Ronald is in the middle, and Dr. Jones picks up Ronald so he can catch a high pass. Dr. Jones continues to invite Bob in, and he joins in the middle. The game continues and gets a little rough, and Dr. Jones comments that he doesn't want to get the ball thrown in his face again. Bob is continuing to play with them. He tries to throw the ball over to David.

RONALD: The ball was mine. John was cheating. [says to Adam] John cheated.	
DR. EDWARDS: Time out, everyone. John, you just threw the ball, time out.	→ Supportive intervention: Suggestion
DR. JONES: How many minutes is that?	→ Statement relating to the treatment
DR. EDWARDS: Three minutes.	→ Statement relating to the treatment

She looks at her watch to begin, and John sits in the time-out chair. The boys continue to play. Bob and Ronald are in a tussle, and Ronald moans on the floor.

DR. JONES: Are you okay, Ronald? Are you faking it, or is it for real?	→ Supportive intervention: Reassurance, Empathy

RONALD: Oh, it hurts.

DR. JONES: For real?   → Directing attention:
                                           "Look-at" statement (in the
                                           present)

RONALD: It hurts.

BOB: Oh, yeah, right.

DR. JONES: [gives Ronald a hand   → Supportive intervention:
  and he gets up and seems fine]   Suggestion
  You guys shouldn't jump on
  each other.

The boys continue with Monkey in the Middle. John and Ronald are in the middle, and Dr. Jones joins them. David and Bob tussle on the floor. Dr. Edwards, the timekeeper, joins the players and tries to throw over Dr. Jones's head. He catches the ball and tells her she is now in the middle. The boys alternate positions, and all are playing. Ronald and Bob tussle with each other on the floor over the ball. Dr. Jones tells John his time-out is over and he can come in now. The boys start jumping on the chairs and tables, but in a playful way. They continue the game and isolate Dr. Jones in the middle.

DR. JONES: I think I'm the only   ⇄* Directing attention:
  one in the middle now.   "Look-at" statement (in the
                                           present)

Dr. Edwards joins him, and Dr. Edwards and Dr. Jones throw the ball back and forth. Bob jumps off the table when Dr. Edwards catches it, and Bob and Dr. Jones are in the middle, then Bob is alone in the middle. Bob and David argue over the ball, and they settle it. Bob is in the middle, and Dr. Edwards and Dr. Jones playfully throw to each other, with the boys trying to intercept. Bob and David pile on the ball on the floor.

DR. JONES: No pile-ups. David,   → Statement relating to the treat-
  get off of it.   ment
                                         → Supportive intervention:
                                           Suggestion

David gets off and picks up a doll. He sits in the chair and tries to break apart the doll.

DR. JONES: [to David] You're determined to destroy the doll,
aren't you?

→ Directing attention:
"Look-at" statement (in the
present)

DAVID: Yeah.

DR. JONES: [takes the doll away]
But it's not your doll to destroy.

→ Statement relating to the treatment

Dr. Edwards continues to play and is in the middle. All the boys stand
on the chairs or the tables trying to throw over Dr. Edwards. Dr. Edwards
tries to catch from John, and they run into each other.

BOB: [about John] He looks at
her sexual organs.

Adam jumps on Dr. Jones's back. Dr. Jones remarks that he can't carry
him, so Adam jumps off. There's more Monkey in the Middle and laughter,
and it's very playful. David is again trying to tear the doll apart.

DR. JONES: You get time-out,
David. Three minutes.

→ Statement relating to the treat-
ment
→ Supportive intervention:
Suggestion

DAVID: Okay.

*The therapists join the children in play as group members. They also model and guide
appropriate social interactions, as when Dr. Jones takes the doll away from David and
clarifies for him that it is not his to destroy. The interaction remains in the educative,
supportive mode during the beginning phase. The possible hidden meaning of the doll
signifying the intrusive curiosity of the youngster about the female therapist is not
discussed, nor is the aggressiveness toward female figures interpreted. Instead, the behavior is contained as socially inappropriate action, and a time-out is given, which David
readily accepts.*

The game of Monkey in the Middle continues until it is time to prepare
for snacks.

DR. JONES: No one gets the ball
until the room gets cleaned up.

→ Statement relating to the treatment

JOHN: I didn't do anything.

DR. JONES: You're part of the group. You have to clean up. David, your time-out is over, so you can help us clean up. [The boys giggle.] John, you're the only one cleaning up here.

→ Directing attention: "Look-at" statement (in the present)
→ Supportive intervention: Suggestion
→ Directing attention: "Look-at" statement (in the present)

RONALD: I would gladly clean up.

DR. JONES: Ronald, why don't you get that stuff off the floor. [The boys are making a lot of noise.] It's impossible to know, to figure out who made what part of the mess.

→ Directing attention: "Look-at" statement (in the present)

RONALD: What do you want me to do?

DR. JONES: You can pick up Mr. Potato Head over here. I just asked you to clean up, not throw it around.

→ Supportive intervention: Suggestion

JOHN: [arguing with David] You took my seat!

DAVID: Tough tittie.

Dr. Jones continues to set limits with the boys and to encourage them to clean up.

DR. JONES: The room is cleaned up, but I need a chair. Adam needs one, and the rest of you who don't have chairs need a chair—which means that this pile of chairs needs to get smaller.

→ Directing attention: Preparatory statement

DR. EDWARDS: I think we're wasting time. We'll only have five minutes for our snack of donuts.

⇄* Directing attention: "Look-at" statement (in the present)

Ronald and John grab each other and kick.

DR. EDWARDS: I wonder if we can settle down. [to Adam and Bob] Come here so we can have our snack. [She points to the circle of chairs.]	⇄* Directing attention: Preparatory statement → Supportive intervention: Suggestion
DR. JONES: Bob, take the two top chairs off.	→ Supportive intervention: Suggestion
BOB: I need help.	

The boys gradually get ready for the snack, with Dr. Jones actively directing them.

DR. JONES: Okay, who will pass out the snack? [Many of the boys yell, "Me!"] Who brought it?	→ Directing attention: Preparatory statement → Facilitative intervention: Invitation to continue
BOB: Me. [He takes it and passes it out.]	

Someone says, "David brought the snack," and someone else says, "No, Bob did." Bob continues to pass out the donuts. Some of the boys ask for seconds, and someone remarks, "Oh, these things are wet!"

DR. JONES: Don't forget to give snacks to Dr. Edwards. She's sitting here, and she's hungry.	→ Supportive intervention: Suggestion ← Directing attention: "Look-at" statement (in the present)
JOHN: Ladies last.	
BOB: [counts the number of people] We all had enough.	
DR. JONES: So, what did you think of group today, John?	→ Directing attention: "Look-at" statement (in the present)
ADAM: [to Bob] You can't count. [to the group] He can't count.	

DR. JONES: How's your spelling, Adam? [Adam sits on Dr. Jones's lap.] Well, some kids do have trouble counting. [Bob gives Adam his second donut.] Someone can have mine, I don't want it. [The others call out, "Me, me, me!"]

→ Supportive intervention: Suggestion

JOHN: I didn't get my second.

DAVID: I didn't get my fourth.

DR. JONES: I think from now on, Dr. Edwards and I should pass out snacks. You guys don't do it fairly. [Several boys say: "I didn't get my seconds."]

→ Statements relating to the treatment

DR. JONES: There are only three left. Maybe Bob should take home the extra.

→ Directing attention: "Look-at" statement (in the present)
→ Supportive intervention: Suggestion

RONALD: I didn't get mine.

DR. JONES: [to Bob] Ronald didn't get his second. Why don't you give me the box, Bob. [Gives a donut to Ronald, who is sitting on a pile of chairs.] You're sitting on your throne, Ronald. Why don't you get down from there? [The other boys indicate that they want some, and the donuts are passed around.]

→ Directing attention: "Look-at" statement (in the present)
→ Supportive intervention: Suggestion
Directing attention: "Look-at" statement (in the present)
→ Supportive intervention: Suggestion

DR. JONES: [to Dr. Edwards] What are your plans for next week when I'm not here?

→ Directing attention:
← "Look-at" statement (in the future)

DR. EDWARDS: Either video or board games. I can't handle other things. [The boys playfully tussle around Dr. Edwards.]

→ Statement relating to the treatment
←* Directing attention: "Look-at" statement (in the present)

DR. JONES: You boys are going to scare Dr. Edwards away from here. [Dr. Jones and Dr. Edwards laugh.]	← Directing attention: "Look-at" statement (in the present)
JOHN: Why are you going away, Dr. Jones?	
DR. JONES: Because I have an appointment Wednesday, somewhere else. And the week after that I'll be on vacation.	←* Directing attention: "Look-at" statement (in the future)
DR. EDWARDS: Do you think we will be able to have group next week? [All the boys are running around Dr. Edwards and end in a pile on the floor.]	→ Facilitative intervention: Preparatory statement
DR. JONES: We'll have to stop in a minute, you guys. Just so you know, you won't have group next week or the week after that if you boys won't behave. Dr. Edwards will have to end the group early if you don't behave yourselves. [The boys continue to throw things, but in a way that doesn't hurt anyone.]	→ Statements relating to the treatment → Directing attention: "Look-at" statement (in the future)
DR. JONES: All right, group's over. Time to end. See you guys in two weeks.	→ Statements relating to the treatment → Directing attention: "Look-at" statement (in the future)

The therapists actively engage the group with suggestions to put the room in order as well as to interact at snack time. Issues of fair share are discussed in regard to who does the cleaning up and who has more or less of the snack. The time in itself provides the structure and the opportunity to observe the group experience. At this juncture it is possible to acknowledge for the first time the impact of Dr. Jones's leaving and to look at the implications of Dr. Edwards' leading future sessions by herself until Dr. Jones returns.

In the next chapter, we will follow the progress of our clinical group, in the middle phase of PGP.

13

The Middle Phase of Treatment

THE major themes of the middle phase in PGP are dependency issues and authority concerns. Although limit setting continues to be needed, the basic framework for treatment is established, and there is a semblance of order for longer and longer periods during the session. Therapists often feel more hopeful as they detect the children establishing an important relationship with them, albeit fraught with ambivalence. On occasion, symbolic play scenarios emerge, which the therapists use to help the children understand their behavior. These occur within the context of both individual and group dynamics. Interpretations can begin to be made in this phase as the children become able to understand them. Peers take on auxiliary therapist roles to help confront members and support interventions made by the therapists.

The establishment of one's role in the group is the focus for each individual member during the middle phase of PGP. A pecking order among the children develops. When focused on in the treatment, the children learn that leadership can shift; some children may be better at one activity than another, and at various times peer leadership can change depending upon the activities of the group.

Development of social skills is another major focus of the middle phase of PGP. As new skills are learned, the children's self-esteem and self-concept improve. These children learn not only how to lead but also how to follow and how to become a team member. Within the therapeutic

232

framework they are able to develop, maintain, expand, and terminate interaction in a constantly shifting field. They learn how to say yes and no to social opportunities. Alternatives to impulsivity, risk taking, and self-defeating behavior are worked on. The children have opportunities to learn to think before acting, to follow rules, to tolerate mistakes and errors in themselves and others, to play a game without cheating, and to lose without blaming others.

The group affords the children the opportunity to learn more adaptive ways to express their aggression. An important part of the children's work is learning to recognize the beginning of aggressive feelings before they turn into impulsive actions, to modulate aggressive feelings by giving oneself time to react, and to channel aggression into words or appropriate competitive activities.

The group can become a benevolent environment for the modification of old behaviors as the child assimilates the input of the therapists and his peers. Submission and rebellion themes become apparent as "we-against-they" themes in the play, and the children coalesce as a group in their rebellion against the therapists. This is a time for the children to establish a balance between peer interactions and interactions with adults. Because these children are already so disappointed in, and cynical about, adults, it is a challenge for the therapists to be seen as protectors and facilitators, rather than as adults who can't be counted on.

It is important to note that in the middle phase one may see or hear about incidents of the children's participating in antisocial behavior outside the group. A penknife may be wielded in the halls of the clinic prior to or following the session; property may be destroyed, windows broken, or threats made to other group members. As the therapists hear about an incident through the parents, the school, clinic staff, or group members, they must bring it back to the group to work on immediately or in the next session. It is a misconception to treat the group as a sanctuary, free from input from the larger milieu. The boundaries of the group should be seen as semipermeable, as input from the outside is integrated by the therapists and handled therapeutically. These children are prone to act out, not to verbalize the difficulties they get into, and it is imperative for the therapist to bring in such material as it occurs. Failure to do so would be collusion with the children and would maintain the split between action and feeling, and also would prevent the negative feelings about the group from being dealt with sufficiently.

If such deviant behavior occurs, the therapists speak with the children involved and then share what happened with all group members. If the event is localized to the environment of the clinic, the group could be told that a member has been involved in discrediting the group and/or endangering others. The children need to know that this behavior poses a risk that the member or members could be expelled from the group. The meaning of the incident must be examined next, in an effort to get the entire group to understand the behavior and, once it is understood, to find alternative ways of behaving. A clinical decision is then made about whether the members can remain in the group.

Working with the Children's Group

In the middle phase of PGP, the therapists' primary role is to facilitate interactions within the group and to offer new models of behavior that can be examined within the group. They continue to demonstrate their presence by providing materials and props and participating in the play. They also carry out a gatekeeping function to maintain group boundaries to allow the process to be carried out within the assigned room and space, with time-out utilized as needed.

Play

At the beginning of the middle phase, structured games, construction sets, and sports activities are utilized. As the group progresses, it is possible to provide less structure and allow imaginative play to unfold. The appearance of symbolic play is a definite sign of improvement. Symbolic play indicates the capacity to sublimate aggressive impulses in fantasy play instead of destructive activity in the external world. For instance, a theme of police and muggers hiding and being sent to prison might develop. Understanding social interactions as they occur and reviewing them for further clarification is an ongoing activity during the middle phase. A videotape camera can be used to record sessions, which the children can then see later to observe further and learn from the interactions. Another technique is to have the children role-play events that occur in the session. The children can switch roles when conflictual behavior is demonstrated to permit different outcomes from member-to-member confrontations to be played out and then discussed during snack period. Role-playing might portray difficulties in sharing or taking turns, bullying or scapegoating phenomena, or virtually any current focused dilemma faced by the children. Puppets can be introduced for similar purposes. Children can reveal the "we-against-they" themes through particular plots. Tables can become fortresses, chairs can become barricades, and toys can become pretend guns as the children assemble as armies of good versus bad guys or policemen versus robbers and portray their concerns symbolically.

Some groups have difficulty using any materials because of continued aggressive and destructive behavior. In such a case, it may be beneficial to remove all supplies from the room and introduce cushions and blankets for pillow play. These materials can help the children express aggressive behavior nondestructively. They stimulate actual contact between members, which is now less threatening than it would have been in the initial phase. They also help to promote contact that is not associated with destructiveness but with playfulness.

Verbal Interventions

The group is more cohesive in the middle phase, and therefore the children are better able to listen to the comments of the therapists than they were in the beginning.

Statements related to the treatment

Although the number of statements related to treatment might decrease, there are points that need to be made and reminders the children need to hear. For instance, the therapists should review the rules about behavioral expectations, inform the group about the planned absence of any member or therapist, encourage group plans for subsequent sessions, and remind the members to review what occurred in the session during discussion/ snack time. The children can be given poster paper to chart their own week-to-week progress, and this chart can be used during the discussion/ snack time.

Requests for factual information

Children are encouraged to share information that is related to recent events and evoked by the group process, rather than past history. For instance, children need to be encouraged to inform the group about relevant data such as where they live, the school they attend, and whether they have brothers or sisters, as well as about critical events going on in their lives outside the group. This sharing of information may have been attempted earlier, but during the initial phase of PGP the children were less able to attend to it. As the children begin to feel more bonded as a group, sharing information takes on new meaning. Moreover, reporting issues outside the group is a way to reinforce ties with the outside world.

Supportive interventions

In the middle phase of PGP there is an increase in supportive statements that educate the children in new ways to handle aggression and impulsivity and suggest ways to improve their social skills.

→   You must say "Hello" when you come in, so that the other kids know you are here.

←   If you say "Hi, Dr.—," I will know you are here and ready to start.

(→) If the blue guys were not so bossy and were able to invite the red guys to join them on the team, they would then be able to have a better team overall.

(→) Let's role-play. You, Peter, can play Andy and Andy can play Peter, and we will be able to review the fight all over again and see if we have a different outcome this time.

←   It would be better if you could tell me about your anger toward me, rather than letting me know by breaking the toys or hitting me.

→   The champion who won this round should have 10 seconds time out before continuing to fight.

The children continue to receive encouragement, reassurance, and empathy from the therapists. These statements support their mastery of new social skills.

→   Wow, you kids are doing great at taking turns!

←   You really noticed I got angry when Johnny hit me with a ball.

(→) The red team need not worry about not having enough time to finish their bridge. We still have 15 minutes left.

Facilitative interventions

Facilitative statements in the middle phase of PGP are similar to those given in the initial phase. The therapists continue to convey ongoing attention and interest in the group.

→   Oh, now we can see. Now we know.

←   What else could you be thinking about me and Dr. Allen?

(→) Hm, the cowboys would like to know more from the Indians.

In this phase of PGP, the use of review statements increases. The group operates as though it has a short memory span, and the children need to have their progress, or their lack of progress, reflected by the therapists.

→ So today you started by saying none of you were going to play. Then you started to wrestle in pairs. Now we are in a wrestling contest.

← Today you kids have been telling us we don't know anything; we don't even know how to play with you, and you can't count on us to be helpful.

(→) The cops have looked in every corner of the room, and they've checked the pockets of every one of the thieves, and they still haven't found anything. What will they do next?

Directing attention

Directing the children's attention helps them to attend to events and to focus their attention on themselves and others. During the middle phase of PGP, the awareness of the group members increases, and these types of interventions become especially useful.

Preparatory statements:

→ We will all have to notice the times when John gets jumped on by the kids. Let's check it on the videotape and then get some ideas about why this happened.

← I have the sense that all of you have some feelings about me.

(→) The clown is up to something today. Let's try to figure it out.

"Look-at" statements (in the present):

→ You kids always seem to pick on James.

← You kids are all trying to pretend the therapists don't exist. Have you noticed that?

"Look-at" statements (in the past):

→ Remember when Billy and Arthur did not feel they could play with us?

← You were quite upset last week when the group began. You were sure we were going to punish you.

($\rightarrow$) Remember when the blue team didn't want to join the red team in fighting the outsiders?

"See-the-pattern" statements (in the past and present):

$\rightarrow$ When we talk about being friends and doing things together, you start beating Tommy up with a pillow.

$\leftarrow$ Today I noticed that first Timmy wanted to talk to me alone; then Peter wanted me to help him in his building project; after that, Mark invited me to play with the darts; and that was followed by Greg getting his finger stuck in the door, so he needed my attention. So, it seems as though each of you wants my individual attention, and you all have a different way of showing me that you need it.

($\rightarrow$) Each time the robbers are about to be caught by the policeman, they change the rules of the game.

Interpretations

Interpretations in the middle phase of PGP are made within the context of how the children behave with others. Focusing upon social skills is especially useful. Clarifications and confrontations about how the children are reacting toward their peers and toward adults and how they perceive others' behaviors and their own intentions are appropriate at this point in the development of the group. The use of interpretations helps to make the children aware of their defenses, affects, and motives. Issues concerning self-image and self-esteem can be a part of the interpretive work, as well as new ways of dealing with stress and alternative solutions to problems concerning social interactions.

Many interpretations are about defenses.

$\rightarrow$ You are all being bullies with each other, in order to make sure no one can hurt you.

$\leftarrow$ You're all throwing the food on the floor and making a mess, instead of telling us how you feel about our not being here next week.

($\rightarrow$) The ghosts are scaring the people so that nobody will guess that even ghosts feel scared.

Other interpretations concern motives.

→ Each time Paul feels excluded he starts fighting, as if he wished to become the center of attention at any cost.

← When you guys threaten to run out of the door, so that I have to stand by the door to keep it shut, it seems that you wished that I would keep everybody safe and together by being the gatekeeper and making sure we don't lose any members.

(→) The burglars want to get their revenge from the cops because they feel they were not treated fairly.

While most interpretations are made on the spot, as incidents occur, they may also be made about past experiences. In this type of group treatment, the past experiences refer to earlier experiences in the group and not to the individual child's biographical past.

→ You may remember that in the beginning you all felt so strongly about not having new members that you barricaded the door, because you weren't sure that we'd pay the same attention to you if we had a new member. I guess the feeling is still around, because we were talking about adding Richard and Steven to the group and then the next thing I knew many of you were putting chairs in front of the door again.

← Remember when we first began, and you thought we would hurt and punish you. Maybe that is why you are still afraid to tell us what the group is planning to do in the hallway after the session.

(→) Do you remember in the summer we played cops and robbers and everyone hid under the table and refused to participate? I have the impression that right now, when we are telling you about our Easter break, the same kids who were playing cops and robbers are hiding under the table and wanting nothing to do with us.

Working with the Parents

In the middle phase of PGP, the parents' group becomes a more cohesive group. The adult members generally attend regularly and demonstrate a willingness to share more of their vulnerabilities as parents with each other and with the group therapist. They begin to reveal their own dependency conflicts *vis-à-vis* the therapist, as well as to describe their children's needs. As the parents ask for practical suggestions and recommendations, the therapist should be directive and educational. Material may be used from Part II, Parent Training, to provide a systematic orientation to understanding and managing problem behaviors. The material from chapter 7 may be copied and distributed, or the material may be introduced verbally into group discussions. As parents give vignettes of their child's behavior, the therapist may use the material to illustrate a particular principle of management. The parents' group leader must have a solid understanding of the materials outlined in the section, Parent Training, in order to present this approach.

Empathy from others in the group who have faced similar predicaments, as well as the group therapist's supportive and clarifying statements, helps the parents to feel more confident. Sharing experiences as they implement the new management techniques described by the group leader is a continuing source of strength to group members. The developing dependency of the parents toward their group therapist is adaptive in that it helps the parents to take in new information and practice improved ways of handling their children.

We have noticed resistance when the parents develop a split transference between the therapist of their group and the children's therapists. Because they sometimes feel neglected and needy, parents may operate to defeat the rival therapists of the children's group by encouraging their children to act out. For instance, if the children act out in the waiting room of the clinic before the group sessions, the parents may make no effort to set limits, claiming that they want the therapists to see the children as they really are. In doing so, however, they deny their responsibility for their children, and that point must be made clear to them.

Issues of resistance need to be worked through by the parents with the parents' group therapist, who should explore the underlying issues while enlisting the parents' support in their mutual endeavor. For instance, in addressing parental passivity about handling the children in the waiting room, the therapist might say, "Now we really understand what you experience with your child. Give us time to figure out together what might be useful." In this manner, the omnipotence the parents attribute to the therapists is diminished and a working-together stance is enhanced. At the same time parents might be helped to express their disappointment about what they feel they are not getting from the parents' group.

An important part of the work with the parents in the middle phase of PGP is to help them see how they contaminate their perceptions of their child with their concerns. The therapist's goal is to help the parents to view their child as a separate individual in his own right. The parents need to explore the gap between their real child and their fantasy child. With the support of the group, they must discover and confront the lacunae in the consistency of their care that are augmenting their child's problems. At times these lacunae have their genesis in the parents' upbringing; they have therefore not been previously perceived on a conscious level. An identification can occur when a parent sees herself reflected in the experience of another parent and can begin to come to terms with the meaning of parenthood. The therapist can be helpful in making connections between parental feelings shared by the group and their behavior with their children. For instance, in a group composed mainly of single or divorced mothers whose sons were in treatment, the parents wanted to discuss how the men in their lives made them suffer. The therapist asked, "You're disappointed in men and have little men around you. How do you let them know of your expectations of them?"

The children's therapists decide whether it would be appropriate for their specific group of children to hold a midyear meeting between the parents' group and the children's group, with all therapists present. The purpose of the meeting would be to enhance the parents' understanding of how the children's group operates and how the parents' group supports the children. The anxieties the meeting would evoke would have to be carefully considered by all three therapists and discussed with the children, should there be a decision to proceed with the joint meeting. An alternative technique for providing feedback to the parents is to invite the co-therapists to participate in a parent meeting. In this instance, the parent meeting is rescheduled to a time that does not conflict with the children's regular PGP session.

If a joint meeting combining parents' and children's groups is deemed appropriate by the therapists, an agenda is prepared in conjunction with the children. One possible activity is for the children to prepare a videotape of their group to be shown at the meeting. This technique enables the parents to see what might be a typical group experience for their children. Since the children prepare the video themselves, confidentiality is not an issue; the children select what they want the parents to see. Alternatively, the group may have its own ideas for an interesting agenda. In addition to activities, snacks should be part of the plan.

Parents are usually curious about what goes on in the children's group, and such a meeting helps to demystify treatment as well as to enhance communication between the two groups. The group therapists reiterate the goals of each group and encourage the children and the parents to report about their own group experience. The anxieties this combined meeting elicits need to be addressed by each group separately in anticipation of the joint meeting. We have found these joint meetings to be an invaluable way to promote a therapeutic alliance in both groups. If a videotape is made by the children, it should be shown during the joint session; it can help organize follow-up discussion in the parents' group. Parents can be asked: "Is what you saw surprising or new?"; "Do you approve of what you saw or were you disappointed by the video?"; "What was acceptable to you?"; "What behavior would you like to see changed?"; "What could you do to change it?" From the discussion that follows the joint meeting, new and useful ideas about childrearing can emerge. The parents' group therapist reviews the topics the parents have chosen to speak about with regard to the tape and continues the discussion in subsequent sessions.

A Middle-Phase Session

As we resume our observation of PGP in progress, we expect to find an emergent identity within the group as a unit, as well as a more defined sense of each individual group member. These themes will be discussed following the excerpt of the group session from the middle phase of PGP.

Present at this session are Dr. Edwards, Dr. Jones, David, Adam, John, Bob, and Ronald. David, John, and Adam enter the room with Dr. Edwards. John picks up a heavy punching bag. David then picks up the bag and throws it to the floor. Dr. Edwards encourages John to bring the toy automated truck that he brought to group into the middle of the room to show it to the other boys. She encourages him to sit in the circle. Dr. Jones soon comes to the group, as does Bob. Adam and David sit in chairs.

Bob: Who brought the toy truck to the group?

Dr. Jones: We'll talk about it. → Supportive intervention: Suggestion

Adam: I brought snacks today.

Dr. Jones: Were you supposed to → Statement about the treatment bring snacks; or was someone else supposed to bring a snack?

Bob: David was supposed to bring a snack. When is the new person coming to our group?

Ronald knocks on the door and enters the group session.

Dr. Jones: Hi Ronald, we've been wondering where you've been. [to Bob] The new person will start in about two weeks.

→ Statement relating to the treatment

Bob: After the parent performance?

Several of the boys talk about what they will bring to the performance. Ronald talks about a recorder. One of the other boys mentions drums.

Dr. Edwards: I want to talk about one thing after the other. Last time we talked about when the new boy was coming, and then Bob remarked, "that's when I leave and come back," as if there was some kind of connection.

→ Facilitative intervention: Review statement
→ Directing attention: Preparatory statement

Adam: Yeah. [points to Bob] And the new person better not act like you.

Ronald: Yeah. Because Bob talks to Dr. Jones alone.

Adam: And he's always sitting near him.

Ronald: But not today.

Dr. Jones: What do you guys make of that?

→ Directing attention: "Look-at" statement (in the present)

Ronald: Today, I haven't seen him talk to him yet.

Dr. Jones: What do you make of that?

→ Directing attention: "Look-at" statement (in the present)

Ronald: Maybe he's changing.

This illustrates how the children have become accustomed to the seating arrangement, which has become part of the format of the beginning of the session. The children are showing their capacity to observe each other and the events of the group.

DR. JONES: Yeah. Sometimes peo-   → Supportive intervention:
ple change if you give them a   Education
chance.

RONALD: And he's been talking
outside, like me and Adam. And
John, yelling and screaming all
the time.

DR. JONES: I know, I've noticed   ⇄* Directing attention:
that, too. Have other people?   "Look-at" statement (in the
You're saying, Ronald, that this   present)
change is good.   → Supportive intervention:
                                           Encouragement

JOHN: If this is not the real Bob, if
this is the happiest Bob, I wonder what the real Bob looks like.

*John's observation that people can present themselves in different frames of mind and still
be the same person reveals great progress. This is an example of the increasing social
awareness of the group members, which is uniformly deficient in the conduct disordered
population.*

DR. EDWARDS: Maybe both are   → Directing attention:
the real Bob.   "See-the-pattern" statement

RONALD: If this is the real Bob
over his old Bob, I don't know,
something is wrong with him.
[Adam and Ronald begin to
arm-wrestle.]

DR. EDWARDS: I would like to   → Facilitative intervention:
know what other people feel   Invitation to continue
about the change in Bob. Obvi-
ously [she points to Adam and   → Directing attention:
Ronald] some people feel a   "Look-at" statement (in the
wonderful change. Does anyone   present)
have any feelings about some-
one new coming to the group?
Obviously, Ronald and Adam
don't want to hear about it.
[These boys are continuing with
their   arm-chair   wrestling
match.]

Bob: It's just going to be harder, really.

Dr. Edwards: It's just going to be harder? Adam and Ronald, do you hear what Bob is saying? You complain that Bob doesn't say anything. When Bob does say something, you don't seem to hear it. Ronald, do you want to know what Bob just said?

→ Facilitative intervention: Invitation to continue
→ Supportive intervention: Suggestion
→ Directing attention: "See-the-pattern" statement
→ Supportive intervention: Suggestion

Ronald: What did you just say?

Bob: It's going to be harder.

Ronald and Adam don't want to hear what was said, as their arm wrestling serves to distract them. The therapist encourages them to look at their interactions to find out their motivations for their interactions. Dr. Edwards suggests they come back to listen to what is being said about Bob. Ronald accepts this.

Bob: [Bob starts counting the boys.] There are already five kids and soon there will be six, and then eight, and it's going to be harder.

Dr. Jones: Although Bob is going to be away two weeks, it's only going to be one group session that he'll miss.

→ Statement relating to the treatment

Dr. Edwards: I didn't realize that.

←* Directing attention: "Look-at" statement (in the present)

Dr. Jones: Part of the time will be midwinter vacation. Two of the mothers are asking whether we would just cancel group at that time.

→ Statement about the treatment.
→ Directing attention: "Look-at" statement (in the present)

Dr. Edwards: Did everyone hear that?

→ Supportive intervention: Suggestion

David: No.

Dr. Edwards: No, what? No, not to cancel?	→ Directing attention: "Look-at" statement (in the present)
	→ Supportive intervention: Suggestion
Dr. Jones: You mean not to cancel the group?	→ Supportive intervention: Suggestion
Boys as a group: Yeah.	
Dr. Jones: [to the group] Should we cancel?	→ Facilitative intervention: Invitation to continue
Boys: No.	
Dr. Jones: Let's count.	→ Supportive intervention: Suggestion
Adam: It's four against three.	
Dr. Jones: Who is the three? How do you know how Dr. Edwards and I would vote? We want to work it out in a way that's good for everybody. People in the group, and their mothers.	⇄ Directing attention: "Look-at" statement (in the present)
	→ Supportive intervention: Encouragement, Reassurance, and Empathy

The addition of new members to the group serves to threaten one's position in the group. The therapists encourage the group to make decisions about itself, such as whether to meet during vacation. This, in turn, helps the youngsters examine their opinions about each other and the meaning the group has for them. However, there are decisions that are the sole authority of the therapists, such as when to admit new members.

Adam: I would be bored if I didn't have group.	
Ronald: I would have my own group.	
Dr. Edwards: [to Ronald] What's wrong with this group?	→ Directing attention: "Look-at" statement (in the present)

Ronald remarks, "nothing," and Dr. Edwards says, "Oh, okay," and some of the boys talk about how they'll be away on vacation. John says that he's serious, that he'll be away on vacation.

Ronald: Maybe you'll see Bob.

John tells the group that he'll be away at his grandmother's house in North Carolina. Dr. Jones tells him to remind them when he will be away. Dr. Edwards comments to Ronald not to throw the ball, as Ronald is tossing a volleyball while he is sitting in his chair. Dr. Jones goes back to the subject about what to do about midwinter break and indicates that he feels that if the mothers can bring the kids, then he and Dr. Edwards would be glad to have group during that time.

DR. EDWARDS: I basically agree, as long as one person can come I think we should have group. ←* Statement relating to the treatment

DR. JONES: I think we should have group as long as we have two or three people. ←* Statement relating to the treatment

The therapists wonder aloud whether Dr. Murphy meets with the mothers this week,† and the boys say, no, next week. The therapists agree that they can wait until next week to find out.

DR. EDWARDS: I notice that none of the boys are sitting near me. [playfully] Is anything wrong with me today? ←* Directing attention: "Look-at" statement (in the present)

DR. JONES: [laughingly] Everyone is moving away from Dr. Edwards. [Bob moves his chair a little bit closer to her as he moves into the circle.] Is it people moving away from you, Dr. Edwards or toward Ronald? ← Directing attention: "Look-at" statement (in the present)

Dr. Edwards's question, "Is anything wrong with me today?" is a "look-at" statement, referring not only to each other but to the therapist. She is modeling for the group members that she, like one of them, could feel rejected.

DR. EDWARDS: That could be a possibility too. Ronald and Adam are putting their back to the camera. → Directing attention: "Look-at" statement (in the present)

---

†The parents' group meets parallel to the children's group, but on alternate weeks.

DR. JONES: Bob will be away on February 12.	→ Statement relating to the treatment
BOB: You mean I will be away from February 12 to the 15.	
DR. JONES: We're going to leave a chair open for Bob. [Ronald gets up from his chair and moves toward Bob, whom he taps with a volleyball.]	→ Supportive intervention: Suggestion

The potential instability of the group is shown when Ronald gets up from his chair and taps Bob. The group has periods of progression and regression, with a trend towards more integrated behavior.

DR. JONES: Do you want to get a time-out, Ronald?	→ Directing attention: "Look-at" statement (in the present)
RONALD: No.	
DR. JONES: Then get back in your chair.	→ Supportive intervention: Suggestion
DR. JONES: The week that Bob is away, we're going to leave a chair for him in group. We're going to leave a place for him in the group, so people will know that he's away.	→ Statements relating to the treatment

The strengthening of the child's individual role and place in the group is one of the therapist's roles.

Bob jumps up and down in his chair and claims it as his own. Bob says to write his name on it. Dr. Jones says, "We'll remember, we don't need to write your name on it." The other boys start jumping up and down in their chairs too, just as Bob did. Dr. Jones remarks, "We've got some kangaroos in here." Dr. Edwards comments, "Bob invented a game, the kangaroo game." David gets up from his chair and starts pounding it on the floor, and Dr. Jones says to him that that's not what the boys are doing. The therapists talk to each other about bringing up more about the new boy. One of the boys asks what the new person's name is, and Dr. Jones replies that he doesn't even remember. Bob remarks that his name is Matthew, and Dr. Jones concurs.

DR. JONES: He'll be coming three times.	→ Statement relating to the treatment
RONALD: Why?	
DR. JONES: To see whether he likes it, and whether he can do well in group.	→ Statements relating to the treatment
ADAM: I hope that when he comes he will stay, so that we can then beat him up. [The other boys laugh.]	
BOB: What grade is he in?	
DR. JONES: You can ask him when he gets here.	→ Supportive intervention: Suggestion

The arrival of the new member in the group brings forth rivalry. The therapists' decision to have an evaluative trial of three sessions for the new member is in keeping with their gatekeeping function and has been made clear to the prospective member and to the group. The ultimate decision about whether the new member remains belongs to the therapists and not to the children.

RONALD: [to John] You start hitting him in the face, I'll start kicking him.

Ronald then punches his volleyball with his fist. Adam goes "boom, boom, boom" as he smashes his fists together. Dr. Edwards notes how everyone has their back to the camera. The boys are getting up from their chairs; Dr. Jones remarks to David that this is a warning. If he gets up from his chair again, he could have a time-out. David starts hitting the punching bag.

DR. EDWARDS: [tries to quiet the boys down and says to Ronald] We really need to talk more. Everybody is turning their backs to the camera. It's like the whole group is saying "no way" to the new member.	→ Supportive intervention: Suggestion → Interpretation: Defense, Motive

Dr. Edwards makes an interpretation addressed to the group, illustrating to the children how they are saying "no" through their different behaviors.

Ronald walks up to the one-way mirror and pretends to be throwing the ball at the mirror.

DR. JONES: I think it's time for   → Supportive intervention:
Ronald to get a time-out. [Dr.   Suggestion
Edwards agrees.]

The boys continue to have a discussion about some of their planned activities.

DR. JONES: The last issue is that   → Facilitative intervention:
John was supposed to bring a   Review statement
snack today for group and he
didn't bring a snack again. I just   ←* Directing attention:
don't understand what's hap-   "Look-at" statement (in the
pening with snacks.   present)
JOHN: I have to be reminded.
DR. EDWARDS: Okay, so we have   → Supportive intervention:
to tell your mother? [John   Empathy, Suggestion
agrees.]
RONALD: Does anybody have a
piece of paper?
DR. JONES: So we can write down   → Supportive intervention:
who needs to bring snack next   Suggestion
week?

Ronald agrees, and Dr. Jones comments that he thinks that's a great idea and that he'll go to his office to get a sheet, and that he'll be back in one half of one minute. When Dr. Jones is out, the boys get up from their chairs and start playing various games. Dr. Edwards reminds them that they're not playing games yet. David knocks a chair over and Dr. Edwards asks whether anyone noticed what happened between David and Bob, that she didn't see it. Did anyone else? Dr. Edwards asks Ronald whether he saw what happened. Ronald throws the ball against one of the other boys. Meanwhile, Bob gets up and moves toward Dr. Edwards and tells her that there was some kicking between the boys.

Ronald tries to organize the snack, which is supported by the therapist. The importance of the male therapist as an authority is illustrated by his brief absence from the room, which triggered a challenge to the authority of the female therapist. This observation is then shared with the children. The therapist could have added that they are not sure she can protect them from each other, because they perceive her as weak. This therapist-related comment (transference) occurs more frequently in the middle phase of treatment.

Dr. Jones returns and gives the sheet of paper to Ronald. With Dr. Jones's help, Ronald organizes when the boys will bring in snacks. David drops the heavy punching bag near Bob, and Bob says "Owww!"—as if it had been dropped on his foot. Adam and John are playing together at a table and Ronald continues to work on organizing for snacks.

RONALD: John, you bring it next
week. [The boys make noise.]

DR. JONES: Ronald, that's just the   ⇄* Directing attention:
problem that Dr. Edwards and I   "See-the-pattern" statement
have. When we try to say some-
thing, all the boys are talking,
and no one listens.

Ronald asks for the ball that David and Bob are playing with, and they throw it to him. Ronald then throws the ball to John and he catches it. Ronald repeats to John, "Bring the snack next week." John turns around and pretends to throw the ball hard at Ronald. Dr. Jones asks John if he'd like to be reminded about next week. Dr. Jones comments that he thinks we should talk about it, if John thinks that we should remind his mother. Dr. Edwards agrees. Adam moves his toy car toward John, and John moves it back into the group room.

Dr. Jones supports the child's self-esteem by suggesting that it is acceptable to have assistance.

DR. JONES: I wonder why Adam   → Directing attention:
keeps bringing the snack every   "See-the-pattern" statement
week and others don't.

Ronald shows his snack list to Drs. Jones and Edwards, and Dr. Jones notices that he left Bob's name out as well as those of Drs. Jones and Edwards, and therefore he asks if they are included. The other boys are playing with a toy car and David is lifting the heavy punching bag.

DR. EDWARDS: David is showing   → Directing attention:
what he can do, lifting, carrying.   "Look-at" statement (in the
      present)

Dr. Jones supports the group as a whole by making sure everyone's name is included in the snack list. The following display of Adam's prowess is a response to Dr. Edwards's previous supportive comment. Adam is now showing his ability as a competent child.

This demonstration of skill spreads to the rest of the group, as the boys then share their national backgrounds.

DR. JONES: David is pretending   → Directing attention:
he is a wrestler.   "Look-at" statement (in the
present)

David throws the punching bag to the floor. David jumps over it. Adam and John take turns lifting it on their shoulders as David had done. Bob tells Ronald his name in Russian.

DR. JONES: [repeating] Roika?   → Supportive intervention:
Wow . . .   Encouragement
Empathy

Bob tells the group that he's not Russian, but that his grandmother is. One of the other boys says that he is German and Irish. John, David, and Adam tackle each other.

Ronald asks Dr. Edwards what the first letter of her last name is, and she spells it for him. Dr. Edwards comments that it looks like Adam and David are asking for a time-out because of their tussling with one another. Bob asks John if he can play with his remote control truck, and John says yes. Ronald plays catch with John. David lifts the punching bag weight from the floor and Bob keeps on playing with the remote control truck. Dr. Edwards and Dr. Jones discuss what they should do with the chart that Ronald has prepared and whether they should tape it to the wall. David asks permission to get a drink, and Dr. Jones replies that he should wait until group is over. David then asks to go to the bathroom and indicates that it is an emergency.

A fragmentation of the group occurs at this point. This is to be expected given the progression/regression cycles of the group.

DR. JONES: Do you boys want to   → Supportive intervention:
play catch around the room?   Suggestion

Dr. Jones suggests an activity to help reintegrate the group, and the children respond positively by playing catch. The aggression continues but in a more playful and acceptable manner.

All the boys then become involved in this game of catch, passing to one another around the circle. Adam starts throwing rougher than the other boys, and then he and Ronald both start getting after John, who is holding the punching bag and using it as a bat.

DR. EDWARDS: Ronald, I think → Supportive intervention:
you need to cool it a little bit,   Suggestion
okay?

Bob and Ronald play catch. Adam moves between them with the punching bag and drops it at John's feet. Adam then tackles Bob, after Bob comes toward him with the ball. John picks up the punching bag and looks as though he's going to drop it on Adam's head. It is all playful, nonetheless.

DR. JONES: No one throws the ← Directing attention:
ball to me!   "Look-at" statement (in the
  present)

David returns and joins the game, and now everyone is throwing to one another and to the therapists. Adam throws behind him, and hits Bob, before Bob notices what is happening. The boys laugh, as does Bob. Adam also tries to remove Bob from the table that he is standing on behind him. The boys then call out, "Monkey in the Middle," and after John has a turn in the middle, they tell Dr. Jones to come into the middle. The game remains playful.

DR. JONES: Just don't hit the mi- → Supportive intervention:
crophone, okay?   Suggestion

The boys continue playing, and even Bob joins in the middle with John at one point. Drs. Edwards and Jones coax David to come into the middle when he has thrown a ball and one of the boys has caught it. He joins in the middle. Ronald at this point is standing on the table that Bob had been standing on at one of the outside posts of the room. All the boys are actively engaged in the game. Adam stands on a table before the one-way mirror and sways his hips so that he partially blocks out the view of the camera. Bob and David tussle over the ball, and Adam and Ronald pile onto the two of them on the floor. Dr. Jones picks up the ball from the boy on the bottom and throws it to Dr. Edwards. He and she throw the ball to one another, and the boys remove themselves from the pile-up. Dr. Jones is in the middle and Adam tries to throw over him. Dr. Jones encourages David to cover some people, so that they can get the ball away from them. The boys continue playing actively and accidentally knock down a shade covering one of the windows in the group room.

DR. JONES: I just want people to know that if you are destroying property, we're going to have to change the rules in here. This is a warning, David.

←* Statements relating to the treatment
→ Directing attention: "Look-at" statement (in the future)

Meanwhile, the boys are getting wilder, and they're beginning to tackle one another.

DR. EDWARDS: Stop, everyone.

→ Supportive intervention: Suggestion

RONALD: Not me.

DR. EDWARDS: Just stop, everyone. [John continues to try to tackle David.]

→ Supportive intervention: Suggestion

DR. JONES: John, take a time-out.

→ Supportive intervention: Suggestion

DR. EDWARDS: [David asks if he may go out for a drink of water.] No, not now, now just cool it. [Everything gets wild.] There will have to be a time-out.

→ Statement relating to the treatment
→ Supportive intervention: Suggestion

Drs. Edwards and Jones become active participants in the game, coming out of that role only when the window shade is accidentally knocked down. Each therapist supports the other in the use of the stop-the-action technique. The therapists also support the children in their appropriate use of this rule to protect the group process.

DR. JONES: [to David] I want to give a special warning to David right now. David, if you go about destroying property in here, we're going to have to change the rules. Do you hear me, David?

←* Statements relating to the treatment
→ Directing attention: "Look-at" statement (in the future)

DAVID: Mmmm hmmm.

DR. EDWARDS: Should we try to fix that thing before we go on? [points to the shade]

→ Supportive intervention: Suggestion

DR. JONES: [The playing continues.] It is snack time.

→ Statement relating to the treatment

DR. EDWARDS: Seven minutes   → Statement relating to the treat-
   left.   ment

Ronald tries to tackle Adam, and Bob takes the ball out of Adam's hands
while Ronald is grabbing Adam. Adam twists Ronald's arm when Ronald
is on the floor.

DR. EDWARDS: I don't think   ←* Supportive intervention:
   they're going to have a snack.   Suggestion
DR. JONES: Then I'm going to get   ←* Directing attention:
   to eat it all by myself.   "Look-at" statement (in the
                               present)

Adam takes the snack bag. One of the boys calls out, "It's fruit." The
boys all sit down, and Dr. Edwards asks them are they curious about what
they are going to have. She then turns to the bag as Adam takes out the
fruit, and she comments that Adam is going to bring good food again.
Adam says, "I'm eating a snack," and he takes his chair and turns it away
from the boys, as though he is going to eat the fruit all by himself.

DR. JONES AND DR. EDWARDS: → Supportive intervention:
   [playfully] Ohhhhhh.   Empathy

Ronald and Bob try to grab Adam, and Adam says, "Okay, okay, I'll
share it!" Then Adam says, "I'm just joking," and walks away from the
chair with the fruit in his hand. Ronald goes after Adam to tackle him. The
therapists remind Adam to pass the food, and Adam teases the boys about
what kind of fruit they want. He gets them to raise their hands as they call
out the various kinds: "Oranges, apples, pears." Adam is slow to pass out
the fruit.

DR. JONES: Give them some fruit   → Supportive intervention:
   already, Adam.   Suggestion
DR. EDWARDS: Come on.   → Supportive intervention:
                               Suggestion

Adam tears the orange into sections and Dr. Edwards comments that he
is doing it in a very elegant way, as Adam then passes sections of the fruit
to the boys. Dr. Edwards asks Bob whether he wants something. He replies
no, because he threw up last night.

The issue of sharing during snack time is now played out as to what kind of snack to have and under what conditions.

The therapists offer Bob some fruit. Bob changes his mind and says he wants some, but that Adam didn't come to him. Adam says, "What do you want?" and then he yells louder. Dr. Edwards comments about how nice the fruit is and that they should all thank Adam's grandmother. Adam comments that he picks the best ones.

Ronald and John playfully make fists at each other. Ronald goes to the lights to turn them out. He does so, and Dr. Jones yells at him to turn them on again. The boys sit around quietly eating. Ronald manages to antagonize Adam, who then goes after him. Bob pulls at John's jacket, and they start fighting. The boys start throwing some food and Dr. Jones tells them to pick it up. Dr. Jones specifies that it is Ronald and Adam who threw the fruit. Dr. Jones notes that whoever it was that spit the pits, either Ronald or Adam, should put them in the garbage. Dr. Edwards tries to encourage the boys to clean up. Adam and Ronald continue to fight with one another.

The boys begin fighting when they notice that the therapists have singled out Adam for his good snack. The therapists did not address this jealousy. They could have said that the group felt he did not appreciate their efforts, and they show this in action by fighting with each other and by throwing food. The many events occurring simultaneously tended to sidetrack the therapists from the issue of sibling rivalry to other apparently disconnected events; for example, Dr. Jones yells to Ronald to turn on the lights again. Dr. Jones tells others to pick up the food, and orders Adam and Ronald to put their pits in the garbage; Dr. Edwards encourages the boys to clean up. These individual commands are not as effective as addressing the group as a whole by pointing out that the boys are reacting to their jealousy and their uncertainty about whether the therapists care about each of them, and they are expressing it through their behavior. In addition, the interactions here are aimed at inducing the therapists to become the critical and bad images that the boys carry within themselves. In other words, they contribute to the actualization of their fear that the therapists are no good and prefer Adam over each of the boys in the group.

In this session from the middle phase of PGP, several themes emerge. The dominant theme is revealed in the discussion of a prospective new member's entering the group. This prospect evokes expressions of underlying group tensions. On an individual level, fantasies of exclusivity and pairing are aroused. "He better not be like Bob," we hear, followed by a chorus expressing resentment that Bob talks to one of the leaders alone and monopolizes his attention. The suggestion that "maybe he is changing," however, alerts us to the possibility of new feelings emerging. Not only does the group demonstrate an increased social awareness of the different aspects of an individual's behavior, but the suggestion here is that the nature of the group may be changing as well. The theme that binds the children together may be transforming from resentment to a sense of shared identity. This sense of cohesiveness is not accepted by all the children in the group. A couple of children "do not want to hear" and continue to fight. A few children respond, "This will be hard." The acceptance of a new member clearly threatens their sense of security and need for dependence. Several children turn their backs on the camera, expressing negativity.

In the middle phase, the sense of the group as a "benevolent mother" is enhanced. Each member belongs to the group and is cared for by the group. This caring is expressed concretely by each member having his or her own familiar seat; a chair is left empty for an absent group member. The group discusses, and plans for, a vacation period. The group shares knowledge of its diverse ethnic backgrounds. There is planning for snacks, with an individual child's competence in sharing serving as a model of competence for the entire group.

The hallmark of the group at this point in therapy is flux and change. Disintegration occurs as a defense against feelings of loss when group cohesiveness is threatened. Thus we witness aggression contained within the context of a game and the use of the "stop-and-go" rule for protection. The feelings about the newcomer reveal tensions that are not resolved, however. Aggression breaks out over the feeling that one child is favored at snack time. Rivalrous feelings incite fighting, and negative feelings are projected onto the therapists, who are perceived as preferring one child over another. In the next chapter, we will see how this underlying group tension, resulting from a combination of individual concerns, is played out in the ending phase of PGP.

14

The Ending Phase of Treatment

AS the year proceeds, the PGP group progresses along a dimension of increased individuation, as well as increased cohesion. The members' sense of unity as a group is enhanced by their improved understanding of themselves as individuals and by each member's contributions to the group as a whole. When we next join our group in session in a later phase of treatment, several new themes are apparent. Belonging is counterbalanced by exclusion as the group struggles with its identity in the face of having to deal with including a new member. Aspects of similarity and difference are defined along parameters of age, geographical locale, and behavior. The children demonstrate more intrusive curiosity about their therapists as they decrease the distance between themselves and their leaders, beginning to relate to them as people with whom they can form identifications. Scapegoating occurs as a form of projective identification. One child is scripted to be "the bad one," and accusations of unacceptable behavior, including cheating and name calling, are made to substantiate this claim. Structure is well integrated into the group's functioning as we notice an increased awareness of rules and responsibilities. Most significant at this later stage in PGP is the capacity of group members to observe themselves and other members, verbalizing these observations and sharing them with each other for clarification and validation.

An Ending-Phase Session

In the ending-phase session that follows, a new boy, Matthew, who is three years younger than the others, has been added to the group. We do not generally add a new member so late in the year; this is an instance of situational need taking precedence over customary guidelines. In this case a three-session trial period was agreed upon because the group was not filled to capacity and a clinical trial could help determine whether Matthew was an appropriate match with the rest of the group. The procedure, although not usual, is well planned and carefully evaluated. The session described is the third of the trial sessions. All of the children, including Matthew, are aware this is a trial assessment period.

As the session begins, all the boys are sitting in a circle. Those present are Bob, Ronald, Adam, Matthew, and John.

DR. JONES: I am wondering where all you kids were, since Matthew was the only one here last week.	⇄* Directing attention: "Look-at" statement (in the past)
RONALD: I had a date.	
DR. JONES: It would have been nice if you told us.	→ Supportive intervention: Suggestion
RONALD: I had a date. I didn't have time to tell you. I was with my date all night long.	
DR. JONES: Where were you, Adam?	→ Directing attention: "Look-at" statement (in the past)
ADAM: I was doing my homework.	
DR. JONES: It still would have been nice if you called us.	→ Supportive intervention: Suggestion
ADAM: [twirling a play gun] My doctor at the group, well, he had cancelled.	
DR. JONES: He had cancelled?	→ Facilitative intervention: Invitation to continue
ADAM: Yeah, he had cancelled.	

Ronald stands up and offers candy to the children. Several of them reach out for it.

DR. JONES: Is there one for me?   ← Directing attention:
Did anyone miss out on candy   "Look-at" statement (in the
who had wanted some?   present)

Ronald says to the new boy in the group, Matthew, that if he gets gum
he can't have candy. Dr. Edwards notes that some of the boys are standing
up from their seats and says that we usually start the group sitting down.

DR. EDWARDS: What are we dis-   → Directing attention:
cussing? Since I haven't been   "Look-at" statement (in the
here for two weeks, and last   present)
week Matthew was the only   ⇌ * Facilitative intervention:
one here. I missed everyone for   Review statement
two weeks, I need to know how   ← * Directing attention:
everyone is.   "Look-at" statement (in the
                                             present)

RONALD: [to Dr. Edwards] Your
hair is messed up.
DR. EDWARDS: My hair is messed   ← Directing attention:
up? Really?   "Look-at" statement (in the
                                             present)

RONALD: Yeah.
DR. EDWARDS: Is it okay?   → Facilitative intervention:
                                             Invitation to continue

RONALD: Oh, I have an idea for
today, we need to go outside.
DR. JONES: Will everyone sit   → Supportive intervention:
down for a minute? We need to   Suggestion
find out. Will you listen to Dr.   → Directing attention:
Edwards and me? We need to   "Look-at" statement (in the
find out why people didn't call   past)
last week when they were out.
ADAM: My grandmother didn't
call. I don't know why.

Dr. Edwards then polls some of the other boys as to why they
weren't here. One boy says he was sick and had to go to a doctor. Ronald reports that his grandmother was out of gas and Dr. Jones asks him
why he didn't call.

ADAM: Kids don't call doctors.

DR. JONES: Well, that's true, kids don't have to call, but there's no rule that they can't.

→ Statements relating to the treatment
→ Supportive intervention: Encouragement Reassurance

The boys then turn to Matthew, the newest member and the youngest, and start being critical of what he's doing, saying "Matthew, don't do that. What are you doing?"

RONALD: Who wants to see Matthew out of this group, raise your hand.

Bob, Adam, and Ronald raise their hands to exclude Matthew. One of the boys shouts, "It's three and three." And they comment that they don't see Dr. Edwards's hand.

DR. EDWARDS: You want to know what Dr. Jones and I think? Is that what it is?

← Directing attention: "Look-at" statement (in the present)

RONALD: [pointing to Matthew] He was exposing his underpants.

DR. JONES: Ronald, you can't speak now, you have to wait for Dr. Edwards to finish.

→ Supportive intervention: Suggestion

DR. EDWARDS: I am waiting to find out what the group wants. I don't feel it's such a good idea that we should say our opinion before the group says its opinion.

←* Directing attention: "Look-at" statement (in the present)

ADAM: Ronald, say your opinion, if you want Matthew or why you don't want him. Why don't you want Matthew to stay?

RONALD: He exposed his underwear to everybody.

One of the boys then asks Bob for his opinion. Bob doesn't give it, and Ronald continues about how Matthew exposes his G.I. Joe underwear.

MATTHEW: That was the first week I came here.

RONALD: That's the problem. He exposed his underwear the first week. Remember, you're supposed to be good the first week.

ADAM: Remember the first week we played ball, he was cheating. We don't like you, Matthew, that's the problem.

RONALD: That's two complaints.

MATTHEW: [to Dr. Edwards] Can I say something?

Dr. Edwards puts her hand supportively on him and says that she would like to hear what the group thinks right now.

DR. JONES: Can I say something? I remember Ronald also struck out a couple of times and he, too, said he didn't get out.

←* Ordinary social behavior
Facilitative intervention:
Review statement

RONALD: That was only once, that was only once.

DR. JONES: Twice.

→ Directing attention:
"See-the-pattern" statement

BOB: That's true, Ronald.

DR. JONES: You see, I happen to like Matthew. I think he's a nice guy. But Matthew has difficulty getting along with you guys, just as you guys have difficulty getting along with each other.

←* Supportive intervention:
Encouragement, Reassurance, and Empathy
→ Directing attention:
"See-the-pattern" statement

MATTHEW: He's older than me.

DR. JONES: That, I think, is the real question. All these guys are a lot older than you.

⇄* Supportive intervention:
Empathy

RONALD: He exposed his G.I. Joe underwear.

Dr. Edwards: I really would like to know what every one of you thinks about it. I would like to know where that comes from, that everyone thinks it's a problem when he exposes his underwear. What I think probably has nothing to do about this.

←* Facilitative intervention: Invitation to continue

Ronald: It's uncomfortable, every time we talk about it, he tries to change the subject.

Dr. Edwards: Ronald, is it sometimes uncomfortable for you when we talk about you? It happens to me sometimes. How about you?

⇄* Supportive intervention: Encouragement, Reassurance, and Empathy

Ronald: Sometimes.

Adam: I have an idea, let's not go outside today. It's cold, and I don't feel good.

Matthew: Let's go outside.

Ronald: Whoever wants to go outside, raise your hand. [John and Matthew raise their hands.]

Bob: I can't go outside, I've got a cold.

Dr. Jones: Yeah, I don't want to go outside.

←* Supportive intervention: Suggestion

The therapists continue to try to get the boys to focus on Matthew. The boys boo him, and Dr. Edwards says that they are talking because it is uncomfortable to talk about the subject. Dr. Jones indicates that the boys, especially Ronald and Adam, may feel that because they think that Matthew is younger, they wonder whether Dr. Edwards and Dr. Jones think that they act like Matthew. The boys are quiet and Dr. Jones goes on to say that maybe Adam's and Ronald's feelings have been hurt. Ronald says, "What do you mean?" Adam bursts out laughing, all the while holding his play gun. Ronald says, "What do you mean?" Meanwhile, Matthew gets up from his seat, and the boys become restless. Bob shouts that there goes Matthew again. Dr. Jones continues to explain his statement that maybe Ronald and Adam think that Dr. Edwards and Dr. Jones feel that they act younger than they are. Adam continues to laugh. Dr. Jones comments that what he said didn't go over very big. Dr. Edwards says that Adam is laughing and she wants to know what he is thinking.

DR. JONES: [to Adam] What do you think, Adam? Were you embarrassed when Matthew came in?	→ Directing attention: "Look-at" statement (in the present)
ADAM: No, I don't like him, that's the problem.	

Dr. Jones comments that he doesn't think there's a problem with Matthew's behavior. Ronald makes reference to the underwear incident. Bob then says the problem in running bases is that Matthew ran so many bases that he was called out, but he wouldn't go out.

DR. JONES: Well, all of you guys have that problem.	→ Directing attention: "See-the-pattern" statement
ADAM: No way.	
RONALD: And then, when he finally gets to play, he throws his ball all over and starts walking across.	
MATTHEW: I don't even know how to play the game.	
DR. JONES: Don't forget, he's brand new. He could learn how to play the game.	→ Supportive intervention: Encouragement, Reassurance, and Empathy

Dr. Jones tries to say something. When Matthew asks if they could go out to play, the boys begin to make noise. Dr. Edwards comments that Adam and Ronald always make noise when she wants to say something. Some of the boys make noise about wanting to go out to play, and Dr. Edwards tries to continue.

ADAM: Okay, go on, I want to listen.	
DR. EDWARDS: Thank you, Adam. I really want to say that I think Matthew has a lot of good qualities. No one says anything about these things.	←* Supportive intervention: Encouragement, Reassurance, and Empathy
	→ Directing attention: "Look-at" statement (in the present)

DR. EDWARDS: [The boys continue with some of their own
activities.] Look at this. The
boys are having their own
group.

→ Directing attention:
"Look-at" statement (in the present)

DR. JONES: They really don't
want to hear about this.

→ Directing attention:
"Look-at" statement (in the present)

The boys continue to interrupt and voice some of their objections to Matthew's being there. Matthew tries to suggest that they go outside and play. The boys continue to talk, and Dr. Jones remarks that they don't seem to be afraid of hurting Matthew's feelings. Matthew tries to get them to go outside. Finally Matthew calls out, "Time!"

MATTHEW: The reason I feel we
should go outside to play is that
when we play inside there's not
enough space to play soccer.
When we go outside there's a
lot of space to play.

DR. JONES: Well, we're not going
outside today. Dr. Edwards, did
you want to say something?

→ Supportive intervention:
Suggestion

DR. EDWARDS: I really didn't finish. It's not much fun to talk
when nobody wants to listen. I
was wondering what everyone
had to say. It seems that people
have trouble hearing that Matthew is maybe a good member
of the group. Every time I want
to say something about this,
people are doing other things. It
must be fairly uncomfortable to
discuss this.

←* Directing attention:
"Look-at" statement (in the present)

→ Interpretation:
Defense

← Facilitative intervention:
Review statement

→ Supportive intervention:
Empathy

Bob then tells John not to put tatoos on his arm, and he and Ronald argue about whether they are poisonous.

DR. JONES: Well, you know, one thing that we haven't said that's important is that David's mother called to say that David isn't coming today.

→ Directing attention: "Look-at" statement (in the present)

BOB: Why not?

ADAM: Maybe he's sick, maybe he's depressed.

DR. JONES: He misses a lot of groups, doesn't he.

→ Directing attention: "See-the-pattern" statement

Ronald starts talking about how the boys should play running bases, and Matthew joins in.

ADAM: Can I say something? I think the reason that David is not coming is because of the way we've been treating him. We used to call him names.

Both therapists encourage Adam.

RONALD: But he wrote on our stuff. He used to do curses.

ADAM: No, he doesn't say more than we say. We can hardly hear David. [Adam points to the other side of the room.] He stays over there, and no one can hardly hear him.

DR. JONES: He does keep to himself, doesn't he.

→ Directing attention: "Look-at" statement (in the present and past)

ADAM: He hardly says anything.

DR. JONES: [to Adam] Sounds like you're feeling that his feelings are hurt.

→ Supportive intervention: Empathy

RONALD: The only thing is that he kills the snack. He kills it.

DR. JONES: He does like the snack, doesn't he.

→ Directing attention: "Look-at" statement (in the present)

DR. EDWARDS: You know, Matthew's hardly saying anything. A lot of people have been saying things, but I wonder how Matthew feels.	→ Directing attention: "See-the-pattern" statement

Dr. Jones tries to draw Matthew out, who at first shrugs his shoulders. Dr. Jones asks him how he feels, and Matthew replies that he has to make a big trip to get here to the group. Bob then comments that he lives nearby. John reports that he lives far away. Dr. Jones says, "Yup, probably John has to come the farthest." Matthew replies that he still lives the farthest, that he has to come from Long Island.

DR. JONES: Well, you know what I think is the hardest? The difference in age.	⇄ * Supportive intervention: Reassurance, Empathy

The boys report their ages: ten and a half, twelve, eleven. Dr. Jones asks Matthew how it feels to be the youngest, and Matthew turns to Dr. Edwards and talks about something else. John shows his tatoo, and John, Matthew, and Ronald get up from their seats. Bob continues to sit next to Adam in the circle with Dr. Edwards and Dr. Jones. The boys ask if they can play now.

DR. JONES: [turns to Dr. Edwards] What do you think?	← Supportive intervention: Suggestion
DR. EDWARDS: I haven't been here for two weeks. I wonder whether there is more that could be said about this.	⇄ Facilitative intervention: Invitation to continue
BOB: I can't hear you.	
DR. EDWARDS: I'm sorry. I'm not going to talk louder. Two weeks ago I hear it was rather difficult. Does anyone have anything to say about that?	← * Supportive intervention: Empathy, Suggestion → Directing attention: "Look-at" statement (in the past)
DR. JONES: Do you boys remember two weeks ago when we had to stop playing early? You boys were getting too wild?	→ Directing attention: "Look-at" statement (in the past)
ADAM: Yeah. That was the first time Matthew was here.	

DR. JONES: Well, I hope it doesn't happen today.	←* Supportive intervention: Encouragement, Reassurance, and Empathy

After the boys make a few of their comments, Dr. Jones says that he wants to ask Bob how things worked out last week, because he remembers then that Bob didn't want to talk to the group—that he came, but he didn't want to come into the group. Bob replies that he doesn't want to talk about it, and Dr. Jones says okay. The boys then start to play and decide that they'll play "O-U-T". Matthew asks how to play and Ronald explains the rules: if you drop the ball, you get an "O," if you drop it again you get a "U," and if you finally get a "T," you have to sit out. Bob points to Matthew and tells him he has to follow those directions—"Okay?" Bob holds the gun as though he's the referee; he holds it up in the air to say when he'll start.

DR. JONES: Now, Matthew, are you going to follow these rules today and obey?	→ Supportive intervention: Suggestion

The sharing of the rules with the newcomer is illustrated when Matthew asks how to play and Ronald and Bob explain how to do so. This sharing is reinforced by Dr. Jones's conveying to the new member the expectation that rules are to be followed in the group.

MATTHEW: Yeah.

They throw to Matthew, who catches and does well, and then Matthew throws and one of the boys doesn't catch. Adam gets the first "O," and Dr. Jones reminds them that if they throw too hard, they get an "O" also. The boys appear supportive and are involving Matthew in the play. Bob remains with the gun as the one to call the rules.

BOB: I'm not playing.	
DR. JONES: I'm sorry that Bob isn't playing.	←* Directing attention: "Look-at" statement (in the present)
BOB: Okay, I'll play a little, but not too much.	

The boys continue to play, but they also jump in the middle as though they are reaching up to touch the microphone. The boys laugh and joke while they play. They then pull a table over to stand on, so they can jump up and try to touch the microphone on the ceiling. Matthew participates along with the other boys.

DR. JONES: I don't think I like this game.	←* Supportive intervention: Suggestion

The boys stop jumping to the microphone and continue with their ballgame. Adam sways his hips a little in front of the one-way mirror. Bob moves the table to the side of the room, and Dr. Jones approves. Matthew gets an "O" and calls out that he has an "O"; later he gets a "U" and says he has an "O, U."

DR. JONES: Be careful, Matthew, you could get out first in this.	→ Supportive intervention: Encouragement Empathy

Matthew gets the "T," so he's out and has to sit some time out.

DR. JONES: Now, Matthew, are you going to have a hard time sitting out while the rest of us play? If you need help sitting on the side, let us know, okay?	→ Supportive intervention: Reassurance, Empathy

Matthew asks Bob for the gun. Bob doesn't want to give it to him, but he gives Matthew the gun when Dr. Jones asks him to do so. Matthew watches the boys and holds the gun as Bob did before, being a commentator for the play and saying "O, U" when one of the boys gets the "U." The boys play nicely. Adam throws the ball behind him as though he's a basketball star, and the boys also involve Dr. Jones in the play. Dr. Jones comments that Adam is playing like one of those well-known players, Kareem Abdul Jabar, and calls Adam, Kareem. The boys are quite involved with the game. Bob throws a shot to Adam, who almost misses. The boys comment that Adam did a good job of catching it. Bob gets an "O" and agrees to accept it. Matthew, holding the gun, repeats what the other boys say.

MATTHEW: You went for it, you got an "O." [Matthew comes over and leans on Dr. Jones.]

DR. JONES: Matthew, would you   → Supportive intervention:
   do me a favor and not lean on   Suggestion
   me like that? I appreciate that   ←* Supportive intervention:
   [as Matthew moves away].   Reassurance,
                                              Empthy

The boys then involve Dr. Edwards more actively, and when she gets
an "O," they start cheering. Dr. Jones joins in. Dr. Edwards comments that
she hasn't seen them for two weeks. One of the boys remarks that they
have to get Adam, and they cheer gleefully when Adam misses the ball.
Adam gets "O-U-T" and has to stay out. Matthew joins the boys and says
that he's in, since Adam's out. Ronald comes over and pushes Matthew
lightly, but Matthew stays in the game and the boys accept him. Ronald
insists, "He's not in." But Dr. Edwards says, "Yes he is." One of the boys
goes out, and he comes in. Bob throws to Matthew, he misses, and Bob
exclaims, "O."

MATTHEW: I didn't go for that
   one, I didn't get it.

Bob and Matthew debate with Dr. Jones whether Matthew gets an "O."
The therapists decide that Matthew should not get the "O," because he
didn't try for the ball. Dr. Jones comments that since Matthew has come
in, no one has thrown him the ball.

DR. EDWARDS: Did everyone hear   → Directing attention:
   that? Dr. Jones is saying that no   "Look-at" statement (in the
   one has thrown the ball to him   present)
   at all.

The game of "O-U-T" continues with Matthew being included in the
group with the support of the therapists. There is laughter and camaraderie
as the children enjoy the game.
   Bob has been standing on the table, even though Dr. Jones has at other
times commented that it isn't a safe place. When Bob starts jumping up
and down on the table, Dr. Jones tells him to come down, and Bob does
jump off. Bob screams, "O-U, O-U, O-U," when one of the boys has that
score, and Dr. Jones says, "Shut up, Bob, you're screaming much too loud."
John mimics Bob, and Dr. Jones apologizes to Bob for saying "shut up."
Adam goes over to Dr. Jones and asks him if he has children. When Dr.
Jones asks him why he asks, Adam replies, "Because you're not even
married, that's why."

DR. JONES: What makes you think I'm not married? [Adam shrugs his shoulders. The play is interrupted.]	⇄ Directing attention: "Look-at" statement (in the present)
DR. EDWARDS: Are we playing, or are we talking about who has children?	⇄ Directing attention: "Look-at" statement (in the present)

At this advanced stage in the group process, there is more curiosity about the lives of the therapists. There is also more investment in what behaviors are needed to be good enough members of the group.

The boys continue playing, getting somewhat wilder. Dr. Jones notes that soon it will be snack time. They prepare for the snack. Matthew helps Dr. Jones put a table in the middle, and the boys pull the chairs into a circle. Matthew has brought the snack, and Dr. Jones notes that this is the second time in a row that Matthew has brought it. He asks who's going to bring it next week, and Ronald says, "Me." Matthew gives each boy two Ring-Dings. The boys seem to enjoy them. Bob says that he's getting tired of these, and Dr. Jones agrees, even though they're a good snack.

DR. JONES: Just so Matthew and everyone else knows: whether or not we decide to have Matthew in group, next week Matthew won't be here, because next week Dr. Edwards and I are going to talk about whether it is going to be best for Matthew to continue or not to continue. Matthew won't be here next week, and if he continues, he'll be here the week after.	→ Facilitative intervention: Preparatory statement
DR. EDWARDS: I wonder how that feels to the group.	←* Directing attention: "Look-at" statement (in the present)
MATTHEW: Why can't I come?	

DR. EDWARDS: Well, Matthew, we said in the beginning you'd come three times and then we'd decide whether you would come to the group after that. The final decision is going to be made by Dr. Jones and myself. The three times you came to the group were to find out how you and the group get along together, because you're three years younger than the other boys. Do you understand that? I get anxious about it, because I think it's a heavy-duty decision for Matthew and for the group, too.

→ Statements relating to the treatment

←* Supportive intervention:
Reassurance,
Empathy

DR. JONES: I remember last year we had a kid in the group named Josh. Bob remembers him. [to Adam] Do you remember him? [Adam nods his head yes.] And do you remember that Josh came to the group for a while and then he stopped coming? We had to ask him not to come to the group. Remember? And it really hurt Josh's feelings. Do you remember how sad he was about leaving? Josh didn't want to leave.

→ Directing attention:
"Look-at" statement (in the past)

→ Supportive intervention:
Empathy

RONALD: How come you let me keep coming?

DR. JONES: How come we let you keep coming? Your behavior was good enough so that you could stay in group.

→ Supportive intervention:
Encouragement, Reassurance, and Empathy

In clarifying for Ronald that he has good-enough behavior to remain in the group, Dr. Jones could have chosen to go into greater detail by reviewing concretely how Ronald came to every session, how he stopped hitting other children, how he was a leader in organizing a schedule for the snack. This more detailed description would demonstrate to Ronald specifically what was meant by "good-enough" behavior.

BOB: Well, last year when I was in Dr. Stephens' group, we had a kid, I think his name was Matthew also, and he kept on bothering us in group. He was kicking people and bothering people, and Dr. Stephens had to ask him to leave, too.

DR. EDWARDS: Well, I don't think we're talking about behavior in Matthew's case. [Matthew walks to the door.] Matthew, you need to stay in group.

⇄* Supportive intervention: Suggestion

BOB: Good-bye, Matthew. [Matthew exits the room.]

Dr. Jones gets up and shuts the door. Adam gets up from his chair and says, "Where's my friend Matthew?"

DR. EDWARDS: Adam, why do you think Matthew walked out just now?

→ Facilitative statement: Invitation to continue

Ronald goes out and says he's going to find Matthew, but Dr. Jones tells him to come back inside. Dr. Edwards continues to ask the boys why they think Matthew walked out. One of the boys suggests Matthew is mad.

A scrutiny of Matthew's behavior in group reveals the progress the children have made in their social awareness and ability to observe. It was possible Matthew was sensing his stay in the group was tentative. He left the room to go to the bathroom but made it appear as if he were leaving the group and enacting the group's ambivalence about whether or not he should be a member. The children notice his behavior and volunteer their understanding of it.

DR. JONES: Matthew will be back.   → Supportive intervention:
He went to the bathroom. He   Reassurance
asked, I said no, and he went   ⇄ Directing attention:
anyhow.   "Look-at" statement (in the
                                             present)

RONALD: You said no, and he
went anyhow? He's going to get
in trouble.

DR. EDWARDS: [to the group]   → Directing attention:
Well, you're really not nice to   "Look-at" statement (in the
Matthew. You're not nice. [to   present)
Bob] Do you think we're nice to   ⇄ Facilitative statement:
Matthew?   Invitation to continue

BOB: Well, he was a pain in the
neck in the beginning.

RONALD: He even exposed his
underwear. Now what does that
mean? [The boys giggle.]

DR. EDWARDS: It's easy to find   → Directing attention:
something wrong with one per-   "Look-at" statement (in the
son.   present)

Adam says that even though Matthew tugged on his ears, Adam
wouldn't be bullied into pulling his pants down; nor would he do it
because Matthew pulled his pants down. Their discussion continues.
When it is time to stop, Dr. Jones tells the group they're going to end
differently today—everyone leaving one at a time.

MATTHEW: I'm going to be first,
because I'm the smallest.

ADAM: Let's start with names,
letter "A."

DR. JONES: Well, Matthew asked,   → Statements relating to the treat-
let's let Matthew leave first.   ment
Matthew, you have to leave
with your mother, then when
you and your mother walk
away, the next person will
leave.

The boys then exit one by one.

Prior to and after the group session two weeks earlier, the arrival of the new member had precipitated acting-out behavior by the children. For example, they threw tennis balls at windows outside the building, stuck chewing gum inside the gasoline tanks of staff members' cars, and threw rocks at cars. This information was brought to the attention of the therapists, who brought it up in the children's group and in the parents' group. The therapists pointed out that the children were again expressing their feelings of anger in destructive acts outside the group, seemingly to protect the group; yet they were actually threatening the group's existence, since vandalism would not be permitted. A memo was also written to each parent and child, informing them that the group would not be continued if there were more vandalism. This limit-setting device of bringing the outside world into the group proved significantly beneficial. As a result of this acting out, the therapists changed the structure at the end of the group session by having them leave the room one by one, with their parents waiting to accompany them out of the clinic.

Special Issues

This session highlights several issues, which include fighting, scapegoating, refusal to attend, relationships with the school, the introduction of new members, removal of members, and emergencies.

Fighting

Fighting among children can be understood in terms of both group dynamics and individual psychopathology. If the fighting persists, the group therapists should reiterate the conditions for belonging to the group as originally stated. The therapists also try to engage the other children actively in a discussion of the aggressive behavior that has taken place and its ramifications for the children involved. The therapists must focus the group on ways to control the fighting and to prevent its recurrence. Separating the fighting children may be a necessary tactical approach. Having a time-out period for the aggressive children may be needed until the children are calm enough to discuss what has occurred. Sometimes group contagion may necessitate curtailment of the session for that day, if the fighting continues to escalate despite the therapists' efforts to verbalize what has occurred and to control the group. A temporary suspension from the group is used as a last resort. If this step is needed, the parents should be involved. In these measures the individuals and the group are told that the therapist's aim is to re-establish control, not to punish.

Scapegoating

The therapists should stop the action and clarify the process as a group defensive maneuver, helping the children understand how the scapegoated child serves the needs of the group at that moment in time. The emphasis at first is upon developing a productive group climate without letting the group fall deeper into the role of blaming the victim; it is, therefore, best not to explore at this time why a particular child is singled out as the group victim. Postponing that issue is also better for the scapegoat, who frequently lacks the capacity for self-observation while being ostracized, and he may be able to reflect on why he was scapegoated only after the group is no longer acting out. For example, one child who was put down and excluded from all games and subgroups encouraged that behavior by never looking the other children in the eyes, doing only "his thing" (videogames), rather than following other children's suggestions. The therapist began by exploring how everyone can feel insecure and how relieved each member is to have someone else as the scapegoat. The therapist then added at a later time that John found pleasure in being special—that is, if not the most popular in the group, then the most unpopular.

Refusal to Attend Sessions

During discussion, the therapists take note of the absence of a child. If frequent absences occur, possible reasons for the absence should be discussed by the group. If a child misses repeatedly, a telephone call and a letter become necessary. The therapists also confer with the parents' group therapist and/or have a special meeting with the parents to explore whether they may be colluding with the child to protect him from his "bad" group. If a child enjoys the group, keeping him out is a means of punishment. The children's group is made aware that an absent member has missed out on new information that was discussed and has also lost his time to speak with—and be spoken to by—other group members. On the other hand, his absence is not a time to talk about him behind his back. The children are encouraged to express their feelings directly to the absent member, if and when he returns.

Contact with the School

School is an important part of the children's lives. Contact with teachers provides extremely useful information for the therapists. At the beginning of the year, the parents' consent for school contacts is requested. Teachers are called for information initially and then again at midyear and during the final phase of the group. Teachers are given the therapists' names and telephone numbers in the event problems arise that require discussion. Communication with the teachers is shared by the children's group therapists and the parents' group therapist. Because all the therapists partake in the information gathering, they make the task less formidable timewise, assuring that everyone receives all information obtained.

Introducing New Members

Ideally, new members should be introduced in pairs to avoid pressure upon a solo newcomer who, by definition, lacks social skills and needs to be supported by the group therapists. The group requires a minimum of two weeks' notice to discuss how the group will change with the addition of new members. This interim period permits the working through of any anxieties aroused by the impending change in group composition.

Removal of Members

Any child unable to abide by the minimal rules of coexistence in a group is considered for removal from the group after a significant clinical trial of four to six weeks. Sometimes the group setting brings out previously undiagnosed behavior, such as severe antisocial behavior that cannot be managed and contained within the group. After careful clinical consideration, the decision may be made to remove a child. In that event, planning for the child, including the provision for other treatment modalities as needed, becomes part of the therapists' clinical responsibility before the child is discharged. These plans must also be worked through with the child's parents. This decision is part of the group process for the children's group as well, because it arouses guilt about extruding a member and fear of being expelled.

Antisocial behavior is also a clinical issue that may warrant removal from the group. It is not an absolute determinant, but this behavior cannot be ignored and must become a critical group issue before a decision is made. Anything that reaches the ears of the therapists, including destruction of property or threats of violence that may occur outside the group, has to be brought to the group for discussion. The therapists inform the group that a member is discrediting the group and that there is a risk the member may have to be expelled from the group. The meaning of the behavior must be understood to enable all the children to work on the problem. According to the response, a clinical decision must then be made as to whether to discharge the member from the group.

Emergencies

An emergency that requires individual attention to a child must be referred to the therapist treating the child individually or to an evaluator assigned to the child. An example is suicidal behavior. If the group therapists uncover suicidal ideation in the session, they should promptly take extra time to explore it. One of the group therapists conducts this exploration in an individual meeting with the child, or the therapist must refer the child for an emergency evaluation.

Ending the Year of Treatment

At least two months in advance of the end of the academic year in June, an announcement is made regarding the last session. This event is marked on a calendar for all the children to see. Information about what the children will be doing during the summer is requested. Children can share plans about summer vacations and any plans to move, as well as information about whether they are continuing with the clinic. The children are informed of the individual meetings that are planned with each of them and their parents after the group sessions have ended. They are told that the purpose of this joint parent-child meeting is to review their progress and to plan for future treatment needs. The children are told what to do in the event of an emergency after the group has ended; they need to know how to reach the clinic and ask for help, even though the group is no longer in session.

Ending treatment for the year gives each child, and the group as a whole, an opportunity to experience separation. Although it is generally difficult for youngsters with socialized conduct disorders to express their attachment to the group, we do see some evidence of it in the ending phase. Terminating the group is viewed not as terminating treatment but as the ending of this particular group. The children generally show signs of improvement, but given the extent of their problematic behavior, further treatment is usually indicated. It is important for the group therapists to realize that they have provided the children with a therapeutic group experience but generally not a completed treatment. Nonetheless, the therapists make clear that the group is ending, despite the fact that some children may continue in treatment. This understanding enables all the children to go through a separation process that strengthens them. These children have usually experienced previous loss and reacted to it in a derivative way, such as acting out, or through accident proneness or somatization, in which grief is disguised.

In a supportive manner, with encouragement and reassurance, the therapists review the group's history and each child's accomplishments within the group. The group therapists also outline areas in which each child needs further progress. All the children are encouraged to contribute to the review of themselves and their peers within the group format. In this manner the children are assisted in acknowledging, and being acknowledged for, their contributions to the group and in planning for and accepting the ending of the group. The children are encouraged to show their reactions to this ending phase in words and play that connote both their positive and their negative feelings.

Some children will terminate therapy. These children will have made gains in social skills and will have become more confident that they can develop friendships outside the group. Their behavior will have progressed toward adaptation to their social surroundings: a significant decline in expressing uncontrolled aggression; improved impulse control; and consequent gains in self-esteem. Identification with group norms and with the group therapists will have moderated their conflicts with authority figures. A capacity for self-awareness, as well as an awareness of the feelings of others, will have widened the range of feelings that they can express, enabling them to experience the ending phase without a major relapse of symptomatology. After the group has ended, a meeting is held with each child and his parents to review the child's progress in meeting the goals delineated at the beginning of treatment. At this time plans for future therapeutic interventions are also formulated.

Working with the Children's Group

Play

In the ending phase of PGP, more initiative as to what is played in the group is left to group members. The materials do not change basically from those of the other phases of treatment, but ending-phase rituals may evolve. The play is likely to contain earlier themes from the history of the group, and the therapists are, of course, responsive to them. Returning to some of the play activities from earlier times might be expected to occur. These regressive concerns are anticipated aspects of the ending phase of treatment. Food becomes especially important, for both supportive and symbolic reasons.

Some ending-phase rituals might include the making of a special scrapbook or mural, which could be a group project to recount the group's history. This activity shows the children concretely that their group treatment has meaning and reflects both continuity and change. Another possible project is to create a map that shows where the children will be in the summer after group treatment ends. Some group therapists enjoy taking the children on a special outing, such as to the snack bar or for a picnic on the grounds. One of our groups elected to visit a dog who had just given birth to puppies and whose owner, a staff member, lived on the hospital grounds. These special events convey nonverbally the children's impending coming out into the world. A good-bye party should be planned for, with everyone contributing something. The children may need to take something from the group, such as plants that were potted earlier or T-shirts or other items they have made, and they should be encouraged to do so.

Verbal Interventions

Within the framework of termination, the therapists will utilize the same types of verbal interventions used all along. We expect to see the children express anger and grief about the ending of the group and the loss of the other members and the therapists. They are also likely to express disappointment about the group, disillusionment about gains not made, and feelings of abandonment. The impending dissolution of the group may need to be defended against. Impulsive behaviors often occur and should be linked to the group's ending. The therapists and group members should review areas where gains in the group could be applied to the outside milieu.

Of the categories of verbal interventions that are utilized, we find that directing attention and interpretations are especially important. Supportive and facilitative comments are of secondary importance. Interpretations and "look-at" statements are useful to clarify and share feelings of rivalry, defeat, and envy among those who have improved versus those who remain behind, as well as overall feelings of loss for the group that is coming to a close. Emphasis is given to clarifying the progress each child has made as well as areas for further work. The children are encouraged to be active participants in this review.

Supportive interventions

Educational interventions are not specifically needed in this phase. If the children want to keep in touch with one another, however, they may need some instruction regarding how to send postcards, how to collect addresses, and so on. Most supportive statements by the therapists concern suggestions about activities and expressions of encouragement, empathy, and reassurance.

→   You kids may want to plan something special for our last session.

←   It would be a good idea to stay in touch with us. Calls are always welcome.

(→) Don't forget to water the plant after you leave here.

→   We have only four weeks left, and you kids seem to be responding to the fact of our ending by acting how you used to act at the beginning of our sessions. This is what happens in the last sessions; things from the beginning of the year come back again.

←   You might as well tell me that you're not so happy with me because the group didn't go as you wanted.

(→) The puppies still need a lot of care if they are to grow up to be strong. But, I am hopeful that they will grow up to be strong, happy dogs.

Facilitative interventions

The therapists facilitate interaction by encouraging the children to continue to express their ideas in the group. Review statements are important as they review the history of the group—how it began, its difficult moments, and achievements. This review may include playing old videotapes, having the therapists recount the history as they remember it, and asking the children what they felt about past sessions.

→   We are going to review the old tapes to see our history, how we began, as well as the changes that we can see in that period.

←   Remember, John and David, when you were afraid that I'd throw you out of the group or that Dr. Edwards would do so? Do you also remember when you were testing us about what is okay and not okay to do in the group? Now you know so much more about what is acceptable for us to do in here. Even Daniel, who didn't believe there were rules, has begun to accept some rules, like not hitting each other in the group.

($\rightarrow$) Do you remember when the chairs were all over the place, and you used to pile them up one on top of the other to see who could make the highest pile? Now all the chairs are in a circle, as if even they have decided to form a group of equals.

Directing attention

The therapists continue to make statements that direct the children's attention to relevant feelings, thoughts, and events.

Preparatory statements:

$\rightarrow$ Let's see what has happened to each of you in this group.

$\leftarrow$ Maybe you have some thoughts about what we have been doing here in the group or how we've done our jobs as therapists over the course of the year.

($\rightarrow$) I wonder where the chairs will be placed at the end of the session.

"Look-at" statements (in the present):

$\leftarrow$ You guys seem to be all in agreement about ignoring us, the therapists. Johnny and Bill are talking with each other, Ed is looking out the window, the three of you are fighting as though we didn't exist.

($\rightarrow$) Now the cowboys and Indians are fighting harder than ever.

"Look-at" statements (in the past):

$\leftarrow$ You guys used to say "hello" to us when we came to the session, and now you don't even acknowledge we are here.

($\rightarrow$) Have you noticed that the cowboys and Indians who used to make peace don't do so anymore?

"See-the-pattern" statements (in the past and present):

$\rightarrow$ Have you noticed that whenever I mention how many sessions are left, all of you make a lot of noise?

←   Dr. Edwards and I will not be meeting with you anymore after June; yet you deal with us as if both of us will continue next year, when actually, only one of us will be here.

(→)   It looks as if the fortress is getting higher and higher when we have fewer sessions to meet.

Interpretations

The therapists also make interpretations about defenses used by the children and the motives behind these defenses.

→   You boys are making so much noise shouting, running all over, as if you want to avoid talking about our last session.

←   You boys are all getting into trouble, as if you are telling us we should start the group all over again.

(→)   Frankenstein is getting beaten up again, so that nobody in the group will be scared of him, and he will never come back again even after the group has ended.

→   Matthew and Steven are building a wall of bricks just to tell us they can do without the group.

(→)   That wall of bricks puts us out of sight, as if out of sight would be out of mind.

Working with the Parents

Feelings in the parents' group often parallel those in the children's group. Ending treatment is an experience that affects both groups simultaneously and can evoke past defensive patterns of response, challenging the groups to arrive at a more adaptive resolution.

An example of this parallel process occurred in the group we have been following, in relation to the incident of vandalism described earlier. The week following the incident a special meeting was called for all three group therapists and the parents, or other caregivers. The group was told that it was known which children had been involved in the vandalism, although there had been varying reports. The therapists stated that this behavior was unacceptable and must not be repeated. The possibility was suggested that the children had perceived the ending of the group as threatening and had responded to the threat with characteristic aggression to fight off feelings of helplessness about the impending group dispersion. At this meeting, the children's therapists reviewed the general progress the children had made during their year together. They also set up the procedure of having each child leave separately in the company of an adult to prevent future occurrences of loss of control.

The incident was brought up again in the following parents' group meeting. The parents' group consisted of one grandmother and two mothers; a fourth member had left the group previously, feeling that her son no longer needed group treatment. During the discussion of the vandalism, the grandmother of the child who was reportedly least involved in the incident appeared upset and withdrawn. The other two women were able to discuss their feelings about the incident openly, but despite encouragement from the others, the grandmother stated that she was too upset and angry to talk about it and alluded to other personal difficulties affecting her at the same time. The following week, as she remained upset, one of the other members inquired whether she thought that her grandson, the only black child involved, was being unjustly accused. The other mother was able to empathize with the grandmother's fears, saying she had seen subtle racist attitudes at work in other such situations. Meanwhile, the boys had already gotten over the incident, even though they felt they had all been scolded equally for an incident they did not perpetuate equally. The therapist pointed out to the parents' group the irony in their harboring a grudge about the incident while the children had already made peace. All the members were able to express regret that the parents' group would end on a rancorous note.

At a subsequent meeting, one of the caregivers informed the group that her child had finally admitted to her that he had been primarily responsible for the vandalism. The withdrawn grandparent was then able to express her anger at her grandson for not speaking up earlier to identify the perpetrators and for allowing himself to be blamed for the incident. Another group member stated that, in fact, her grandson had not been speechless, as in the past, but did speak up to protest his innocence. A discussion ensued, and the grandmother was able to maintain eye contact with the other group members. Plans for the summer were exchanged, as well as inquiries about plans for future treatment. All three women were able to participate in the discussion regarding termination. The history of the group and its evolving closeness were reviewed, and separation was accomplished. The members agreed to maintain informal contacts from time to time on their own initiative.

These developments revealed that the group was sufficiently cohesive to contain the intensity of hurt feelings aroused by the vandalism incident and to examine the parallels with the feelings their children might have been experiencing. On a larger scale, they were able to understand the children's acting out with aggression when confronted with the pain of separation and their own reactions of anger at being victimized. The structure of the group enabled a positive resolution of this conflict to occur, obviating the need to resort to former defensive maneuvers of attack and counterattack.

In summary, as the parents' group nears its end, the therapist for the group reviews the history of the group. He discusses what has been facilitated and achieved, and helps the parents deal with their own reactions to the termination of this particular group. By this time, the group will have become a support group for the parents. They also need to know in advance, as do the children, when the group will finish. A two-month period to work on these issues is suggested for the ensuing grief work to be accomplished. The issues that arise during the ending phase of PGP are similar to those encountered in the final sessions of parent training. Chapter 10 on ending parent training should be reviewed for further discussion of these issues.

Parents require education about what to expect from their children as the children's group ends. They need to be informed of the possible reappearance of symptoms in response to termination and to be reassured that this is a temporary phenomenon and that all the gains their child has made will not be lost. The therapist helps the parents to be empathic with their child during this time of stress. He discusses the general areas of concern that remain for all the children in the group. He also prepares them in advance for the individual meeting that each of them will have with the child's group therapists to review their child's progress.

Although the ending of PGP is determined, in part, arbitrarily by the close of the school year, the group experience attains a sense of closure for both parents and children. Each member of each group comes to comprehend his or her place within the group and to begin to apply these new understandings to life in the world outside the clinic.

BIBLIOGRAPHY

Achenbach, T. M. (1982). *Developmental Psychopathology*, 2d ed. New York: Wiley.

Achenbach, T. M. (1978). The Child Behavior Profile: I. Boys Aged 6 through 11. *Journal of Consulting and Clinical Psychology* 46:478–488.

Achenbach, T. M., and Edelbrock, C.S. (1981). Behavioral Problems and Competencies Reported by Parents of Normal and Disturbed Children Aged Four through Sixteen. *Monographs of the Society for Research in Child Development* 46 (188).

Aichorn, A. (1935). *Wayward Youth.* New York: Viking.

American Psychiatric Association. (1980). *Diagnostic and Statistical Manual of Mental Disorders,* 3d ed. Washington, D.C.

American Psychiatric Association. (1987). *DSM-III-R.* Washington, D.C.: American Psychiatric Association.

Annesley, P. T. (1961). Psychiatric Illness in Adolescence: Presentation and Prognosis. *Journal of Mental Science* 107:268–278.

Anthony, E. J. (1964). Communicating Therapeutically with the Child. *Journal of the American Academy of Child Psychiatry* (3):106–125.

Anthony, E.J., and Benedek, T., eds (1970). *Parenthood: Its Psychology and Psychopathology.* Boston: Little, Brown.

Azima, F. J., and Richmond, L. (1989). *Adolescent Group Psychotherapy.* Monograph 4. *American Group Psychotherapy Association Monograph Series.* Madison, Conn.: International Universities Press.

Barkley, R. A. (1981). *Hyperactive Children: A Handbook for Diagnosis and Treatment.* New York: Guilford.

Bates, J. E., and Baylis, K. (1988). Attachment and the Development of Behavior

Problems. In *Clinical Implications of Attachment,* ed. J. Belsky and T. Nezworski, pp. 253–294. Hillsdale, N.J.: Lawrence Erlbaum.

Becker, W. C. (1971). *Parents Are Teachers: A Child Management Program.* Champaign, Ill.: Research Press.

Bennis, W., and Shepard, H. (1956). A Theory of Group Development. *Human Relations* 9:415–437.

Bion, W. R. (1959). *Experiences in Groups.* New York: Basic Books.

Blechman, E. A. (1985). *Solving Child Behavior Problems at Home and at School.* Champaign, Ill.: Research Press.

Bowlby, J. (1958). The Nature of the Child's Tie to His Mother. *International Journal of Psychoanalysis* 39:350–73.

Bowlby, J. (1973). *Attachment and Loss: Vol. 2. Separation.* New York: Basic Books.

Bowlby, J. (1980). *Attachment and Loss: Vol. 3. Loss, Sadness and Depression.* New York: Basic Books.

Bowlby, J. ([1969] 1982). *Attachment and Loss: Vol. 1. Attachment,* 2d ed. New York: Basic Books.

Bracklemanns, W. E., and Berkovitz, I. H. (1972). Younger Adolescents in Group Psychotherapy: A Reparative Superego Experience. In *Adolescents Grow in Groups,* ed. I. H. Berkovitz, pp. 37–48. New York: Brunner/Mazel.

Bretherton, I., ed. (1984). *Symbolic Play: The Development of Social Understanding.* Orlando, Fl.: Academic Press.

Bretherton, I., ed. (1985). Attachment Theory: Retrospect and Prospect. In *Growing Points of Attachment Theory and Research,* ed. C. Bretherton and E. Waters. *Monographs of the Society for Research in Child Development* 50 (209), pp. 3–38.

Bretherton, I., McNew, S., and Beeghley-Smith, M. (1981). Early Person Knowledge as Expressed in Gestural and Verbal Communication: When Do Infants Acquire a "Theory of Mind?" In *Infant Social Cognition,* ed. M. E. Lamb and L. R. Sherrod, pp. 333–373. Hillsdale, N.J.: Lawrence Erlbaum.

Bruner, J. S. (1983). *Child's Talk: Learning to Use Language.* New York: Norton.

Bruner, J. S., Jolly, A., and Sylva, K., eds. (1976). *Play: Its Role in Development and Evolution.* New York: Basic Books.

Call, J. D. (1980). Some Prelinguistic Aspects of Language Development. *Journal of the American Psychoanalytic Association* 28:259–290.

Campos, J., and Stenberg, C. (1980). Perception of Appraisal and Emotion: The Onset of Social Referencing. In *Infant Social Cognition,* ed. M. E. Lamb and L. R. Sherrod, pp. 273–314. Hillsdale, N.J.: Lawrence Erlbaum.

Catterall, C. D., and Gadza, G. M. (1977). *Strategies for Helping Students.* Springfield, Ill.: Charles C. Thomas.

Cerreto, M. C., and Tuma, J. M. (1977). Distribution of DSM-II Diagnosis in a Child Psychiatric Setting. *Journal of Abnormal Child Psychology* 5:147–155.

Chazan, S. (1989). "Some Comments on the Treatment of Borderline Children." In *Current and Historical Perspectives on the Borderline Patient,* ed. R. Fine, pp. 377–392. New York: Brunner/Mazel.

Clifford, M., and Cross, T. (1980). Group Therapy for Severely Disturbed Boys in Residential Treatment. *Child Welfare* 59:560–565.

Cohen, D. (1987). *The Development of Play.* New York: New York University Press.

Conger, J. J., and Miller, W. C. (1966). *Personality, Social Class, and Delinquency.* New York: Wiley.

Conners, C. K. (1969). A Teacher Rating Scale for Use in Drug Studies with Children. *American Journal of Psychiatry* 126:152–156.

Conners, C. K. (1970). Symptom Patterns in Hyperkinetic, Neurotic and Normal Children. *Child Development* 41:667.

Conners, C. K. (1973). Rating Scales for Use in Drug Studies with Children. *Psychopharmacology Bulletin,* Special Issue Pharmacology of Children, pp. 24–84.

Dangel, R. F., and Polster, R. A., eds. (1984). *Parent Training.* New York: Guilford.

Daunton, E. (1980). Communication and Interpretation in the Opening Phase— Illustrated from the Analysis of an Eight-year-old Boy. *Journal of Child Psychotherapy* 6:93–105.

Demos, V. (1984). Empathy and Affect: Reflections on Infant Experience. In *Empathy,* ed. J. Lichtenberg, M. Bornstein, and D. Silver, pp. 9–34. Hillsdale, N.J.: Lawrence Erlbaum.

Donnellan, G. P. (1989). Borderline Children and the Dilemma of Therapeutic Efficacy. *Contemporary Psychoanalysis* 25:393–411.

Dunn, J. (1988). *The Beginnings of Social Understanding.* Cambridge, Mass.: Harvard University Press.

Dunn, J., Bretherton, I., and Munn, P. (1987). Conversations about Feeling States between Mothers and Their Young Children. *Developmental Psychology* 23:132–139.

Edelbrock, C., and Achenbach, T. M. (1980). A Typology of Child Behavior Profile Patterns: Distribution and Correlates for Disturbed Children Aged 6–16. *Journal of Abnormal Child Psychology* 8:441–470.

Emde, R. N. (1983). The Prerepresentational Self and Its Affective Core. *Psychoanalytic Study of the Child* 38:165–192.

Emde, R. N. (1989). Toward a Psychoanalytic Theory of Affect: I. The Organizational Model and Its Propositions. In *The Course of Life: Psychoanalytic Contributions Toward Understanding Personality Development,* ed. S. Greenspan and G. Pollock. Vol. I. *Infancy and Early Childhood,* pp. 165–193. Madison, Conn.: International Universities Press.

Emde, R. N., and Sorce, J. E. (1983). The Rewards of Infancy: Emotional Availability and Maternal Referencing. In *Frontiers of Infant Psychiatry,* ed. J. D. Call, E. Galenson, and R. Tyson. Vol. 2, pp. 17–30. New York: Basic Books.

Erikson, E. H. (1940). Studies in the Interpretation of Play. *Genetic Psychology* Monograph 22:557–671.

Erikson, E. H. ([1950] 1963). *Childhood and Society,* rev. ed. New York: Norton.

Ezriel, H. (1950). A Psychoanalytic Approach to Group Treatment. *British Journal of Medical Psychology* 23:59–74.

Fonagy, P. (1989). On Tolerating Mental States: Theory of Mind in Borderline Personality. *The Bulletin of the Anna Freud Centre,* 12, Part 2. London: Anna Freud Centre.

Forehand, R., and Atkinson, B. M. (1977). Generality of Treatment Effects with

Parents as Therapists: A Review of Assessment and Implementation Procedures. *Behavior Therapy* 8:575–593.

Forehand, R., Griest, D., and Wells, K. C. (1979). Parent Behavioral Training: An Analysis of the Relationship Among Multiple Outcome Measures. *Journal of Abnormal Child Psychology* 7:229–242.

Forehand, R., and McMahon, R. J. (1981). *Helping the Noncompliant Child: A Clinician's Guide to Parent Training.* New York: Guilford.

Fraiberg, S., Adelson, E., and Shapiro, V. (1975). Ghosts in the Nursery: A Psychoanalytic Approach to the Problems of Impaired Infant-Mother Relationships. *Journal of the American Academy of Child Psychiatry* 14:387–421.

Frank, M. M., (1976). Modifications of Activity Group Therapy: Responses to Ego-impoverished Children. *Clinical Social Work Journal* 4(2):102–109.

Freud, A. (1965). *Normality and Pathology in Childhood.* New York: International Universities Press.

Freud, A., and Burlingham, D. (1944). *Infants Without Families.* New York: International Universities Press.

Gadza, G. M. (1978). *Group Counseling: A Developmental Approach.* Boston: Allyn and Bacon.

Galenson, E. (1971). A Consideration of the Nature of Thought in Childhood Play. In *Separation-Individuation: Essays in Honor of Margaret S. Mahler,* ed. J. McDevitt and C. Settage, pp. 41–59. New York: International Universities Press.

Garvey, C. (1977). *Play.* Cambridge, Mass.: Harvard University Press.

Goldstein, A. P., and Simonson, N. R. (1971). Social Psychological Approaches to Psychotherapy Research. In *Handbook of Psychotherapy and Behavior Change,* 1st ed., ed. A. E. Bergin and S. L. Garfield. New York: Wiley.

Greenacre, P. (1952). Infant Reactions to Restraint: Problems in the Fate of Infantile Aggression. In *Trauma, Growth and Personality,* ed. P. Greenacre, pp. 83–105. New York: Norton.

Greenberg, M. T., and Speltz, M. L. (1988). Attachment and the Ontogeny of Conduct Problems. In *Clinical Implications of Attachment,* ed. J. Belsky and T. Nezworski, pp. 177–218. Hillsdale, N.J.: Lawrence Erlbaum.

Greenspan, S. C. (1981). Interviewing the Parents: Selected Comments. In *The Clinical Interview of the Child,* pp. 172–192. New York: McGraw-Hill.

Gresham, F. M., and Lemanec, K. L. (1983). Social Skills: A Review of Cognitive-Behavioral Training Procedures with Children. *Journal of Applied Developmental Psychology* 4:239–261.

Griest, D. L., Forehand, R., and Wells, K. C. (1981). Follow-up Assessment of Parent Behavioral Training: An Analysis of Who Will Participate. *Child Study Journal* 11:221–229.

Griest, D. L., and Wells, K. C. (1983). Behavioral Family Therapy with Conduct Disorders in Children. *Behavior Therapy* 14:37–53.

Grunebaum, H., and Solomon, L. (1982). Toward a Theory of Peer Relationships: On the Stages of Social Development and Their Relationship to Group Psychotherapy. *International Journal of Group Psychotherapy* 32(3):283–307.

Harter, S. (1982). The Perceived Competence Scale for Children. *Child Development* 53:87–97.

Hartmann, H. (1958). *Ego Psychology and the Problem of Adaptation.* New York: International Universities Press.

Hartmann, H., and Loewenstein, R. M. (1962). Notes on the Superego. *The Psychoanalytic Study of the Child* 17:42–81. New York: International Universities Press.

Henn, F. A., Bardwell, R., and Jenkins, R. L. (1980). Juvenile Delinquents Revisited: Adult Criminal Activity. *Archives of General Psychiatry* 37:1160–1163.

Hoffman, M. L. (1978). Toward a Theory of Empathic Arousal and Development. In *The Development of Affect,* ed. M. Lewis and L. A. Rosenblum, pp. 227–256. New York: Plenum.

Horwitz, L. (1986). An Integrated Group-Centered Approach. In *Psychotherapy Casebook,* ed. I. L. Kutash and A. Wolf, pp. 353–363. San Francisco: Jossey-Bass.

Jacobson, E. (1964). *The Self and the Object World.* New York: International Universities Press.

Jastak, S., and Wilkinson, G. G. (1984). *Wide Range Achievement Test-R.* rev. ed. Wilmington, Del.: Jastak Associates.

Kagan, J. (1981). *The Second Year.* Cambridge, Mass.: Harvard University Press.

Kagan, J. (1984). *The Nature of the Child.* New York: Basic Books.

Katan, A. (1961). Some Thoughts About the Role of Verbalization on Early Childhood. *Psychoanalytic Study of the Child* 16:184–188. New York: International Universities Press.

Kazdin, A. E. (1985). *Treatment of Antisocial Behavior in Children and Adolescents.* Homewood, Ill.: Dorsey.

Kazdin, A. E. (1987). *Conduct Disorders in Childhood and Adolescence.* Newbury Park, Calif.: Sage.

Kendall, P. C. (1984). Cognitive-Behavioral Self-Control Therapy for Children. *Journal of Child Psychology and Psychiatry* 25:173–179.

Kendall, P. C., and Braswell, L. (1985). *Cognitive-Behavioral Therapy for Impulsive Children.* New York: Guilford.

Kendall, P. C., and Hollon, S. D., eds. (1979). *Cognitive-Behavioral Interventions: Theory, Research and Procedures.* New York: Academic Press.

Kennedy, H., Moran, G., Wiseberg, S., and Yorke, C. (1985). Both Sides of the Barrier: Some Reflections on Childhood Fantasy. *Psychoanalytic Study of the Child* 40:278–283. New Haven: Yale University Press.

Kernberg, O. F. (1977). *Object Relations Theory and Clinical Psychoanalysis.* New York: Jason Aronson.

Kernberg, P. F. (1983). Issues in the Psychotherapy of Borderline Conditions in Children. In *The Borderline Child,* ed. C. Robson, pp. 223–234. New York: McGraw-Hill.

Kernberg, P. F. (1985). Verband der Wissenschaftlichen Gesellschaften Osterreichs. *Die Beendigung der Kinderpsychoanalyse* 5:71–89. (Termination in Child Psychoanalyis: Criteria from within sessions)

Kernberg, P. F. (1989). The Forms of Play. Paper delivered at the annual meeting of the American Academy of Child and Adolescent Psychiatry, New York, October 14, 1989.

Kernberg, P. F. (1989). Narcissistic Personality Disorders in Childhood. *Psychiatric Clinics of North America* 12:671–694.

Kernberg, P. F., et al. (1985). Cornell Interview of Children's Perceptions of Friendships and Peer Relations. In *Proceedings for the Papers and New Research Posters,* ed. L. Greenhill, presented at the 32d annual meeting of the American Academy of Child and Adolescent Psychiatry, San Antonio, Texas, October 23, 1985.

Kernberg, P.F., Cohen, J., Saunders, S. Frankel, A., Scholl, H., Chazan, S. (1986a). The Global Verbal Interventions Scale. A workshop on the differences and similarities between child psychoanalysis and child psychotherapy. Conducted at the annual meeting of the American Psychoanalytic Association, New York, December 18, 1986.

Kernberg, P.F., Liebowitz, J. Frankel, A., Scholl, H., Kruger, R., Chazan, S., Saunders, S. (1986b). Therapists' Verbal Interventions: A Scale. Workshop conducted at the annual meeting of the American Academy of Child and Adolescent Psychiatry, Los Angeles.

Kernberg, P. F., and Rosenberg, J. Play Group Therapy for Children with Socialized Conduct Disorders. In *The Expanding World of Group Psychotherapy: Essays in Honor of Saul Scheidlinger, Ph.D.,* ed. S. Tuttman. Monograph 7. American Group Psychotherapy Association. New York: International Universities Press (In Press).

Kolvin, I., Garside, R. F., MacMillan, A., Wolstenholme, S., and Leitch, J. M. (1981). *Help Starts Here: The Maladjusted Child in the Ordinary School,* pp. 218–221. London: Tavistock.

Lewis, M. (1974). Interpretation in Child Analysis. *Journal of the American Academy of Child Psychiatry* 13:32–53.

Loewenstein, R. (1957). Some Thoughts on Interpretation in the Theory and Practice of Psychoanalysis. *Psychoanalytic Study of the Child* 12:127–150. New York: International Universities Press.

Lorber, R., and Patterson, G. R. (1981). The Aggressive Child: A Concomitant of a Coercive System. *Advances in Family Intervention, Assessment and Theory* 2:47–87.

Luborsky, L. (1984). *Principles of Psychoanalytic Psychotherapy: A Manual for Supportive-Expressive Treatment.* New York: Basic Books.

Luborsky, L., and DeRubins, R. J. (1984). The Use of Psychotherapy Treatment Manuals: A Small Revolution in Psychotherapy Research Style. *Clinical Psychology Review* 4:5–14.

Maenchen, A. (1970). On the Technique of Child Analysis in Relation to Stages of Development. *Psychoanalytic Study of the Child* 25:175–208. New Haven: Yale University Press.

Maenchen, A. (1984). The Handling of Overt Aggression in Child Analysis. *Psychoanalytic Study of the Child* 39:393–406. New Haven: Yale University Press.

Mahler, M. (1975). Verbal Communication to Paulina Kernberg, M.D.

Mahler, M., Pine, F., and Bergman, A. (1975). *The Psychological Birth of the Human Infant.* New York: Basic Books.

Markwardt, F. C., Jr. (1989). *Peabody Individual Achievement Test—Revised.* Circle Pines, Minn.: American Guidance Service, Inc.

McMahon, R. J., and Forehand, R. (1988). Conduct Disorders. In *Behavioral Assessment of Childhood Disorders,* 2d ed., ed. E. I. Mash and L. G. Terdal, pp. 105-153. New York: Guilford.

McMahon, R. J., Forehand, R., and Griest, D. L. (1981). Effects of Knowledge of Social Learning Principles on Enhancing Outcome and Generalization in a Parent Training Program. *Journal of Consulting and Clinical Psychology* 49:526–532.

Meeks, J. E. (1981). What Did the Therapists Say? What Did the Therapists Do? *International Journal of Psychoanalytic Psychotherapy* 8:233–241.

Moran, G. S., ed. (1987). Some Functions of Play and Playfulness: A Developmental Perspective. *Psychoanalytic Study of the Child* 42:11–29. New Haven: Yale University Press.

Moran, G. S., ed. (1988). International Scientific Colloquium on Playing: Its Role in Child and Adult Psychoanalysis. *The Bulletin of the Anna Freud Centre,* 11, (97), Part 2, London: Anna Freud Centre.

Morris, H. H., Escoll, P. J., and Wexler, R. (1956). Aggressive Behavior Disorders of Childhood: A Follow-up Study. *American Journal of Psychiatry* 112:991–997.

Ollendick, T. H., and Cerny, J. A. (1981). *Clinical Behavior Therapy with Children.* New York: Plenum.

O'Neal, P., and Robins, L. N. (1958). The Relation of Childhood Behavior Problems to Adult Psychiatric States: A Thirty-year Follow-up Study of 150 Subjects. *American Journal of Psychiatry* 114:961–969.

Osofsky, J. D. (1988). Attachment Theory and Research and the Psychoanalytic Process. *Psychoanalytic Psychology* 5(2): 159–177.

Padawer, W. J., Bupan, B. A., and Kendall, P. C. (1980). *Developing Self-Control in Children: A Manual of Cognitive-Behavioral Strategies,* University of Minnesota.

Parens, H. (1979). *The Development of Aggression in Early Childhood.* New York: Jason Aronson.

Patterson, G. R. (1974). Intervention for Boys with Conduct Problems: Multiple Settings, Treatments and Criteria. *Journal of Consulting and Clinical Psychology* 42:471–481.

Patterson, G. R. (1975). *Families.* Champaign, Ill.: Research Press.

Patterson, G. R. (1976). The Aggressive Child: Victim and Architect of a Coercive System. In *Behavior Modification and Families,* ed. E. J. Mash, L. A. Homerlynch, and L. C. Handy, pp. 267–316. New York: Brunner/Mazel.

Patterson, G. R. (1982). *Coercive Family Process.* Eugene, OR: Castalia.

Patterson, G. R., Reid, J. B., Jones, R. R., and Conger, R. W. (1975). *A Social Learning Approach to Family Intervention.* Eugene, OR: Castalia.

Peed, S., Roberts, M., and Forehand, R. (1977). Evaluation of the Effectiveness of a Standardized Parent Training Program in Altering the Interaction of Mothers and Their Non-Compliant Children. *Behavior Modification* 1:323–350.

Pine, F. (1984). The Interpretive Moment—Variations on Classical Themes. *Bulletin of the Menninger Clinic* 48(1): 54–71.

Prelinger, E. (1989). The Function of Aggression: Old Concepts and New Thoughts. *The Austen Riggs Center Review* 1, no. 2 (Spring): 4–7.

Pritchard, M., and Graham, P. (1966). An Investigation of a Group of Patients Who Have Attended Both the Child and Adult Departments of the Same Psychiatric Hospital. *British Journal of Psychiatry* 112:603–612.

Puig-Antich, J. (1982). Major Depression and Conduct Disorder in Prepuberty. *Journal of the American Academy of Child Psychiatry* 21:118–128.

Quay, H. C. (1977). Measuring Dimensions of Deviant Behavior: The Behavior Problem Checklist. *Journal of Abnormal Child Psychology* 5:277–287.

Radke-Yarrow, M., Zahn-Waxler, C., and Chapman, M. (1983). Children's Prosocial Dispositions and Behavior. In *Handbook of Child Psychology,* ed. P. H. Mussen, vol. 4. New York: Wiley.

Rapoport, J. L., and Ismond, D. R. (1984). *DSM-III Training Guide for Diagnosis of Childhood Disorders.* New York: Brunner/Mazel.

Reister, A. E., and Kraft, I. A. (1986). *Child Group Psychotherapy Future Tense.* Monograph 3. American Group Psychotherapy Association. Madison, Conn.: International Universities Press.

Ricks, M. H. (1985). The Social Transmission of Parental Behavior: Attachment Across Generations. In *Growing Points of Attachment Theory and Research,* ed. I. Bretherton and E. Waters. *Monographs of the Society for Research in Child Development* 50 (209), pp. 211–230.

Risley, T. R., Clark, H. B., and Cataldo, M. Y. (1976). Behavioral Technology for the Normal Middle-Class Family. In *Behavior Modification and Families,* ed. E. J. Mash, L. A. Homerlynch, and L. C. Handy, pp. 34–60. New York: Brunner/Mazel.

Roberts, M. W., McMahon, R. J., Forehand, R., and Humphrey, L. (1978). The Effect of Parental Instruction-Giving on Child Compliance. *Behavior Therapy* 9:793–798.

Robins, L. N. (1970). The Adult Development of the Antisocial Child. *Seminars in Psychiatry* 2:420–434.

Rosen, V. H. (1974). The Nature of Verbal Interventions in Psychoanalysis. *Psychoanalysis and Contemporary Science,* ed. L. Goldberger and V. Rosen, pp. 189–209. New York: International Universities Press.

Rosenberg, J., and Cherbuliez, T. (1979). Inpatient Group Therapy for Older Children and Pre-Adolescents. *International Journal of Group Psychotherapy* 29:393–405.

Ross, A. A. (1981). *Child Behavior Therapy: Principles, Procedures, and Empirical Basis.* New York: Wiley.

Rutan, J. S., and Stone, W. N. (1984). *Psychodynamic Group Psychotherapy.* Lexington, Mass.: D. C. Heath.

Rutter, M., Birch, H. G., Thomas, A., and Chess, S. (1964). Temperamental Characteristics in Infancy and the Later Development of Behavioral Disorders. *British Journal of Psychiatry* 110:651–661.

Rutter, M., Cox, A., Tupling, C., Berger, M., and Yule, W. (1975). Attainment and Adjustment in Two Geographical Areas. The Prevalence of Psychiatric Disorder. *British Journal of Psychiatry* 126: 493–509.

Rutter, M., and Garmezy, N. (1983). Developmental Psychopathology. In *Handbook of Child Psychology*, 4th ed., ed. P. H. Mussen, vol. 4, pp. 776–911. New York: Wiley.

Rutter, M., and Giller, H. (1983). *Juvenile Delinquency: Trends and Perspectives.* New York: Penguin.

Rutter, M., Tizard, J., and Whitmore, K., eds. (1970). *Education, Health and Behavior.* London: Longmans.

Rutter, M., Tizard, J., Yule, W., Graham, P., and Whitmore, K. (1976). Research Report: Isle of Wright Studies, 1964–1974. *Psychological Medicine* 6:313–332.

Safer, D. J., and Allen, R. P. (1976). *Hyperactive Children: Diagnosis and Management.* Baltimore: University Park Press.

Sandler, J. (1960). On the Concept of the Superego. In *Psychoanalytic Study of the Child* 15: 128–162. New York: International Universities Press.

Sandler, J., Kennedy, H., and Tyson, R. (1980). Clarification and Confrontation. In *The Technique of Child Psychoanalysis*, Chap. 18–20, pp. 170–187. Cambridge, Mass.: Harvard University Press.

Sandler, J., and Rosenblatt, B. (1962). The Concept of the Representational World. *Psychoanalytic Study of the Child* 17:128–145. New Haven: Yale University Press.

Sarnoff, C. (1976). *Latency.* New York: Jason Aronson.

Schaefer, C. E., and O'Connor, K. J. (1983). *Handbook of Play Therapy.* New York: Wiley.

Scheidlinger, S. (1974). On the Concept of the "Mother-Group." *International Journal of Group Psychotherapy* 24:417–428.

Scheidlinger, S. (1980). *Psychoanalytic Group Dynamics: Basic Readings.* New York: International Universities Press.

Scheidlinger, S. (1982). *Focus on Group Psychotherapy: Clinical Essays.* New York: International Universities Press.

Schiffer, M. (1977). Activity-Interview Group Psychotherapy: Theory, Principles, and Practice. *International Journal of Group Psychotherapy* 27:377–388.

Selman, R. L. (1980). *The Growth of Interpersonal Understanding.* New York: Academic Press.

Sherif, M., and Sherif, C. (1969). *Social Psychology.* 3d ed. New York: Harper and Row.

Shraga, S. (1986). Therapeutic Implications of Games with Juvenile Delinquents. In *Game Play: Therapeutic Uses of Childhood Games*, ed. C. Schaefer, pp. 311–330. New York: Wiley.

Siepker, B. B., and Kandaras, C. S. (1985). *Group Therapy with Children and Adolescents: A Treatment Manual.* New York: Human Sciences Press.

Slavson, S. R., and Schiffer, M. (1975). *Group Psychotherapies for Children: A Textbook.* New York: International Universities Press.

Solnit, A. J., ed. (1987). Psychoanalytic Views of Play. *Psychoanalytic Study of the Child* 42: 3–223. New Haven: Yale University Press.

Spear, D. C. (1971). The Behavior Problem Checklist (Peterson-Quay): Baseline Data from Parents of Child Guidance and Nonclinic Children. *Journal of Consulting and Clinical Psychology* 36:221–228.

Spitz, R. (1957). *No and Yes.* New York: International Universities Press.

Spitz, R. (1958). On the Genesis of Superego Components. *The Psychoanalytic Study of the Child* 13:375–404. New York: International Universities Press.

Spitz, R. (1959). *A Genetic Field Theory of Ego Formation.* New York: International Universities Press.

Sroufe, L. A. (1988). The Role of Infant-Caregiver Attachment in Development. In *Clinical Implications of Attachment,* ed. J. Belsky and T. Nezworski, pp. 18–40. Hillsdale, N.J.: Lawrence Erlbaum.

Sroufe, L. A., and Waters, E. (1977). Attachment as an Organizational Construct. *Child Development* 48:1184–1199.

Stern, D. N. (1985). *The Interpersonal World of the Infant.* New York: Basic Books.

Thomas, A., and Chess, S. (1977). *Temperament and Development.* New York: Brunner/Mazel.

Thomas, A., Chess, S., and Birch, H. G. (1968). *Temperament and Behavior Disorders in Children.* New York: New York University Press.

Turecki, S., and Tonner, L. (1985). *The Difficult Child: A Guide for Parents.* New York: Bantam.

Weathers, L. R., and Liberman, R. P. (1977). Modification of Family Behavior. In *Child Behavior Therapy,* ed. D. Marholin, pp. 150–186. New York: Gardner.

Weissman, M. M., and Klerman, G. L. (1984). *Interpersonal Therapy for Depressed Patients.* New York: Basic Books.

Wells, K. C. Coercive Family Process: A Review and Overview of Patterson's Recent Work, n.d. Paper presented at the Children's Hospital Medical Center, George Washington University School of Medicine, Washington, D.C.

Wells, K. C., and Forehand, R. (in press). Conduct and Oppositional Disorders. To appear in *Handbook of Clinical Behavior Therapy with Children,* ed. P. H. Bornstein and A. E. Kazdin. New York: Dorsey.

Wells, K. C., and Forehand, R. (1981). Child Behavior Problems in the Home. In *Handbook of Clinical Behavior Therapy,* ed. S. M. Turner, K. Calhoun, and H. E. Adams, pp. 527-567. New York: Wiley.

Wells, K. C., Griest, D. L., and Forehand, R. (1980). The Use of a Self-Control Package to Enhance Temporal Generality of a Parent Training Program. *Behavior Research and Therapy* 18:347–353.

Willock, B. (1986). Narcissistic Vulnerability in the Hyper-Aggressive Child: The Disregarded (Unloved, Uncared-For) Self. *Psychoanalytic Psychology* 3:59–80.

Willock, B. (1987). The Devalued (Unloved, Repugnant) Self: A Second Facet of Narcissistic Vulnerability in the Aggressive, Conduct-Disordered Child. *Psychoanalytic Psychology* 4:219–240.

Winnicott, D. W. (1965). *The Maturational Processes and the Facilitating Environment.* New York: International Universities Press.

Winnicott, D. W. (1971). *Playing and Reality.* New York: Basic Books.

Winnicott, D. W. (1984). *Deprivation and Delinquency,* ed. C. Winnicott, R. Shepherd, and M. Davis. London: Tavistock.

Wittes, G., and Radin, N. (1968). Parent Manual on Child Rearing. Manuscript. (Available from Ypsilante Early Education Program, Ypsilante, Michigan.) Cited in *Helping the Noncompliant Child,* ed. R. L. Forehand and R. J. McMahon. (1981). New York: Guilford.

Wolff, S. (1967). Behavioral Characteristics of Primary School Children Referred to a Psychiatric Department. *British Journal of Psychiatry* 113:885–893.

Wolff, S. (1971). Dimensions and Clusters of Symptoms in Disturbed Children. *British Journal of Psychiatry* 118:421–427.

Yalom, I. (1970). *The Theory and Practice of Group Psychotherapy.* New York: Basic Books.

INDEX

Acceptance, 28, 138–39, 141

Achenbach Behavior Check List (1978), 25

Adaptability (temperamental trait), 135

Adaptation, 17, 135, 136

Adolescence, 3, 136

Affection, 121, 124, 127. *See also* Love

Aggression, 18, 114–16; discharging of, and play, 10; earliest manifestations of, 6–7; and emotional development, 114–15; induced as a secondary reaction, 5; "irritable," 154; and overidentification, with the child, 169; and PGP, 233, 234, 235, 236, 257, 275, 279, 284–85; and problems between parents, 116; and punishment, 141, 154; and SEPP, 25, 26–27, 29–33, 37, 39, 56, 96

Alone, capacity to be, 157–58

American Psychiatric Association, 2

Anger, 41, 90, 95; the child's, identification with, 115; and countertrans-ference, 39; and provocations, 25, 26; and SEPP, 39, 40, 90, 95, 106

Anxiety, 95, 96, 203; disorders, 2, 3, 25; separation, 153, 166, 174–75, 197; and SEPP, 23, 25, 27, 35, 60; tolerance for, 5; about treatment, 60, 109, 120, 194, 195, 241

Approach/Withdrawal (temperamental trait), 135

Athletics, 79

Attachment, 64–65, 67, 117; figures, therapists as, 120, 121–22, 123, 128–29, 165, 167–72, 175–76; and individuation, 121, 134; insecure, 8, 113, 115, 119; parental, 95, 129, 130, 166–67, 177; -seeking behavior, 153; and SEPP, 64–65, 68; theory, 8, 9; Winnicott on, 114

Attention Deficit Disorder, 3, 5, 183

Authority figures, 2, 129; negative reaction to, 183; and PGP, 193, 194, 195, 232; teachers as, 182